ALSO BY GÖTZ ALY

Into the Tunnel:
The Brief Life of Marion Samuel, 1931–1943

Hitler's Beneficiaries:
Plunder, Racial War, and the Nazi Welfare State

Architects of Annihilation:
Auschwitz and the Logic of Destruction
(with Susanne Heim)

WHY THE GERMANS?

WHY THE JEWS?

WHY THE GERMANS?

WHY THE JEWS?

ENVY, RACE HATRED, AND THE
PREHISTORY OF THE HOLOCAUST

GÖTZ ALY

TRANSLATED BY JEFFERSON CHASE

METROPOLITAN BOOKS   HENRY HOLT AND COMPANY   NEW YORK

Metropolitan Books
Henry Holt and Company, LLC
Publishers since 1866
175 Fifth Avenue
New York, New York 10010
www.henryholt.com

Metropolitan Books® and m® are registered trademarks of
Henry Holt and Company, LLC.

Originally published in Germany in 2011 under the title
Warum die Deutschen? Warum die Juden? by S. Fischer Verlag, Frankfurt am Main.

Library of Congress Cataloging-in-Publication Data

Aly, Götz, 1947– author
  [Warum die Deutschen? Warum die Juden? English]
  Why the Germans? why the Jews? : envy, race hatred, and the prehistory of the
Holocaust / Götz Aly ; translated by Jefferson Chase.
       p. cm.
  Includes bibliographical references and index.
  ISBN 978-0-8050-9700-9 (hardback)—ISBN 978-0-8050-9704-7 (electronic
book) 1. Jews—Cultural assimilation—Germany—19th century.   2. Jews—
Cultural assimilation—Germany—20th century.   3. Jews—Germany—Identity—
19th century.   4. Jews—Germany—Identity—20th century.   5. Jews—Germany—
Social conditions—19th century.   6. Jews—Germany—Social conditions—20th
century.   7. Antisemitism—Germany—History—19th century.   8. Antisemitism—
Germany—History—20th century.   9. Germany—Ethnic relations.   I. Chase,
Jefferson S., translator.   II. Title.
  DS134.25.A59 2014
  943'.004924—dc23   2013042037

First U.S. Edition 2014

Designed by Kelly S. Too

Printed in the United States of America
1 3 5 7 9 10 8 6 4 2

CONTENTS

ACKNOWLEDGMENTS

The S. Fischer Foundation in Berlin generously supported this book, as did the International Institute for Holocaust Research at Yad Vashem, Jerusalem. My work there was underwritten by the Baron Friedrich Carl von Oppenheim Stipend for Research on Racism, Anti-Semitism, and the Holocaust. My research was made a lot easier and a lot more pleasant by my helpful and welcoming colleagues at Yad Vashem, who took an interest in my work and were always ready to discuss it.

The editor of this book in the original German was Walter Pehle. In his thirty-five years at the S. Fischer publishing house, Pehle brought out more than 250 books on the history of National Socialism and the persecution of European Jews. He always advised his authors with patience, conviction, and understanding. Pehle produced books about horrible crimes yet never lost his sense of humor. The manuscript for this volume was the last one he worked on before reluctantly retiring, at the age of seventy. As always, he checked every comma, and occasionally, as was his wont, he would ask me, "What is the author trying to say here?"—before remarking, "Maybe we'd better take that out." He has my heartfelt gratitude for that and for our two decades of working together.

I'd also like to express my gratitude to my editor at Metropolitan Books, Sara Bershtel, for her courage in taking on such a challenging project and her efforts to better present my ideas to an English-language audience. My thanks as well to Roslyn Schloss and Grigory Tovbis for their work. Finally, I'd like to thank my translator, Jefferson Chase, for his love of the German and English languages. He repeatedly queried the exact meanings of words and phrases, and undercovered some minor mistakes in the German original—something only the best translators do.

TRANSLATOR'S NOTE

In the interests of making an extraordinarily complex historical investigation more comprehensible to an American audience, Götz Aly's German original has been revised for this edition. All changes have been made in consultation with the author.

WHY THE GERMANS?

WHY THE JEWS?

THE QUESTION OF QUESTIONS

WHY THE GERMANS? WHY THE JEWS?

Why did Germans murder six million men, women, and children who were guilty of nothing other than being Jews? How was this possible? How could a civilized, culturally diverse, and productive people release this sort of massive destructive energy?

In the nineteenth century, Jews who emigrated to Germany from neighboring countries in Eastern Europe felt great relief when they crossed the border. They appreciated the legal protections, economic freedom, and educational opportunities offered first by Prussia and later by the German Empire. Anti-Jewish pogroms, which continued well into the twentieth century in Eastern and Southeastern Europe, had died out in Germany, while the absence of governmental restrictions helped make the country a magnet for Jewish migration. By 1910, Germany had twice as many Jews as England and five times as many as France.

In 1919, when post–World War I Germany was forced to cede the province of Posen to Poland, most of the region's German Jews quickly fled to Berlin. They had, as sociologist Alfred Marcus wrote in 1931, "an almost pathological fear of the new Polish powers-that-be."[1] And as Siegfried Lichtenstaedter—a retired Bavarian civil servant and author who spent much of his life pondering his dual identity as German and Jew—wrote in 1937, anyone who had prophesied in 1900 that thirty-three years later thousands of Jews would flee Germany for Palestine "would have been considered ripe for a lunatic asylum."[2] So why the Germans? Why the Jews? The fact that Jews felt welcome and safe in pre-Nazi Germany precludes any simple answer to this unsettling, historically urgent double question.

We tend today to focus on and identify with the victims, not only in our memorials but also when it comes to research on the Holocaust and literary and educational treatments of it. At the same time, we tend to cast the perpetrators as bizarre, almost alien figures. In a fashion that often belies their own family histories, Germans prefer to speak from a remote distance of "the Nazis," "Hitler's henchmen," "the regime," "the fanatic racist ideologues"—or, even more abstractly, of "racist populism" and "the paranoid worldview of anti-Semites." Such generic terms tell us little. This book is an attempt to show what lies behind the abstractions, by looking in detail at the period from 1800 to 1933—that is, the prehistory of the Holocaust.

The various theories we have about fascism, dictatorship, and the logic of inclusion and exclusion serve to keep the Holocaust at arm's length. Vague theoretical constructions cloak the phenomenon of racist murder in quasi-Marxist inevitability or diminish its significance by portraying it simply as a regression into barbarism. The idea of a special German path through history—fixed and neatly definable—transfers too much responsibility from individuals to ideology or a proclivity for totalitarianism. And it does not truly explain why German history culminated in genocide.

To understand the origins of the Holocaust, we first need to stop dividing up its prehistory into "good" and "bad" lines of development. Historical optimists favor such straightforward binary distinctions because they regard present-day society as the pinnacle of civilization.

They appeal to their audience with the illusion that everything that seems right or wrong today was equally right or wrong in the past. Analytically, this conception of history leads nowhere. It creates distance and fails to explain anything. Nor is it useful to divide historical figures into "bad" conservatives and "good" liberals.* Conservatives weren't the only ones guided by hostility toward and even hatred of Jews. Reformers and pioneers of political liberty often were as well. We must look for explanations elsewhere.

Life was hardly rosy for the vast majority of European Jews prior to 1806, the year that Napoleon emancipated their coreligionists from most legal restrictions in the western German territories bordering France. In the medieval era Jews had faced draconian restrictions on where they could live and what professions they could pursue and had been expelled from England, France, Spain, and Portugal. Jews were blamed for plagues and crises, believed to engage in obscure evil practices such as poisoning wells and sacrificing Christian children, and subjected to recurrent and horrific pogroms. Jew hatred was overwhelmingly religious in nature and began to wane only in the age of enlightened absolutism in Western and Central Europe. Still, Gentiles and Jews had extremely limited contact in society. Jews had to live in ghettos in some cities and were entirely forbidden from even entering certain others.

That situation gradually changed in the nineteenth century with Jewish emancipation and entrance into mainstream society. Now Jews were regarded less as adherents of an alien, barbaric faith and more as members of a secular socioeconomic group that disproportionately profited from modern life. Social anti-Semitism, with its far greater degree of internal logic, however misguided, came to replace religious Jew hatred, which was vitriolic but unsystematic. The language

---

* Translator's note: the terms *liberal* and *liberalism* are used throughout this book in their European sense as referring to an ideology that promotes personal liberty and free markets, and not in the often pejorative American sense of "left-wing."

directed against Jews became less crass and wildly emotional, but the implications that Jews were somehow destroying mainstream native society now ran deeper and were more potentially damaging. Beliefs of this kind, spreading through all social strata, became a mass phenomenon and paved the way for the racial anti-Semitism at the core of the National Socialist worldview.

In 1933, Lichtenstaedter tried to predict the future for German Jews. For years, he had been studying the *Völkischer Beobachter* newspaper, which he described in 1922 as "the widely read organ of the National Socialist German Workers' Party," or NSDAP.[3] Lichtenstaedter asked himself why such hatred was being directed against Jews. After all, he noted, German Jews were very similar to the majority population in terms of their behavior, appearance, and religion. At the same time, however, they did possess a distinguishing "collective ego." A movement directed against left-handed people, Lichtenstaedter speculated, would be doomed to failure because the common characteristics of such a group are otherwise too vague to justify the idea of a collective ego. With Jews, the commonalities were just strong enough to produce a compact image of a group to which other characteristics could then be ascribed.[4]

Lichtenstaedter saw the NSDAP as a party of social climbers, and that view informed the prognosis he made for himself and for German Jews in general. On average, Jews in Central and Western Europe occupied relatively high social positions—a fact held against them by Gentiles who had not achieved similar social mobility. Jewish success was thus a goad to their adversaries. In Lichtenstaedter's view, virulent anti-Semites regarded Jewish religious tradition as "practically irrelevant." Instead, they hated Jews because Jews were competition for "survival, honor, and prestige." Anti-Semitism owed its aggressive force to competition and the desire for social betterment. If Jews as a group were perceived as being "disproportionately happier" than other groups, Lichtenstaedter wrote, "why shouldn't this give rise to jealousy and resentment, worries and concerns about one's own future, just as is all too often the case between individuals?"[5]

Instead of simply demonizing National Socialists, Lichtenstaedter analyzed the political situation, which posed an existential threat not just to him and his coreligionists but to everyone who was considered a member of the Jewish race. He wanted to understand the National Socialist environment around him in order to anticipate what was coming and figure out how to react. He acknowledged that Hitler saw Jews as "a people with special innate characteristics" that "set them apart from all other peoples living on the earth."[6] But in his view, German anti-Semitism was nourished not by an ideology based on specific Jewish traits but rather by more generic material conflicts and interests. In other words, Nazism was propelled by the least pleasurable of the seven deadly sins: envy.

Envy dissolves social cohesion. It destroys trust, creates aggression, promotes suspicion over proof, and leads people to bolster their sense of self-worth by denigrating others. Those who achieve success, especially if they are also outsiders, are invariably subjected to sidelong glances, malicious rumor, and libel. At the same time, as enviers know only too well, jealous people gradually poison themselves, becoming ever more dissatisfied and bitter. Thus they tend to conceal their shameful, base resentment of others behind supposedly more sophisticated arguments—for example, those of racist theory. Enviers brand those more intelligent than they are as clever but not profound. Upset by others' success, they dismiss those they envy as immoral, egotistical, and despicable, while they themselves pose as respectable moral authorities. They pass off their own failure as modesty of ambition while accusing those they dislike of always pushing to get ahead.

The envier doesn't necessarily seek to emulate the object of his envy; indeed, often he very vocally refuses to do so. As Immanuel Kant observed, the envious instead devote their energy to "destroying the happiness of others." The envier feels deep satisfaction and enjoys expressing his scorn and schadenfreude whenever others lose their advantages. Do those envied deserve assistance or even pity? No, answers the envier. They always thought they knew better. They were always pushing to get ahead. So let them fend for themselves. Such logic assuages the envier's moral scruples, allowing him to do nothing and play the innocent even in the face of gross injustice. If others are harassing the object of his envy, the envier concludes that it's none of his business. His conscience remains clear. He isn't the one doing the actual persecution.

What are the sources of envy? They include weakness, timidity, lack of self-confidence, self-perceived inferiority, and excessive ambition. And many prominent observers have ascribed just such characteristics to the German people. "The German is always at pains to emphasize how German he is," complained Julius Fröbel, a delegate to the National Assembly in Frankfurt in 1848–49, the gathering that failed to establish either a German democracy or a German nation-state. "The German spirit, so to speak, always stands in front of a mirror admiring itself, and even if it has looked itself over a hundred times and become convinced of its perfection, it still harbors a secret doubt, which is the hidden core of vanity."[7]

The English, the French, and the Italians all followed a very different trajectory. The Italians, for instance, established their nation-state in 1870 after three wars waged in their own country against the foreign powers of France, Austria, and the Papal States. Moreover, they confirmed that nation-state with a popular referendum. Roughly at the same time, between 1854 and 1870, an alliance of German states led by Prussia invaded Denmark, Austria, and France without any true provocation—merely in order to achieve a sense of national self-confidence. The conservative nationalist historian Heinrich von Treitschke may have crowed that "war is the best medicine for a people," but national unity achieved through military aggression remained fragile. In 1933, the Italian diplomat Carlo Sforza observed: "The Germans are still constantly asking themselves what German-ness is and what it's not."[8]

The innate insecurity of German national identity produced no shortage of jingoistic boasting between 1800 and 1933. One remarkable example was the proclamation of the German Empire in 1871, which was staged in the Hall of Mirrors at Versailles—on the territory of Germany's archenemy—because Germany itself did not possess any popularly acknowledged main city. Another example is the statement with which Kaiser Wilhelm II dispatched German sailors to put down a rebellion in China in 1900: "If you encounter the enemy, strike against him so that never again will a Chinese dare to look askance at a German."[9] At the public celebrations of Hitler's forty-fourth birthday on April 20, 1933, Germans were delighted to hear themselves described as the "premier people on earth."[10] A nation that feels the need to boast like this lacks inner equilibrium.

CRAVING EQUALITY AND FEARING FREEDOM

People driven by envy always go on about how disadvantaged they are. Those who despise others see themselves as vulnerable and seek official protection. When the French Revolution adopted *liberté, egalité,* and *fraternité* as its motto, the word *egalité* meant nothing more and nothing less than the equality of French citizens before the law. Yet long before anti-Semitism developed into a political movement, the vast majority of Germans had abandoned faith in this crucial idea, demanding instead that the state act as a paternal protector to guarantee *material* equality. Cries went up at every possible opportunity: "That's unjust. We, too, deserve our place in the sun." Germans luxuriated in the feeling of being eternally cheated of their just deserts. The more this notion of equality took over the popular imagination, the more importance Germans attached to what writer Arnold Zweig called the "discriminating affect," the exclusion of unequal groups, especially those characterized by flexibility, wit, cleverness, and success. The reverse side of the German notion of equality was, in Zweig's words, a "centralization affect"—overemphasizing the self-proclaimed mainstream.[11]

In addition to their particular notion of equality, early revolutionary German nationalists also maintained a strangely collective and negative idea of freedom. Many Germans understood freedom not as a matter of individual liberty but as liberation from real or putative enemies. Hitler, for instance, described his radically destructive aims as a "movement of liberation" from the shackles of the 1919 Treaty of Versailles. In summer 1922, the future German chancellor titled one of his crude and incendiary anti-Semitic rants "The Free State or Slavery?" An early Nazi newspaper in the industrial regions of western Germany edited by Joseph Goebbels was entitled *Popular Freedom* (*Völkische Freiheit*), and in 1926 Goebbels founded a Nazi "Freedom Association" in Berlin.[12] A collection of Hitler's wartime speeches was entitled "The Greater German Battle for Freedom," and Nazis often described themselves as pursuing the "freedom" for "self-defense," "food-procurement," and "living space." What they really meant, of course, was war, genocide, and the colonization of places like Ukraine with their vast agricultural and natural resources.

The growing intensity of politically active anti-Semitism in Germany around 1880 revealed both the level of popular resentment against Jews and the political shortcomings in German society: Germans' fear of true freedom and daring and their tendency to attribute their own failings to others. A green-eyed monster was seeking sacrificial lambs. Particularly during times of crisis, Germans tended to associate personal liberty with feelings of discomfort, uncertainty, and helplessness, whereas equality signified for them protection, financial security, and minimal individual risk. Such an attitude prevented Germans from becoming politically mature, and the idea of freedom withered in the shadow cast by communal values. The desire for social equality is at the heart of the German brand of anti-Semitism, along with envy and fear of personal freedom. Thus these three things will be our main focus.

A NOTE ON METHOD

The term *Holocaust* paradoxically obscures the full extent of what Germans did, which was to drive all the European Jews they could into ghettos and concentration camps. Hundreds of thousands of them starved there or died from cold and illness. Germans and their helpers transported the others—by foot, truck, and rail—to remote destinations where the victims were shot or gassed to death. Some of those condemned to die were forced to dig mass graves and stuff bodies into crematorium ovens.

Sometimes, and increasingly frequently toward the end of the war, SS men, administrative officials, and doctors would select the most physically fit among the deportees for forced labor. As a result, tens of thousands of people survived a time of horror. Hundreds of thousands of others were able to go underground or to flee at the last minute or were concealed by people in their hometowns. That was particularly the case in countries where, for various reasons, the German stranglehold over daily life was incomplete: Denmark, France, Hungary, Romania, Belgium, Italy, and Bulgaria. Nonetheless, within the space of only three years, Germans murdered 82 percent of the Jewish populace in the areas under their control. The final total was around six million people.[13]

By now, tens of thousands of prosecutors, criminal investigators, judges, journalists, historians, and survivors and witnesses have greatly added to our knowledge of the Holocaust. Most of those who research, and ponder the significance of, this massive crime no longer quarrel about the major facts and particular details. The most immediate reasons the German leadership under Hitler decided to pursue the "final solution to the Jewish question" are more or less clear. Some differences of opinion exist about how much weight to give individual factors, but all those who participate in research and discussions about the Holocaust agree on its significance as a historical watershed. What remain contentious are questions of its ultimate meaning and deeper causes. The answers will, no doubt, continue to be fragmentary. Nonetheless, historians have a duty to seek them.

The analysis in this book is based almost exclusively on sources that appeared in print in the nineteenth and twentieth centuries—polemics, petitions, memoirs, journalistic articles, and parliamentary protocols. As diverse and often contradictory as these documents are, they have one thing in common: the authors did not know what Germans would do to European Jews between 1933 and 1945. No matter whether they wrote in 1820, 1879, 1896, or 1924 and no matter whether they praised German anti-Semitism, propagated Jew hatred and promoted the Aryan race, or sounded warnings about the impending political consequences of the Great Depression and the popular appeal of Hitler and the Nazi Party, none of the authors cited in this book knew the outcome of history. Unlike us today, no one who lived, observed, and made judgments back then had to explain a crime that beggars description. That's what makes these sources so valuable.

I have also used unpublished sources drawn from my private family archive, a twenty-foot-long corpus of letters, diaries, reminiscences, and photos that I inherited and cataloged four years ago. If German anti-Semitism was a mass phenomenon, unchecked by social disapprobation, during the nineteenth and early twentieth centuries and if people before 1933 had little reason to conceal anti-Semitic attitudes, one would expect to find those attitudes expressed in personal correspondence and family memoirs. In fact, I did find examples of them in the material left behind by my forebears, and I have used them as sources for this book. As is now widely acknowledged, German Jew hatred and anti-Semitism were not restricted to certain institutions or to well-known anti-Semites.

By themselves, of course, isolated statements of hostility toward Jews tell us nothing about the prehistory of the Holocaust. To understand anti-Semitism within Germany's Gentile majority, one has to talk about the skills, educational fervor, and rapid social rise of striking numbers of German Jews. Only then will the contrast emerge between them and the relatively lethargic German majority, revealing why anti-Semitism could gain so large a foothold in German society. Only then can we see anti-Semites as people motivated in large part by jealousy and resentment.

Anyone who wants to understand the past has to reconstruct the social conditions and habits of thought that prevailed in earlier historical epochs. This process allows us to trace how different historical

factors, both positive and negative, interacted and sometimes reinforced one another. For that reason, I am interested not just in the
specific history of Jewish emancipation and advancement in Germany
but also in the mental world of early-nineteenth-century German
nationalism, the demise of liberalism, and the triumph of collectivism.
I also devote attention to the consequences of wars, crises, and economic challenges, as well as to the reforms of the Weimar Republic.

I have limited the scope of my investigation to modern German history, so I begin around 1800 and trace the relations between German
Jews and German Christians for the following 130 years. I touch only
briefly on anti-Semitic associations and regulations in other German-
speaking countries of the period. The point is not to ferret out every
anti-Semite I could find but rather to examine how and why a particularly virulent form of anti-Semitism developed in Germany and
attracted so many supporters throughout all strata in German society.
How, when, and why did Germans—broadly speaking—become anti-
Semites, willing to put their beliefs into practice? Those who merely
hand out blame, in an attempt to feel as though they are on the right
side of German history, will never be able to explain how a majority of
Germans came to support the official state goal of getting rid of Jews.
As German president Theodor Heuss said in 1949, the question is why
so many people abetted the "cold brutality of rational pedantry" and a
"biological materialism that recognized no moral categories."[14]

Investigating the development of German anti-Semitism is made
more complicated by the fact that during this time terms like *Germans*
and *Jews* were used somewhat haphazardly and without a single fixed
meaning. By 1933, more than 80 percent of Jews residing in Germany
were German citizens: that is, they were Germans. They saw themselves
as, and were usually quite proud to be, German. While a distinction
can be made between Jewish Germans and Christian Germans on the
basis of religious tradition, this was not the only sense in which the
term *Jewish* was used during this era, and to focus on it exclusively
would contradict the self-definition of increasing numbers of people
who did not consider themselves religious at all.

The cluster of related German words translated as "Jewry" originated in medieval times as a social group designation, akin to the word *peasantry*. In the course of the nineteenth century, these words evolved to encompass a religious distinction (Judaism as opposed to Christianity) and a national-identity distinction (Jewishness as opposed to Germanness). Because of this gradual evolution, many people who used those terms between 1800 and 1933 did so in different ways and rarely with any degree of strictness. In this book I have tried to remain faithful to these varying perspectives, instead of imposing a linguistic precision, however theoretically desirable, that would be foreign to the period.

At no point were Germans predestined to follow a path that ended in the abyss of inhumanity, but ultimately that was indeed the path they went down. The goal of my work is not to stir up academic controversies about specific details or isolated issues. Rather, I am trying to comprehend the overall internal logic of a historical process that led to the German reign of terror from 1933 to 1945 and the murder of millions of innocent people. My hope is to make some progress, at least, toward answering the double question that has elicited so much bewilderment: Why the Germans? Why the Jews?

1

JEWISH EMANCIPATION

A HALFHEARTED INITIATIVE FROM ABOVE

On August 6, 1806, the Holy Roman Empire of the German Nation disappeared from the face of the earth. It had survived for a thousand years, but in the end it collapsed with barely a whimper under the pressure of the French Revolution and the Napoleonic Wars. Goethe succinctly noted: "Despite everything, [its death] produced a sad sensation in me." Contemporaries didn't know it at the time, but they were standing on the threshold of a stormy epoch. Before long, people would be ripped out of the usual patterns of their lives, and age-old knowledge, artisan skills, and established customs would become worthless. Hundreds of small duchies and autonomous territories would be dissolved with the stroke of a pen. Interdependence established over generations would cease. Common people would become less and less religious, and the church's influence on everyday society would fade.

Secularization proceeded rapidly in the south and west of German-speaking Europe. The dismantling of religious institutions such as monasteries would later be described as a "benevolent [form of] vio-lence" and seen as part of the Enlightenment reform movement, a view that ignored the countless and sometimes crude cases of disap-propriation benefiting university libraries, portrait galleries, and state coffers—as well as ordinary people. In Bavaria, tradesmen and farm-ers built spacious houses from the bricks of demolished convents, monastery chapels, and other buildings. At the same time, enlightened aristocrats and the bourgeois modernized legal codes and advanced economic change. The Vienna Congress of 1814–15 temporarily put the brakes on innovation, shored up traditional authorities, and pro-tected agricultural, artisanal, and patrician conservatism in the face of Western European modernism. Yet this only delayed the Industrial Revolution in Germany, and when it did get under way, it was all the more turbulent, sealing the demise of many older traditions.

Compared with progress in the the Habsburg Empire and Russia, the emancipation of German Jews began early. Yet unlike in France, this emancipation was not enacted on a single day but rather was drawn out over the span of more than a hundred years, from 1806 to 1918. What was particularly German about this process was that Jewish emancipation remained a topic of debate for so long. German society took one step back for every two steps forward. There was also a discrepancy between the legal situation and the reality, espe-cially when it came to government and military service. In a certain limited sense, this stop-and-go process can be compared to the eman-cipation of African Americans during and after the Civil War in the United States. Things were made immeasurably more complex, how-ever, by the fact that Germany did not even exist as a nation-state until 1871. Rules and regulations governing Jews differed wildly in the thirty-seven individual states that made up the German Confederation, as well as within the (partly overlapping) Kingdom of Prussia and from city to city.

Prussia exemplifies both the drawn-out nature of Jewish emanci-pation and the reasons why the general population often greeted it with resistance. After Prussia came under Napoleonic domination, the Cities Ordinance of November 19, 1808, lifted guild restrictions and guaranteed all citizens the right to pursue the trades of their choice, regardless of class, birth, or religion. Laws drafted by Prussian reformer Karl August von Hardenberg and enacted on November 2, 1810, and September 7, 1811, bolstered those rights. Such laws were aimed at unleashing entrepreneurial spirit, encouraging competition, and mobilizing capital, yet according to historian Friedrich Meinecke they "were vehemently opposed by those who were supposed to benefit from them."[1] Far from welcoming the reforms, most German Christians considered them "a plague." Jews, however, seized upon their new freedom to practice trades of their choice and to better themselves economically.

Longstanding prejudices barred Jews from running apothecaries or operating public scales, but those trades turned out to be less and less significant as time went on. Thus, even at this early stage, a peculiar situation arose. Most Jews were enthusiastic about change, while most Christians viewed it with hesitancy. Traditionally submissive to feudal lords and clergymen, German Christians were far less able to exploit the state's encouragement of personal initiative than their Jewish peers.

The contrast between Jewish entrepreneurial spirit and Christian readiness to obey authority was similar to that between Jews' desire for freedom and Christians' fear of it. Taking risks is part of freedom, and precisely that frightened the Christian majority. Old certainties collapsed under the massive force of economic freedom and the Industrial Revolution, and most Germans experienced legal and material progress as personal loss. By contrast, Jews had little to lose from the dissolution of the old world of guilds and castes, pastors and patricians, the mob and the aristocracy—and everything to gain from a new, wide-open future. Despite starting from a position of material poverty, they put their faith in their intellectual assets and attained material success with admirable speed. To speak in everyday language: they got somewhere in life.

On March 11, 1812, as Prussia was preparing to enter the military coalition that would eventually throw off the yoke of Napoleon, King Friedrich Wilhelm III signed an edict, drawn up by Enlightenment intellectual Wilhelm von Humboldt, entitled "Concerning the Civic Relations of Jews." Against "the stubborn resistance of the monarch," his chancellor of state, Karl August von Hardenberg, pushed through the reform and was "pleased" to announce it to the Jews of Prussia. They, in turn, somewhat optimistically saw the new law as "a complete declaration of liberty" and celebrated it "with ceaseless jubilation."[2] The edict granted Jews citizenship and the right to serve in Prussia's armed forces. It also reaffirmed that they could work in trades of their choosing and could own property. But Jews remained excluded from the officer ranks in the military and were restricted in the governmental and electoral functions they could perform. Paragraph 3 of the law also mandated that they adopt last names. Some chose traditional Jewish tribal and caste names (Levi, Cohn); other used the places from which they hailed (Bamberger, Sinzheimer); others were simply given animal designations (Wolf, Katz, Kuh) by Prussian bureaucrats with a fondness for the "cruel popular humor of the Germanic tribes." No small number of Jews followed romantic fashion and took names that paid tribute to the beauties of nature (Feilchenfeld, Silberklang, Rosenzweig, Lichtblau, or Blumenthal).[3]

If we compare Jewish emancipation in Germany not with France but with neighboring Russia, which encompassed much of what is today Poland, progress was quick. For Jews living in the Russian Empire, who were restricted in their freedom of movement and subject to recurring pogroms, post-1812 Prussia was a near paradise of legal guarantees and social opportunity—even though advances there were not without setbacks. During the post-Napoleonic Restoration, starting with the Congress of Vienna in 1814, the Prussian government retightened some of the restrictions. In 1822, for example, Jewish citizens were prohibited from teaching school "because of the infelicities that have been shown when they do so."[4] Still, in the unrest from 1830 to 1849, Prussia again reversed course and loosened some of the constraints.

In some German-speaking states, the first steps toward full equality for Jews under the law began only after 1860. On July 3, 1869, the Alliance of Northern German States adopted the Law concerning the Equality of Confessions, and it was binding for the united German nation created in 1871. Its two key sentences read: "All still-existing restrictions on civic and citizenship rights based on differences of religious creed are hereby revoked. In particular, eligibility for participating in local and national political representation and holding public office is declared to be independent of religious creed."[5]

Consequently, the 1870s saw some movement toward accepting Jews into public service and the higher ranks of the military, though it diminished by 1880. Ten years later, Paul Nathan—one of the leading Jewish political activists in the late Wilhelmine period—determined that most government administrations no longer had any Jewish members. In 1901, Prussian minister of justice Karl Heinrich Schönstedt was called before parliament to explain why he had yielded to conservative pressure and was no longer appointing any Jewish notary publics. He justified himself by claiming the judicial administration was "the only one that hired Jewish assessors at all." "All other state administrations," he said, "refuse to take on Jewish gentlemen." At that juncture, there was not a single Jewish career officer in the Prussian military, nor had any Jew been promoted to officer rank in the reserves since 1886. In 1911, the secretary-general of the Association of German Jews, Max Loewenthal, again tried in vain to find a single Jewish officer in the Prussian army. A scandal comparable to France's Dreyfus affair was impossible in Germany. There were no such Jewish officers whom German anti-Semites could have denounced, degraded, and hounded from the service.[6]

As documents from the various parliaments and governmental administrations amply demonstrate, tacit discrimination had become part of the German civil service, even though it officially contradicted the letter of the law. Those in power during the Wilhelmine era (1870–1918) publicly denied discriminating against Jews, even as they encouraged the practice everywhere in the everyday running of government offices. Here and there, they may have tolerated a "concessional Jew"—a term that was actually used. But as a rule, they behaved as the city fathers in the town of Ueckermünde did in 1904, when they failed to fill a vacant teaching spot. In the words of the town chronicle: "No appropriate candidate answered the announcement, only a Jew. As this was not desired, the town faced a desperate situation."[7]

Still, as hesitant as Christians were to accept Jews as full-fledged fellow Germans, Jews were protected from violence and economic discrimination. That aided their rise between 1810 and 1870 from underprivileged subjects to active and successful citizens. One powerful symbol of Jews' increasing status was the New Synagogue in the central part of Berlin. The building was completed well before full legal emancipation was achieved, and its golden dome complemented those of the royal palace and the still rather modest Protestant cathedral. No other major European metropolis featured a comparable architectural expression of Jewish self-confidence. ("The biggest and most splendid 'church' in the German capital is a synagogue!" hissed Heinrich von Treitschke in 1870.) The royally appointed architect August Stiller had overseen the beginning of its construction in 1859, and the opening ceremony on September 5, 1866, was attended by city and state elites, including Prussian prime minister Otto von Bismarck. It was an uplifting and inspiring ceremony, with only one prominent, and telling, absence: His Christian Majesty King Wilhelm I. Judaism was not deemed equal to the Christian faiths, as it was, for example, in the Netherlands. Nor would it be granted the status of a *Religionsgemeinschaft*—a kind of state sanction for religions deemed to be legitimate—until after 1918. From 1871, German legislation guaranteed individual Jews equality before the law. But as a group bound by their religion, they were still only tolerated.

SELF-EMANCIPATION VIA EDUCATION

The start-and-stop emancipation of Germany's Jewish minority matched the sluggishness of German reforms in general. Yet in contrast to the majority of Christians, who tended toward passivity, German Jews actively emancipated themselves, and they did so with remarkable speed, identifying and using what opportunities there were as they became available. With its halfhearted reforms, its slow economic growth before 1870, and its strong legal protections, Germany was a place that rewarded individual initiative and the spirit of entrepreneurship.

Unlike in the agrarian past, when people's social status usually remained constant, modern men needed curiosity, inventiveness, cleverness, adaptability, social intelligence—and, above all, education. From the very beginning of the nineteenth century, it was obvious that Jewish pupils had a relatively easy time acquiring the skills that would be necessary in the new culture: reading, writing, and mathematics. Unlike most Christians their age, Jewish boys learned to read early on, even if it was usually religious texts in Hebrew. They were born, so to speak, not with a silver spoon in their mouths but with an intellectual legacy. "A village without a school should be abolished," reads the Talmud. Thus, in 1911, Arthur Ruppin could write of impoverished Eastern European Jews: "Even among the poorest classes in Eastern Europe, the necessity of learning and knowledge, at least for a family's sons, is so accepted that there are thousands of poor artisans and merchants in Galicia who spend one-tenth to one-sixth of their weekly income (from one to six guilders) on the *melamed* (teacher of Hebrew and other basics)."[8]

The thirst for knowledge was a by-product of the Jewish religion and a response to centuries of legal disempowerment. Young Jews learned how to think abstractly, pose critical questions, and ponder various possibilities. They honed their intellects on books, by communally reading, interpreting, and debating Holy Scripture. The practice of their religion was a form of mental exercise, and thus they became mature in Kant's political sense. In addition, most Jews could speak two or three different languages with various forms of grammar and expressive subtleties, and they frequently used both the Hebrew and the Latin alphabets. Young men who had been schooled this rigorously possessed a broad, expandable intellectual basis that allowed them to use education to climb the social ladder. In 1743, as a fourteen-year-old boy growing up in the city of Dessau, the philosopher Moses Mendelssohn not only knew how to read and write but was fluent in Yiddish, Hebrew, Aramaic, and German. In the fall of that year, Mendelssohn moved to Berlin, following his beloved teacher, Rabbi David Fränkel. Legend has it that when the watchman who admitted him to the city asked what he intended to do in Berlin, his reply was: "Learn." (The watchman, for his part, noted: "Today six oxen, seven pigs, and a Jew passed through Rosenthal Gate.") Mendelssohn went on to achieve wealth as a silk manufacturer and fame as a man of letters.[9]

Representatives of the Jewish community were quick to realize how important systematic instruction would be for future generations. They placed great emphasis on Jewish children's learning good German and founded commercially oriented Jewish schools in cities like Berlin, Breslau, Hamburg, Dessau, Seesen, and Frankfurt am Main. These institutions shared the main goal of "reducing the misery and contempt under which we suffer and sigh."[10]

The attitude of Christian clergymen was very different. They emphasized rote memorization of canonical beliefs, dismissed debate as Satan's work from which they had to protect laymen, and rarely showed much interest in the systematic education of members of their flocks. A Christian family of peasants, in which few members could read and write, would typically need two or three generations of elementary education before the first member would succeed in gaining an academic degree, and even then it would be decades before that person and his offspring would feel comfortable with their new social position. As late as the twentieth century, it was still common for Christian parents to warn their offspring: "Reading is bad for your eyes!"

In contrast to Jewish educational institutions, German public schools long lacked a solid material and intellectual foundation. Friedrich Wilhelm I may have introduced compulsory education in

Prussia in 1717, but the initiative, underfunded, would not bear any real fruit until the second half of the nineteenth century. Classrooms were overcrowded, and incompetent teachers were interested more in pocketing school fees than in passing on knowledge. Decommissioned and invalid soldiers, building superintendents, aging carriage drivers, and failed artisans often took up "the career of the beater," as it was known, enforcing their wills with cane blows and boxed ears. Instruction under such headmasters in the countryside, as one contemporary observed, "rarely went beyond learning how to spell."[11]

At the First General German Teachers' Conference, held in Erfurt in 1876, the chairman, Julius Berger, called for universal corporal punishment. Punitive pedagogy, he argued, was necessary to overcome "roughness and wild spirits, laziness and dissipation, the presumptuousness of adolescents and their precocious maturity." A contemporary critic noted: "I knew that the pedagogy of school beatings had many advocates in Germany. But only in Erfurt did I realize that almost everyone supported it. Children are educated not to be free but to submit."[12]

Many Christian parents, together with leading clergymen in both of the main Christian denominations, rejected the idea of children's receiving public education. Aristocrats feared that it might prompt their subjects to rebel. Community mayors opposed compulsory education "partly because of poverty, partly because of greed, and partly because of their own crude intellects." Never a great friend of public education, King Friedrich II decided in 1779 that Berlin should import some dedicated schoolmasters from abroad, as long as they weren't "too expensive." In the countryside, though, it was enough for children to be able to read and write a bit. "If they know a lot," the king reasoned, "they will run to the cities and want to become state secretaries or something."

Friedrich soon sacrificed his subjects' public education in favor of building up Prussia's military might. A series of educational initiatives were launched in Prussia at the beginning of the nineteenth century, but they were restricted to universities and university-track academies (*Gymnasien*). Expansion of public schools and systematic training for teachers never got beyond the initial stages, and as of 1840, Prussia once again began to sink in a reactionary swamp. A few statistics suffice to illustrate the state of education in Christian Prussia in 1870. Of thirty-six thousand school teaching positions, three thousand were unoccupied, and twenty thousand were paid worse than those of court bailiffs or train station attendants. Meanwhile, the average class size was eighty pupils per teacher, twice what it was in Switzerland.

In 1848, delegates to the Frankfurt Assembly—the constitutional gathering at which representatives from the various German states had tried and failed to unify Germany as a democratic nation—made a series of educational demands. "Knowledge and its teaching are free," one statement had read. "Instruction and education are the province of the state and are, with the exception of religious instruction, to be raised above the supervision of clergymen. No fees should be levied for instruction in public schools."[13] But it took several decades for actions to be taken toward realizing this ideal; the expansion of the public education system began to slowly make progress only in 1872, as Prussia tripled its expenditures for schools, teacher salaries, and training seminars. And it took even more time for the belated state initiative to produce concrete results. In 1886, educational reformer Eduard Sack determined that 14 percent of Prussians over the age of ten had never seen the inside of a classroom. And most of those who had received instruction, he claimed, "could only read and write at remedial levels." Basing his findings on official sources from 1876, Sack estimated the percentage of pupils capable of basic mathematics and elementary reading and writing skills as "20 percent at the most."[14]

Even at a glance, school statistics highlight the contrast between Christian neglect of education and the energetic, even aggressive Jewish approach to learning. In 1905, the edition of a journal put out by the newly founded Office of Jewish Statistics in Berlin was titled *The Role of Jews in the Instructional System in Prussia*. One of the authors was Arthur Ruppin, who in 1904 founded the Association for Jewish Statistics and published a number of studies about the demographic and social life of German Jews. He continued to explore the theme in the second edition of his book *Jews Today* (*Die Juden der Gegenwart*), published in 1911.

The statistics concerning Prussian schools and universities that Ruppin collected and analyzed in the early twentieth century yield a clear picture of the differing speeds at which German Christians and Jews took advantage of education. In 1869, 14.8 percent of pupils at university-track secondary schools came from Jewish families, while 4 percent of the population said they were of Jewish faith. In 1886, 46.5 percent of Jewish pupils in Prussia earned degrees above those of simple trade schools. By 1905, that number rose to 56.3 percent. The comparable figures for Christian pupils in the same period were just 6.3 and 7.3 percent, respectively. Thus, compared with their Christian peers, Jewish pupils were around eight times more likely to earn a better class of secondary-school degree. Gentile pedagogical reformers like Friedrich Dittes praised Jews' "excellent talent and lively interest in intellectual work" and their "extremely enthusiastic" participation in educational issues: "Parents stress the importance of learning to their children and carefully monitor their progress. Not infrequently, those children are well ahead of their Christian schoolmates in terms of intellectual curiosity and persistent diligence."[15]

What also clearly emerges from the statistics is how concerned Jewish parents were that their daughters be educated as well. In 1901, in terms of their proportion of the overall population, 11.5 times as many Jewish girls went on to higher grades as their Christian counterparts. Depending on their ages, the former often behaved in "unruly and precocious fashion" and received middling marks for diligence and conduct. Many teachers complained that their Jewish pupils were too interested in "social diversions." But they studied hard and ended up with excellent marks.

The statistics cited above reflect average differences in education among Christians and Jews in German society. In some districts of

Berlin, the provinces of East Prussia, Posen, and Silesia, and in the Prussian part of Saxony, the percentages of Jewish and Christian students at *Gymnasien* and university diverged much more widely. For instance, in 1910, the vast majority of sixth-grade pupils at the Mommsen *Gymnasium* in Berlin were of the Jewish faith. "Intellectual arrogance was not entirely absent, but there was good camaraderie," philosopher Rudolf Schottlaender recalled. "The teachers, too, avoided any anti-Jewish remarks, although almost all of them were Gentiles."[16]

Naturally, pupils who did well at *Gymnasien* often continued to have success at university. In 1886–87, Jews accounted for 10 percent of Prussia's university students, although by then Jews made up only around 1 percent of the total population. Official statistics also showed that Jewish students had the lowest average age, while Catholic students had the highest, with Protestants in the middle. Prussian statisticians did not comment on this striking finding other than to note: "Jewish students seem on average to have better abilities and develop more diligence than Christians."[17]

In 1902, the confessional makeup of Prussia's students also attracted the attention of the educational reformer and philosopher Friedrich Paulsen. In terms of educational zeal, Paulsen determined, Catholics lagged more than 50 percent behind their Protestant peers, and Jews were far ahead of both. "The causes for the disproportional participation of the Jewish population at university are obvious," Paulsen wrote. Among Jews, he said,

> there is a strong urge to improve one's social position, and a university education is the most readily available, indeed the only way forward, since careers in the army are forbidden. One should also not overlook the fact that the Jewish population possesses intellectual curiosity and excellent strength of will, paired with a talent for accepting sacrifices in pursuit of a goal. Thus it is that they send a

disproportionate contingent to secondary schools and universities, even though they subsequently encounter difficult and sometimes insurmountable obstacles in their chosen careers, particular in the civil service. As a consequence, those who are rejected push their way into the careers that are open to them, becoming doctors, lawyers, and academics.[18]

Jewish enthusiasm for education was noticeable not only in Germany. The picture was similar at *Gymnasien* in Prague. There, too, even relatively impoverished Jewish merchants strove to give "the best possible education to their sons." This, recalled philosopher Hans Kohn in his memoirs, was "characteristic of Jewish parents and indicative of their respect for learning."[19] The same hunger for knowledge could be observed in Vienna, Kaunas, Budapest, and the parts of Russia in which Jews were allowed to settle. In 1870, when the first classical academy opened in Mykolaiv, Ukraine, 38 Christian and 105 Jewish pupils passed the entrance examinations. Around the same time, it was reported from Odessa: "All the schools are full, bottom to top, with Jewish pupils, and to be honest, the Jews are always the best in their class."[20]

Thinking back on his adolescence in the town of Motol, near the Belarusian city of Pinsk, the first president of Israel, Chaim Weizmann, recalled that education was not compulsory for the children of Russian peasants around 1880. Some attended school every once in a while, while others didn't go at all. Jews, however, sent all of their sons to school so that they "achieved a high level of formal education." Weizmann concluded: "The non-Jewish population simply didn't possess the overwhelming thirst for knowledge that made Jews constantly pound on schoolhouse doors."[21] Weizmann himself, who came from a desperately poor family, got his secondary school degree in Pinsk, before studying chemistry at the University of Darmstadt in Germany.

Around 1900, the Russian Jewish writer Sholem Aleichem had one of his most well-loved heroes, Tevye the Milkman, say of his daughter Hodel: "She gleams like a piece of gold, and to my misfortune, she also has a keen mind. She writes and reads Yiddish and Russian and consumes books as though they were dumplings. You'll be asking yourself: How does Tevye's daughter get hold of books, when her father deals in butter and cheese?" Tevye also relates anecdotes about other young people, the children of tailors and cobblers, who attend *Gymnasium* and university: "You should see the endurance and diligence they display when studying. . . . They live in attics, eat pestilence and bad luck for lunch, and then have sickness for dessert. They don't see a scrap of meat for months. And if there's a party, six of them will chip in and share a roll and a herring."[22]

During the 1913–14 school year, a Viennese teacher named Ottokar Němeček looked into the relative educational success of Christian and Jewish students. He didn't investigate what percent of each group went on to study at the next level—the trend was too obvious. Instead, he looked into what specific areas each group excelled in. He evaluated the grades received by 1,539 male and female students at three Vienna secondary schools. In addition, he conducted various tests with several hundred pupils to determine their cognitive abilities, in particular their verbal skills, memory, and the speed with which they could draw associations and put them into writing.

Jewish students excelled at the tests, while their marks for conduct were below average. The reason for this, Němeček concluded, resided in "the greater liveliness of Jews, who, as every teacher will attest, are much more prone than Christian pupils to chatter and cause disturbances." Likewise, the marks Jewish students received for diligence were significantly worse than those given to their Christian classmates, and yet there was a higher percentage of Jews than Christians (26 to 16) among those who had received an overall grade of "very good" or "good." Jews were hardly represented (4 versus 23 percent) among students who had been deemed merely "passable." Jewish pupils consistently achieved better results in German, French, English, and history, and that pattern was the same in math, chemistry, and physics, as well as commercial and legal subjects.

For Němeček, these were the subjects that primarily tested pupils' intelligence, and he saw as the explanation for the divergence "the greater maturity of Jewish pupils' ability to think abstractly" together with their quickness of wit, speed in writing, larger vocabularies, and greater emotional alertness. The only subjects in which Christian pupils did better than their Jewish peers were drawing, penmanship, and gymnastics. Němeček was interested more in collecting data than in investigating the reasons behind them. But he did note what he felt were the main possibilities suggested by his findings: "It cannot be determined here whether we are dealing with an innate proclivity or the product of a milieu in which some children are from an early age witness to and participants in a more lively intellectual exchange."[23]

No matter what experts saw as the root cause of Jews' educational advantage, non-Jews sensed the difference and reacted with displeasure. In 1880, liberal Reichstag deputy Ludwig Bamberger noted Jews' "unusual thirst for learning" and "obvious haste" to catch up on what had long been forbidden to them and concluded: "It is certain that the revival of hateful behavior toward them is closely connected to these things."[24]

We can get an idea of how that connection played out in everyday school life from an anecdote related by writer (and later Nobel Peace Prize laureate) Bertha von Suttner in 1893. In an open letter, she described an incident she witnessed at a family friend's house: Leopold—a pupil in a comprehensive secondary school—comes home with his report card, telling his parents, "Oh, I'm so happy." They ask why, and he says, "Because I'm alive in the world, and the world is lovely, and I'll go far. I'm top of my class again." Some time later, Leopold comes home with a long face, sobbing. It isn't that he has gotten bad marks—on the contrary. But a lazy bully, the son of an ox-headed anti-Semite, got hold of his cleverer classmate and said: "Hey, Jew boy, why are you working so hard? You'll never get anywhere. You're just another lousy Jew!"[25]

Although it never completely disappeared, the old-fashioned religious idea of Christian-Jewish rivalry faded significantly over the course of the nineteenth century. Rationalism gained the upper hand, and not just as an intellectual ideal but as a real product of the triumph of empirical sciences. Jews began to adapt their appearance and dress to the societies in which they lived. Some married Christians, converted, or became atheists, although among the converts there were those who changed religion only nominally so as to be able to "remain Jews in peace."[26] More and more frequently a Samuel Kohn would become a Siegfried Konitz, a Baruch a Bernhard, or an Esther an Else. New bourgeois social conventions, rapid economic mobility, and gradual legal emancipation broke down the boundaries of traditional religious segregation.

Jews had neither invented the mechanical loom nor sparked the French Revolution nor thought up the *code civil*, but they identified with progress, industrialization, and the idea of liberalism. For Jews, such things meant economic and political liberty both for themselves and for Christians. In premodern Christian Europe, as nineteenth-century historian Isaak Markus Jost characterized the situation up until 1800, Jews had been able to hope for little more than "protection from violence and permission to live." In return, they had to provide the entity that granted those with "money and gifts" and beseech to be allowed to perform "pathetic forms of trade," a concession that their Christian masters could always revoke on a whim.[27]

In 1832, the German Jewish political writer and democratic activist Ludwig Börne quipped that for centuries Christians had kept Jews in a hole in a cellar, which was full of dung but warm, while they themselves, "freely exposed to the frost," had practically frozen in place. Amid an emancipatory thaw, Börne looked forward to the coming competition with confidence: "When spring is here, we shall see who blossoms first, Jew or Christian." Jews would have to overcome no small number of hurdles and obstacles. Stubborn trade masters and professors, many of whom in Germany, sadly, "clung all the harder to their prejudices," rejected Jewish legal equality. But Börne was sure that such opposition would not deter "talented young men" but rather would spur them on "to do everything to pass every test." In fact, young Jews did begin to climb the social ladder at above-average speed. In 1808, Jews in Prussia had almost nothing. By 1834, 13 percent of them were part of the nascent upper middle class, while more than 50 percent were firmly middle class.[28]

Jewish Germans proved to be less cautious, stolid, and obedient than Christians. They were bolder and more flexible, and, statistically speaking, the average Jewish family led an easier and healthier existence than the typical Christian one. In 1840, twenty-one of every hundred newborn Christian infants died within a year, compared with only fifteen of every hundred Jewish babies. The Royal Prussian Office of Statistics attributed the discrepancy to the fact that "the Jewish wife does not have to do heavy labor outside her home, better preserves her energy when pregnant and while breast-feeding, and can keep a closer eye on her child." Jews also outlived Christians—a fact that statisticians attributed to unhealthy Christian eating habits as well as to Jewish temperance "in the enjoyment of spirits."[29]

As Jews rose in society, the walls of their "inner ghettos" began to fall. The man who personified the enlightened reform of Jewish religious rituals and rules was David Friedländer. A silk manufacturer in Berlin and a friend of Moses Mendelssohn's, Friedländer encouraged Jews to use the German language. He published a German reader for Jewish children and established the liberal-progressive movement within German Judaism. One of its aims was to ensure that "excessive religion" no longer hindered Jews' opportunities to demonstrate their abilities in art and science. The constant questioning of what was and wasn't allowed within Orthodox Judaism, which insisted on the maintenance of 248 commandments and 365 prohibitions, had kept Jews from applying the intellectual abilities they acquired through religious study to the secular world. Arthur Ruppin illustrated this idea with an anecdote about a young Jewish fellow from Galicia who sees a man looking in utter rapture at the full moon. Instead of joining in admiration of nature's beauty, the youth, who had been given a strict religious upbringing, asks: "Are we allowed to stare at the moon?"[30]

Freed from external and internal constraint, the Jews of Western and Central Europe gladly embarked on the journey into modernity. Thanks to their qualitative and quantitative educational head start, more and more Jews turned toward well-paying forms of intellectual labor or seized the entrepreneurial initiative. By 1895, half of all working Jews were self-employed, twice the percentage of their Christian peers. Statistics of this nature in rural areas are misleading since farmers were also classed as self-employed, but data about trade and commerce in cities yield striking insights into the connections between work and religion. In 1907, only 4.5 percent of Protestants working in these areas were self-employed. Among Catholics it was only 3 percent, compared with 37 percent for Jews.

The increased division of labor and the global expansion of trade also created the need for office and administrative workers, logistics experts, departmental directors, and financial comptrollers. Around 1900, only 3 percent of Christians belonged to the new social class of office workers, compared with 11 percent of Jews. Conversely, 25 percent of Christians earned their keep as uneducated laborers, in contrast to only 3 percent of Jews.[31]

Jews were often pioneers who put their faith in the future. "In contrast to the Christian," observed one contemporary, "the Jewish entrepreneur represents progress in the area of social life." Jews recognized the advantages of innovations more quickly and made them accessible to their customers.[32] Tax records show this difference quite clearly. In Frankfurt in the early twentieth century, the average Jew paid four times as much in taxes as the average Protestant and eight times as much as the average Catholic. In Berlin, Jews accounted for 30 percent of city tax revenues, although Jews constituted only 15 percent of the tax-paying population and only 5 percent of the population as a whole. In the economically backward region of Posen, the 4.2 percent of the population that was Jewish paid 24 percent of the taxes. The picture was similar in the towns of Beuthen, Gleiwitz,

Magdeburg, Breslau, and Bromberg as well as in the Grand Duchy of
Baden, Denmark, Hungary, and Italy. In Prussia in 1852, 22.5 percent
of door-to-door salesmen were Jewish. By 1895, that figure had
dropped to 8.8 percent, and by 1925 it was only 4.7 percent. In 1934,
sociologist Jakob Lestschinsky noted that "the golden times of the first
blossoming of capitalism" had brought to German Jews "more advantages than the comparable classes in the non-Jewish population." There
have been some disagreements about statistics concerning income
and wealth. Nonetheless, critical studies have concluded that prior to
World War I, German Jews earned five times the income of the average Christian.[33]

The discrepancies may not have been equally obvious throughout
the country, but they were registered everywhere. In 1894, historian
Theodor Mommsen wrote that the root cause of the anti-Semitic
"affliction" was "envy and the basest instincts, . . . a barbaric hatred
for education, freedom, and humanism." In 1918, looking back on
twenty-five years of activity, the Central Association of German Citizens of the Jewish Faith summed things up with these words: "Political and scientific anti-Semitism would have remained insignificant
without economic anti-Semitism. The economic rise of Jews was the
main reason that hatred for Jews became part of the culture of the
broad masses."[34]

Such transformations were particularly striking in rural parts of
Germany. One remarkable example was the southern German town
of Gailingen, which had an unusual but telling situation. In 1875,
seven hundred of the seventeen hundred inhabitants were Jewish, and
the town also had a Jewish mayor, Leopold Guggenheim, from 1870
to 1884. An inspection report filed with the regional office of the
Grand Duchy of Baden on September 12, 1878, found: "Whereas
forty or fifty years ago, the vast majority of the Israelites belonged to
the poorer segments of the population, they now significantly over-
shadow Christian citizens in terms of income." The report also analyzed the causes of the divergent social fortunes of Jewish and Gentile
inhabitants: "Almost all of [the Jews] live off trade (primarily the

trade in livestock) while the Christian residents are almost exclusively dependent on agriculture and day labor. Almost all the larger houses are owned by Israelites." The local hospital in the region was built as an Israelite institution and paid for with money from Jewish citizens. The hospital, of course, also admitted Christians, and the inspector noted that "Israelite generosity also attracts a lot of people who simply exploit it." Summarizing the state of affairs in Gailingen, he wrote: "Because of this gradually growing inequality in wealth, it is no wonder that there is a certain palpable tension between the two confessions."[35]

THE POWER OF FEAR

In the nineteenth century, the Christian majority may still have used the word *Jewish* pejoratively, but its connotation was different from what it had been before. Now it stood for quickness and eagerness for change. The accusation implicit in this usage reflected the unease with which Christians reacted to the dissolution of their comfortably familiar world order. Retreating into smug provincialism, Germans began to accuse Jews of rootless cosmopolitanism and a desire to destroy venerable traditions.

Reactionaries Karl Graf Finckenstein and Ludwig von der Marwitz had made such accusations as early as 1811, denouncing Hardenberg's reforms as an attempt to make "a new-fangled Jew state out of honorable old Brandenburg Prussia." A year later, political scientist Adam Müller painted a dark picture of what could come of the general desire for reform: "The aristocracy and the peasant class will fall, and in the end, there will only be merchants, artisans, and Jews."[36] Even Wilhelm von Humboldt, who otherwise vigorously supported Jewish emancipation and defended the cause against his hatefully anti-Jewish wife, Caroline, wrote that he was not fond of "new-fangled Jews."[37] In a similar instance of neurotic association, Friedrich Wilhelm IV dismissed Schiller's drama *William Tell* as "a play for Jews and revolutionaries."

The French Revolution made the masses a factor in politics. Henceforth, regardless of whether citizens had the right to elect parliaments, the populace influenced the course of events. In Germany, the innovative ideas emerging from France as of 1789 had strengthened elites' commitment to reform, including the integration of Jews into society. On the other hand, the same democratic element that brought about revolutionary change in other areas was skeptical of practical measures aimed at giving Jews equal legal rights. Enlightened statesmen and princes were forced to institute Jewish emancipation from above, often acting against the popular will. For reasons already described, most of society did not want emancipated Jews. The foundation of the emancipation movement thus remained weak.

At the Congress of Vienna, the representatives of the burgher-run cities of Frankfurt, Hamburg, Bremen, and Lübeck, together with many representatives from southern German cities, faced off against the aristocratic advocates of Jewish emancipation. "People fought for equality before the law and for human dignity," historian Fritz Schnabel wrote about the stunted ideas of freedom and equality in German culture. "They wanted to remove the barriers that restricted people's freedom to practice the trades of their choice. But they also attacked door-to-door merchants, tried to keep Jews in their place, and thought corporal punishment was an essential part of the legal system."[38] As soon as French influence started to wane, Jews were expelled from Bremen and Lübeck and excluded from all the important social associations in Frankfurt, be it the Scholars' Association, the Society for Museums of Art and Science, the doctors' and lawyers' trade associations, the Reading Society, or the Society for the Promotion of Practical Arts.[39]

The people who fueled the anti-Semitic "Hep, Hep" riots in southern Germany in 1819 and 1820 feared for their positions in society. They were craftsmen, students, small shop owners, and merchants. Philologists have never definitively determined the origins of the slogan "Hep, Hep" as an anti-Semitic rallying cry—some say it was short for *Hierosolyma est perdita*, "Jerusalem is lost"—but its practical meaning is beyond question. It was an insult and a threat. In his 1819 hate pamphlet *Der Judenspiegel* ("The Jew Mirror"), writer Hartwig von Hundt-Radowsky laid out the rationale behind the anti-Jewish actions: "With the rights granted to Israelites in many states, their duty toward Christian citizens has been violated. Those rights lead to the poverty and malnourishment that prevails in many regions since Jews choke off all the trade and industry of the Christian populace." The chamber of commerce in the city of Cologne described Jews collectively around this time as "winding weeds that latch on everywhere."[40] Hundt-Radowsky suggested that Jews should be "driven out," after first being stripped of their possessions: "We Christians are fully entitled to do this. Everything the Hebrews possess they have grabbed from us and other peoples." Hundt-Radowsky railed against the success that Jews recorded "in all profitable businesses ever since several states, guided by a misunderstood humanism, accorded them the freedom to choose their own trades, which is also a license to plunge Christians into misery." The situation was getting worse and worse, Hundt-Radowsky argued, since Israelites possessed a "boundless rabbitlike drive to reproduce themselves."[41]

Most Christian Germans of the time were less extreme than Hundt-Radowsky and worried primarily about Jewish competition. The nationalist economist Friedrich List typified this attitude; in 1820, he suggested keeping Jews under state control in order to soothe the Christian citizenry, who were increasingly fearful for their future. List saw national unity as "primarily a process of social integration," and that, combined with the fact that many Christian Germans regarded Jews "as a possible threat" to their own social prospects, meant that the state had a duty to protect the Christian majority.[42] In 1830, he remarked: "No community should be burdened with certain classes of people whose religion or general character is incompatible with upstanding society, i.e., Jews, separatists, etc." With that, Jews were lumped together with evildoers, revolutionaries, and enemies of unity who conspired to sow dissent among right-minded Germans.

At the 1848 Frankfurt Assembly, one of List's most prominent allies, the moderately leftist delegate Moritz Mohl, urged the body to exclude Jews from a catalog of basic German civil rights it had just approved. The constitutional committee at the assembly had demanded universal equality of everyone before the law, but Mohl suggested adding a caveat: "The special situations of the Israelite tribe are subject to special legal codes and can be regulated by the empire."[43] Mohl had no success with his proposed amendment, but then again neither did the constitution proposed by the assembly.

It's clear that fear of competition was at the root of resistance to emancipation and was present right from the beginning. In 1845, various Jewish communities throughout Prussia drafted petitions asking for full legal equality, which were then submitted to leaders on regional councils. The representatives were elected according to various class-specific rules, and when they discussed the issue of Jewish equality, a topic that had occupied them occasionally in the past, they reached divergent conclusions. In the Catholic Rhine region and in Westphalia, which were oriented toward France, the majority voted for the emancipation of the Jewish minority. But the situation was different in the Prussian province of Saxony (not to be confused with the state of the same name). People from towns there feared Jewish competition and "the influx, which is certainly not desirable, of Jews from overcrowded neighboring countries." Only four of sixty-six representatives voted for the emancipation petitions. Petitions in eastern and western Prussia were also rejected by a margin of roughly two to one. Likewise, representatives from Silesia voted no, concluding that "the masses are by no means free-minded enough to wish for Jewish emancipation." Representatives in Berlin and Brandenburg supported the measures out of political opportunism, while representatives from Pomerania simply ignored them.

Special circumstances applied in the provinces of the Grand Duchy of Posen, where a disproportionate number of Orthodox Jews lived. The Prussian emancipation edict of 1812 only partially applied to them, although a temporary order of June 1, 1833, had lifted some further restrictions. The political climate was complicated by quarrels with ethnic Poles, who made up more than 50 percent of the population, and the fact that the region was economically backward. A citizens' committee on Jewish affairs opined that after the easing of restrictions in 1833, "the Jews emerged from the confines where they had been kept in our towns and villages." Jewish "property and possessions" had dramatically increased, and it had not taken long for Jews "to take over high roads and market squares and dominate commerce and industry." If they were given full citizenship rights, the committee argued, "almost all the towns and villages in the Grand Duchy would come under the exclusive administration of Jews." (At the time, voting rights were tied to property ownership and membership in one of the Christian denominations; these were restrictions the petitions aimed to lift.) The chairman of the committee also pointed out what he saw as "the disproportionate wealth and power" of Jews in Posen. While the rural aristocracy was divided on the issue, the representatives of the towns unanimously rejected full emancipation. Instead, they supported a compromise that included the longest possible transitional period. The plan allowed individual Jews to achieve full citizenship if they served three years in the military or attended a secondary educational institution, including technical and trade academies, and received good marks in "mores and maturity."[44]

In 1848, a year when revolution threatened to break out in most German states, a student of Jewish theology at Heidelberg University named Israel Schwarz argued that the introduction of democratic procedure was the main obstacle to long-overdue legal reforms: "Many a [German] state would have already granted Jews equal rights, if it did not fear the unenlightened, raw, fanatical masses." The *Allgemeine Zeitung des Judenthums* ("General Jewish Newspaper") diagnosed a similar situation in Austria a year later: "Let us not forget Tyrol, or Hungary, where the powers that be had to postpone equality because of the popular mood, or Prague and its persecution of Jews."[45]

The building social unrest in the years preceding 1848 did not help the cause of emancipation, as the examples of Bavaria and Saxony show. In Bavaria, the conservative Ludwig I was forced in 1848 to abdicate in favor of his enlightened son Maximilian II. Supported by first minister Gustav von Lerchenfeld, he declared Jewish emancipation a major goal of his reign. It didn't take long for a poster caricaturing Maximilian as the "King of the Jews" to appear on the walls of Munich's Theatine Church, which also served as the church of the royal family. The general populace also vented their frustration with some six hundred petitions, containing nearly eighty thousand signatures.[46]

In the Kingdom of Saxony, too, the general populace pressured the royal family to maintain anti-Jewish restrictions. In 1840, there were only five Jews per ten thousand Christians in Saxony, or just over eight hundred in total. A small number lived in Dresden and a few more in Leipzig, where they fulfilled important roles in organizing foreign commerce and finances for the two cities' famous trade fairs. But they were forbidden from becoming everything from booksellers to bakers. The 1838 law that regulated the status of Jews in Saxony, which had been debated and approved by the representatives of both chambers of the Saxon parliament, was full of protective clauses inserted at the insistence of representatives from merchant and trade guilds. Jews were prohibited from working in Chemnitz, which had undergone early industrialization, and in the Saxon flatlands. They were also denied the right to vote or hold public office and to become small tradesmen. Jewish master artisans were allowed to take only Jewish apprentices and to sell wares they made themselves, and their number was required to be strictly proportionate to the Jewish presence in the overall population. In Dresden and Leipzig, Jews could own only one piece of real estate; elsewhere, property ownership was completely forbidden. Moreover, Jews could sell their property only after having owned it for a minimum of ten years. Dresden allowed "at most" four Jewish merchants, lest commercial streets "swarm with Jewish salesmen and trade fall into Jewish hands." Local civic leaders painted nightmare scenarios of "Jews inundating the entire country so that soon farmers wouldn't be able to sell a single calf without Jewish involvement." Reacting to a petition by local Jews to ease the discriminatory restrictions, a parliamentary representative named Dr. von Mayer simply answered: "We don't want to." The parliamentary expert on the issue, a man named von Gablenz, accused the petitioners of social presumption. "You'd like to be generals but not simple foot soldiers," he wrote, adding: "There's no such thing as Jewish common people or Jewish artisans." That flew in the face of the facts, but such statements reflected the general population's fears of how Jews might change society.[47]

As soon as the revolutionary spirit of the time led to relaxed state restrictions, prejudice and often violent anger broke out toward Jews. In late February 1848, self-proclaimed representatives of the winds of freedom that had blown into Dresden from Paris decided to "let off steam." The guild of tailors, for example, "whipped up a small mob to storm the shop of a small Jewish merchant who had attracted the ire of traditional tradesmen with his ready-made wares."[48]

Among those who took to the barricades in the popular uprising in Dresden in 1849 were Mikhail Bakunin and Richard Wagner. Wagner, in particular, was a paradigmatic example of the way that resentment provoked hatred for Jews among German intellectuals and artists. In 1850, when Wagner published his polemic *Judaism in Music*, he had yet to achieve recognition as a composer. Wagner wrote: "In the current state of affairs in the world, the Jew is more than emancipated. He already rules and will rule as long as money remains the force in the face of which everything we do loses its strength." Wagner called for "campaigns of liberation" against the "Jewification" of German music as a way of getting rid of competition. The composer asserted that Felix Mendelssohn-Bartholdy, who had died a few years before and was still quite popular, owed his status to "the incomprehensively barbarian confusion of the luxurious musical taste of our age." Wagner also accused him of plagiarism. Whenever Mendelssohn wanted to put "profound and powerful sensations of the heart" into music, Wagner claimed, he had no other option than to "seize hold of the styles" of his Gentile predecessors, the "true musical heroes."

But the main object of Wagner's vitriol was Giacomo Meyerbeer, "a composer known far and wide today." Wagner fumed: "With his productions, he has turned to a segment of the public whose confusion as to anything resembling musical taste he needed only to exploit." Meyerbeer, in Wagner's eyes, had made opera houses into mere "amusement locales" and owed his success to his ability to serve the public's need for distraction with trivialities: "These days that's the surest way to achieve artistic fame without becoming an actual artist." Wagner pilloried Jews, greedy for money and hungry for fame, as an "entirely foreign element" that "with the frenetic activity of worms" had swarmed over the "decaying" corpse of German musical excellence. This behavior, Wagner claimed, was analogous to "the impious distractedness and indifference of a Jewish community in a synagogue during the musical portion of the services."[49] Still, none of Wagner's assorted justifications could disguise the personal economic interest that clearly lay behind his animosity.

Also in 1848, the first volume in an encyclopedic series entitled *The Present Day* featured a lengthy article on "The Civic Circumstances of Jews in Germany," in which the anonymous author began by discussing "the causes of the most recent persecutions of Jews" in Germany and elsewhere. The article dismissed religious fanaticism as irrelevant, stressing instead the new social tensions that had resulted from Jewish economic success: "In our age [it is] the tendency toward wealth, and Jews' particular ambition in pursuing profitable business, that has made them a target for attacks from those classes of people that feel threatened by their ambition." The author deemed anti-Jewish feelings of this sort "more pardonable" than religious anti-Semitism, since more than a few Jews had "elicited rage against themselves by usurious domination and exploitation of rural folk." Christians, the author asserted, were increasingly impoverished as a result of massive economic changes, lacking orientation and often squandering their money on ill-advised investments. "By contrast," wrote the author, citing the procurator-general in Cologne, "Jews who lugged their wares from place to place ten years ago are the owners of luxurious estates."[50]

The political writer Gabriel Riesser likewise considered envy to be at the heart of Christian animosity toward Jews, arguing that anyone paying attention would perceive that "ninety-nine out of a hundred expressions of resentment against Jews have this as their basis." Riesser went on: "The man who has to compete with Jews in his trade believes he is being treated unjustly. . . . Here envy, which otherwise conceals its ugly face from others' scrutiny, is displayed nakedly and shame-lessly." Freed from their scruples, the majority of Germans were utilizing "the magnifying glass of greed" to focus attention on a few Jews, while "eagerly seizing every pretense" to conceal their own base material motivations. To this end, and in an effort to keep denying their fellow human beings full rights as citizens, they talked a lot about "public interests, nationality, and enlightenment." Riesser cited the example of a movement in southern Germany, led by an apothecary, that made no secret of the fact that "the exclusionary laws were a means of reining in competition."[51]

In 1927, the philosopher Julius Goldstein would express his bewil-derment at how quickly the German middle classes were identifying with ethnically tinged Nazi collectivism. It was a mystery to him why Germans, with their "ideas of equality and freedom," would fall under the sway of such crassly antirepublican notions. Goldstein missed the point. The German middle classes did not, as Goldstein supposed, need to "betray their own legacy" in order to follow Hitler. They had always taken an opportunistic approach to basic civil rights such as individual liberty and equality before the law. By the time of Hitler's rise, the betrayal of the fundamental principles of liberalism had long been established as part of the unwritten political consensus among Germans.[52]

2

THE ANXIETY OF GERMAN NATIONALISM

THE ORIGINS OF INFERIORITY

The Germans' lack of confidence and their resistance to progress should not be attributed to some sort of abstract national character. These characteristics have concrete historical roots in the territorial fragmentation of Germany into small states and its religious split between Protestantism and Catholicism. On the one hand, such divisions produced the diversity that even today is one of Germany's most highly prized qualities. The price, though, was a seemingly endless series of dynastic and religious wars, resulting in tremendous self-inflicted economic damage and mass poverty. In the collective German consciousness, the Thirty Years' War of 1618–48 was the murderous low point in a family feud. In the horrors of that conflict, Germany's urban populations declined by 35 percent, and rural populations shrank by a full half. Innumerable farmers' fields were destroyed, while hundreds of cities and thousands of towns were left in smoke and rubble. It would take decades for the survivors and their children to recover economically and regain a measure of prosperity.

The Thirty Years' War was a dramatic setback for Germany vis-à-vis its neighbors, and it left a persistent sense of trauma. It was no accident that in a 1947 letter to Thomas Mann, historian Friedrich Oertel referred back to the suffering and collective self-mutilation of that war as a key to understanding Germany's recent past. "Two German characteristics remain the lack of feeling for the *liberalitas* of internally confident people and the lack of appreciation for *dignitas*," Oertel wrote. "The legacy of the Thirty Years' War is still a tragic burden upon the history of our people and has prevented us from reaching maturity. When will its shadow ever fade? When will we catch up on what we missed?"[1]

In addition to the defining experience of the Thirty Years' War, Germany also suffered greatly 150 years later as a result of the wars between revolutionary France and the other European powers. The new social order Napoleon instituted in many German states contributed to new divisions. Victorious France played diverse regional and dynastic interests within Germany against one another. States in western and southwestern Germany came away clear winners, while Prussian and clerical interests lost out, as did the southern German states, which were at war for twenty years. Napoleon demanded massive war contributions, costly quarters for his troops, deliveries of food and animal feed, and tens of thousands of horses. He also set up a comprehensive system of spies. Blacksmiths, weavers, tailors, cobblers, tanners, furriers, and saddlemakers worked almost exclusively to meet the needs of the Grande Armée. Soldiers plundered civilians, raped women, and burned down houses. For the vast majority of Germans, the French occupation was a time of executions and murders, inflation, and lasting economic devastation. More than a few communities were still paying off debt accumulated during that period in the late nineteenth century; some wouldn't succeed in clearing the books until the rampant inflation of 1923.

The French emperor required a steady stream of German reinforcements for his army. Hundreds of thousands of young men from Württemberg, Thuringia, Prussia, and Bavaria were conscripted and met their deaths in Napoleon's campaigns in Spain and Russia. Even today, there are no reliable figures for the number of casualties in this twenty-year European war. They number at least three million, and some estimates put the total as high as five million, not including the hundreds of thousands of civilians who starved to death or succumbed to diseases that the troops brought to various regions of Europe.

In the winter of 1813–14 in the garrison town of Mainz, for example, eighteen thousand soldiers in the Napoleonic army died of typhus. The disease also killed twenty-five hundred local residents, a tenth of the city's civilian population. Historian Rudolf Virchow cited similarly appalling figures from the town of Torgau to illustrate the deadly scope of what was known as "garrison fever." There, he said,

> 8,000 horses and 35,000 men were crammed into a small city with a normal population of 5,100. In the period from September 1, 1813, to the surrender of the fortress on January 10, 1814, more than 20,000 people died—some 19,757 soldiers and 680 civilians. The total number of civilians who died in the sixteen months between January 1, 1813, to the end of April 1814, was 1,122, almost a quarter of the town's population. That same year, two-thirds of the French occupying forces and a quarter of the civilian population died of infectious diseases.[2]

The philosopher Johann Gottlieb Fichte was among those who succumbed to typhus in January 1814. His wife, Johanna, had picked up the disease while nursing wounded soldiers and passed it on to her husband. She herself survived.

The philosopher Charles de Villers, who emigrated from France to Germany in 1794, wrote a detailed letter, published in 1807, about how French soldiers conquered the northern German city of Lübeck. The military action lasted from November 5 to 8, 1806, and the soldiers promptly began making life a living hell for the civilians. "People were stopped and stripped of their clothes," de Villers wrote. "Those who dared show their faces in the streets were mistreated." The town herald was stabbed to death, most of the city's houses were plundered or ransacked, and official army requisitions were carried out "slam-bang with familiar French haste." Villers quoted the marauders: "'In the name of the emperor, give me your purse!—your watch!—your shirts!—your wife!—hand over all your money or you'll be killed!' These demands were usually backed up by a rifle, the tip of a saber or the barrel of a pistol. Some unfortunate people were strangled because they failed to react quickly enough." Villers also wrote about an eighteen-year-old girl who was raped by twenty-two soldiers: "The house, which I have seen with my own eyes, is located near the pond that forms part of the city wall. The monsters threw the unfor-tunate girl out into it as far as they could. But because the water was low, she got stuck in the reeds and mud of the pond's bank, where, after a few hours, she breathed her last."[3]

Horrors like this happened in thousands of German communities during the French occupation. In the wake of such experiences, republican, pro-French groups in Germany often turned into Franco-phobe secret societies, while cosmopolitan reformers became guer-rilla propagandists. The dramatist Heinrich von Kleist was one of these: his 1808 play *Die Hermannsschlacht* ("The Battle of the Teu-toburg Forest") is a quickly composed piece of agitprop. In it, Rome is a barely concealed cipher for Paris, which Arminius calls on his troops to annihilate: "For I see that the sphere of the world will not / Attain any rest from this brood of murderers / Until this nest of rob-bers is completely destroyed / And nothing but a black flag / Waves from its desolate heap of ruins." As long as the enemy, this "scornful brood of demons," is in Germania, Kleist has his hero intone, "hate will be my office, and revenge my virtue."[4]

Napoleon was not only a modernizer and a bearer of Western European ideas. For most of the Germans who lived through his reign, he was a force of destruction, a pitiless master who sent enormous numbers of young men to bleed to death in his battles. And it was precisely during this era—and at Napoleon's instigation, no less—that many Jews in parts of Germany were granted economic liberty and civil rights. In the eyes of most Christian Germans, Jews were among the winners of an age that knew a far greater number of losers.

The practices of Bonapartist military dictatorship partly account for German nationalism's innate hostility toward foreigners and its skepticism toward modernity. French troops left behind fertile soil for the resentments of nationalist intellectuals. Objectively speaking, Napoleon paved the road forward. But subjectively, most Germans associated the period of French occupation not with the advance of liberty, equality, and fraternity but with despotism, destruction, exploitation, starvation, misery, disease, and the deaths of a whole generation of young men. Even today, memorials in many German churches attest to the great numbers of men who died in the two final battles against Napoleon. In the northern German village of Priepert, for example, fifty men fell in 1813 and 1814, compared with nineteen villagers who would die in World War I and twenty-eight in World War II. In the nearby community of Menz, the figures are fifty-seven, twenty-eight, and thirty-nine, respectively.

The struggle against foreign domination by Napoleon permanently poisoned the German version of democratic ideals; from early on, values such as the division of governmental power, individual freedom, and bourgeois equality were all regarded with suspicion. With Napoleon as the backdrop, German democratic nationalism soon began going around in circles, developing its particular combination of weakness, timidity, self-doubt, resistance to progress, pent-up aggression, and xenophobia.

In 1806, Germans were less a people than a collection of peoples, cleft by the existence of numerous small states, each with its own history. Germans lived between the Curonian Lagoon, on the eastern Baltic Sea, and the Vosges Mountains in Alsace, between the Belt and Scheldt Rivers in the Netherlands and the Bohemian Forest and Salorno in Southern Tyrol, and a long way up the Danube River into

Eastern Europe. They formed the largest cultural, linguistic, and ethnic group in Europe. Located exactly in the middle of the continent, German territory was the scene of various migrations, wars, and religious conflicts. Consequently, Germans were the most mixed and diversely branched people in Europe, as well as the hardest to define.

A unified German people was a long-standing wish, which may help explain why so many ideas bubbled up about how this end was to be achieved. In any case, German nationalist revolutionaries had to focus both on overcoming an outmoded legal system that granted few social and political rights and on erasing traditional borders in the interests of national unity. For that reason, they had little choice but to invoke putative commonalities of language and history, German essence and blood.

German territory was shot through with a rich variety of border and transitional areas, and the difficulty of defining precisely what "Germany" was promoted both hypersensitivity toward minorities and foreigners and an obsession with melding the state and the people into a single unit. The lack of shared myths brought forth an often ridiculous emphasis on tales involving the Germanic tribes: Arminius's battle against the Romans in the Teutoburg Forest, the saga of the Nibelungs, Friedrich Barbarossa slumbering within the Kyffhäuser Mountain waiting to be awakened. Mythic importance was also attached to Martin Luther, various German-language thinkers and poets, and the 1813 Battle of Leipzig, although it was actually an international force that had defeated Napoleon there. Dedicated historians and scholars of German literature were charged with "discovering"—or, to be more accurate, artificially constructing—national historical sagas and folktales. This work was happening during a period when elsewhere myths were being discredited and rationalism was on the rise. It was an enterprise that could easily go awry.

The cultural obsession with questions of what should be considered German reflected Germans' lack of self-confidence. Ludwig Bamberger hit the nail on the head when he remarked in 1880 that "the incomplete emancipation of the German nation itself accounts for the obstacles Jewish emancipation must combat."[5]

As early as 1810, significant parts of the German nationalist movement had already started heading down an unhappy path. One of the first centers of intellectual hostility toward foreign elements of all kinds was the so-called German Table Society (Deutsche Tischgesellschaft). Founded in January 1811, on the initiative of Romantic poet Achim von Arnim, it was aimed at overcoming "outmoded" traditions and strengthening Prussian and German national sentiment in the face of Napoleonic rule. Frenchmen, "philistines," women, and Jews (including converted Jews) were forbidden from joining this boozy club. Partly seriously, partly in the spirit of an off-color joke, Arnim included a poem in the association's founding document: "The German table camaraderie / Defends itself with equal glee / Against the philistine and the Jew / So it will flourish through and through."

He prefaced this statement of intent with a couplet—"A Jew has, as everyone knows / Above all, a very, very clever nose"—and with a ballad about a fictional Jew from the entourage of a Baron Falckenstein, who is accused of some sort of misdeed and sentenced to "swing from the picturesque heights of the gallows so that his wife and children can see him." But this is just a threat intended to scare the Jew into reforming his ways, and the story has a "happy ending." The delinquent is pardoned, his beard is shaved off, and he converts to Christianity. He swears to desist from all forms of Jewish treachery and burns all the promissory notes he's collected. Arnim celebrates the figure's conversion with these words: "To the honor of Falckenstein / I drink a brimming glass of wine / And sing this song with all my might. / He who hasn't, once or twice, / Rubbed pig's fat in a Jewish beard / Knows nothing at all of Attic spice / And cannot love what is Antique."

Fellow Table Society member Peter Christian Beuth, a passionate supporter of trade guilds in Prussia, had fun imagining what would happen if Jews were given full equality before the law and allowed to own property and therefore enjoyed the right of patronage. It could happen, Beuth reasoned, that a poor Christian clergyman would then be called upon to circumcise the patron's son. Nonetheless, there was a "consoling" silver lining to this cloud. Since Christian clergymen could hardly be expected to have mastered the skills of circumcision, Beuth wrote, the logical and "desirable" result would be that many a young Jew would bleed to death.

Other members of this primarily anti-French club were the theorist of war Carl von Clausewitz, the authors Heinrich von Kleist and Clemens Brentano, musician and Goethe intimate Carl Friedrich Zelter, legal expert Carl von Savigny, and political philosophers Adam Müller and Johann Gottlieb Fichte. In 1812, when he was named the society's spokesman, Fichte tried to put an end to such xenophobic posturing, with its overtones of violence. In a critical speech before the group, Fichte argued that cheap jokes made at the expense of others only proved the crudeness of those directing the barbs. "Let philistinism and Jewry / Remain unscoffed at before me," Fichte concluded in a poetic couplet.[6]

On the surface, Beuth's and Arnim's outbursts seem like expressions of jingoism and racism, but they were manifestations of fear. The members of the Table Society were afraid of Jews because, as they saw it, Jews—with their "restless feet"—were trying to "slime, push, and force" their way into the sciences, arts, and society at large. The Hebrew infiltrators were making their presence felt in an uncertain epoch of fundamental change, "when the rules of our fathers are largely being overturned, when what is venerable and holy is being buried in the same grave as pigheaded insistence on outmoded tradition, when some are trying to bring about a massive confusion and mixing up of everything from laws to classes to religions." The members of the Table Society, as one of Arnim's friends explained in 1811, felt that the Jews' "curiosity and desire for renewal" made them into "critics of all existing orders." Accordingly, the society justified its exclusion of Jews as a "fundamental protest at the ephemeral novelties of the present day."[7]

Readers of Arnim's 1820 novella *Primogeniture* quickly get the sense that the author attributes his rage at Jews' mobility and adaptability to his lack thereof. In the novella, the eldest son of an aristocratic family lives abroad with his mother, as the family estate stands abandoned for thirty years because "the wealthy owners rarely enjoyed their wealth, while others looked up at them with envy." After his mother's death, Jews exploit the old man's weaknesses; they are personified by an unscrupulous shrew, the Jewess Vasthi, who murders her Christian foster child without remorse. (Clearly, some aspects of the ancient religious forms of anti-Semitism had not vanished entirely.) Arnim describes Vasthi as "a fierce Jewess with a nose like an eagle's, eyes like carbuncles, skin like a smoked breast of goose, and a belly like a mayor's." The French Revolution and the Napoleonic domination of Germany had allowed Jews to freely pursue their chosen trades, while the government and elites were also pro-Jewish. "Old aristocratic concessions were discontinued, and the Jews freed from their narrow ghetto street. . . . There was a lot of covert trading on obscure, dubious paths, and Vasthi was said to have used her time productively enough to curry favor with the government and buy the estate for a pittance in order to establish a salmiac factory." She quickly recovers the price of purchase by selling off some of the aristocrats' ancestral portraits, which are for Arnim a symbol of the decline of aristocratic power. In the now empty estate, a Jew—and a woman, no less!—produces a foul-smelling substance for use in modern industry. Ruthless, she sacrifices the beauty of the past for profit, replacing "tradition" with "credit."[8]

Arnim himself had inherited a hopelessly debt-ridden family estate in the village of Wiependorf in Brandenburg, and he never succeeded in getting his personal finances under control. His income was barely sufficient to pay the interest on loans he was forced to take out. He tried his luck growing fruit but was rarely solvent and could never provide his wife, Bettina, with an appropriately aristocratic lifestyle. At one point, he even had to let go his one remaining servant. In 1809, summing up what motivated the political and literary efforts of Arnim and consorts, the Bavarian governmental reformer Johann von Aretin wrote: "Behind the mask of hypertrophic German-ness simmers the rage over the loss they feel they have suffered."[9]

The attitudes of the Table Society were conservative-reformist, romantic-nationalist, and patriotic toward the Prussian state. Early revolutionary democrats—often dismissively termed demagogues in the parlance of the time—were completely different. They opposed aristocratic privilege, the political power of the church, and foreign domination. They rejected men like Arnim as remnants of an era of "silly aristocratic pride," which they wanted to end sooner rather than later. But in one respect the thinking of revolutionary and romantic nationalists converged: they tried with all their might to hinder Jewish emancipation. The hostility is evident throughout the political pamphlets and patriotic poems of men like Ernst Moritz Arndt, Friedrich Ludwig Jahn, Jakob Friedrich Fries, and, somewhat later, Heinrich Hoffmann von Fallersleben, who wrote the lyrics to Germany's past and present national anthem.

As a young man, Arndt had courageously opposed serfdom and advocated an international convention of the rules of war that would save countless civilian lives when it was finally adopted a century later. He has been honored as a vanguard proponent of German national unity and popular sovereignty by subsequent generations of democrats, as well as Nazis, East German Communists, and representatives of the Federal Republic of Germany. But this national hero cherished his anti-Jewish prejudices. The statutes of the revolutionary patriotic "German Societies" propagated by Arndt allowed only Christians, not Jews, to become members. A year after Napoleon's defeat in 1814, university students in the city of Jena, inspired by Arndt, formed the first of Germany's nationalist fraternities, changing the bylaws of predecessor organizations so that "only Germans and Christians" could join.

The practices of these fraternities, including their public festivals, confirm the pessimistic conclusions that German Jewish writers like Saul Ascher and Heinrich Heine drew about their democratically inclined Christian contemporaries. Arndt may not have wanted to see Jews cast back into their former condition of legal helplessness, but he never tired of warning against the dangers of Jewish equality. For Arndt, Jews were a "foreign plague and excretion" that threatened the alleged purity of German lineage: "Inconstant of mind and impulse, vagabond, opportunist, treacherous, criminal, and groveling, the Jew tolerates all manner of insults and misery rather than perform steady, hard work of the sort that ploughs fields, clears forests, breaks rocks, and makes things in workshops. Like flies and mosquitoes and other pests, he flits around here and there, always on the lookout for easy short-term profit, which he clutches in his bloody, pitiless claws whenever he succeeds in getting hold of it."[10]

Arndt dismissed his archenemies, the French, as a "greedy and mischievous people of Jews" who were forever trying to ruin Germans with "Jewish tricks and touches."[11] He warned against "poisonous Jewish humanism" and urged Germans to oppose it with "what is singular and German about us."[12] He suspected that cosmopolitanism was but a smoke screen intended to "reduce [us] to the level of Jews" and to "convert Germans into run-of-the-mill Jews as found throughout the world." He therefore demanded of his followers that they "once and for all divorce what is foreign from what is native."[13]

In the 1840s, as an old man, Arndt continued to rail against "the terrible equalizers and destroyers" of the industrial age, complaining about "steamboats, steam-powered wagons—soon there will be aerial machines speeding over your heads." In the same breath, he carped about the "entrepreneurial agitation, presumption, and activity of unruly, inquisitive Hebrews who stick their fingers in everywhere and upset everything." Right up to his last days, Arndt would call for the "impure flood from the East" to be contained.[14] He also called for Germans to come together as a national people, to "eradicate everything small-minded and foreign and reinvigorate what was great and native." To this end, he demanded that everyone "from princes to beggars be suffused with the great sense that the fatherland belongs to all of us, and that all of us belong to the fatherland."[15]

In 1847, he explicitly rejected the liberal idea that the German people would benefit from being mixed socially and by marriage with Jews. Arndt spilled enormous amounts of ink attacking humanists for the opinion that "there could be no greater blessing to the stupid, sleepy-headed German people" than having "a quick and imaginative element mixed with its own slow, ponderous nature."[16] Continuously repeating the same buzzwords, Arndt turned Jews' alleged cleverness into an accusation, pillorying their "sharpness, pointedness, intellect, slyness, and wittiness." He contrasted those characteristics with so-called German virtues like loyalty, simplicity, orderliness, and piety. Arndt and his followers glorified slow, measured qualities, and legitimized the hatred of the stupid and resentful for everything lively and quick.[17] They created fertile ground upon which anti-Semitism could grow. Theirs was a monotone nationalist mantra, full of envy of those with the imagination to seize the day and prosper in a variety of novel ways.

Friedrich Ludwig Jahn's gymnastics movement offered yet another outlet for nationalist ambitions in the period between 1815 and 1848. On the whole, the members of German athletic clubs were a fairly ragtag bunch, nonconformist and freedom-seeking, who typically sported full beards (at the time a sure sign of seditious thinking) and wore berets, open collars, and black suits. Fresh, pious, cheerful, and free, they set about shaking up the self-satisfied, apolitical, submissive subjects of the various German crowns. Led by Jahn, the fraternity brothers and gymnasts railed against "salacious foreigners" and "the dirty and poisonous French language." They defaced French signs and inscriptions on buildings and chanted things like "Poles, French, priests, aristocrats, and Jews are Germany's misfortune." If they encountered a well-turned-out, stylishly attired Jew, "the unruly youths would form a circle around the object of their horror, stick out their index fingers, and cry: Hey, hey." Jahn himself was known for throwing cow dung in the faces of those he considered his enemies. Within their own circles, Jahn's disciples maintained an ostentatious camaraderie. Thomas Mann would later describe the activities of "people like Jahn" as a jingoistic "mob democracy."[18]

On October 18, 1817, several hundred fraternity brothers and like-minded young men staged the "Wartburgfest," a celebration of what they trumpeted as "the double rebirth of the fatherland." The event conflated Napoleon's defeat at the Battle of Leipzig four years previously and the three hundredth anniversary of the Reformation into a stylized commemoration of Germany's internal liberation by Luther and its external liberation by German military victory against French occupiers. The festivities were full of displays of religious fervor for the German nation, cries of "Heil," and, of course, beer. Decked out in armbands and cockades in black, red, and gold, the colors of revolutionary German nationalism, the celebrants marched from the central market place in the city of Eisenach up to the top of Wartburg Mountain. There they built a bonfire. A brother speared a number of writings they found inimical to their movement on a pitchfork, showed them to the crowd, and then heaved them into the flames. The offending publications included a copy of the Napoleonic Code and an edition of *The History of the German Empire* by August von Kotzebue, a diplomat and author considered a monarchist stooge, as well as books and pamphlets by all "loudmouth and tacit enemies of the German gymnastics movement" and newspapers "that damaged and distorted the fatherland." A gendarme's baton from Austria and other attributes of backward-looking conservatism were also consigned to the flames.

Another publication the nationalist hotheads ceremonially burned was Saul Ascher's pamphlet *Germanomania*, whereupon the crowd bellowed, "Misery upon the Jews!" Ascher had accused "Germanomaniacs" of corrupting universal republican principles so that they applied only to Germans. In the minds of fraternity brothers and gymnasts, Ascher had written, Jews "were neither Germans nor Christians and thus could never become German." Indeed, Jews were considered the antithesis of Germans and would be tolerated only "as long as they did not get in the way of Germandom."[19]

Jakob Friedrich Fries—Karl Marx's dissertation supervisor—was among the professorial agitators at the Wartburg festival. A radical democrat known for his inflammatory speeches and publications, he was stripped of his professorship in philosophy in 1819. One of the reasons was a political pamphlet he had published in 1816. In it, Fries had called for "bourgeois freedom" and "social equality" and excoriated "the small-minded spirit of pastors and the idiotic pride of aristocrats, . . . forces that wish to keep the people in a state of ignorance." Fries favored eradicating class distinctions and ensuring that all Gentiles with talent had access to means of economic and intellectual development. He laid out a number of steps toward a state of law and social equality: "1. Work should receive its just reward. 2. Every citizen should be able to find sensible work. 3. Those who have no property and cannot work should not remain without any means at all." Fries demanded "prosperity, education, and justice" for all but added that justice was of paramount importance.[20]

Around the same time as this pamphlet, and shortly before the Wartburg festival, Fries published another political polemic, disguised as a book review. It was entitled "On the Endangerment of the Prosperity and Character of the Germans by the Jews." On the topic of prosperity, the author accused Jewish merchants of exploiting their widespread connections so that "the Christian merchant, who stands alone, has no hope of competing." And on the topic of pernicious Jewish influence on German character, Fries admitted that Gentiles also sometimes acquired wealth by dubious means, but he dismissed them as the "scum of Christian society that has been polluted by Jews." Citing the example of Jews in the city of Frankfurt, who had been freed from the ghetto in 1796 and had risen up in society, he warned: "Allow them to continue for a mere forty years more, and the sons of the best Christian houses will have to hire on as their manservants."

Fries demanded that the "Jewish caste" be torn out "by root and stump." He was advocating not annihilation but rather limits on further Jewish immigration and marriages, restrictions on which trades Jews could practice, and compulsory Christian education for Jewish children. In addition, he wanted Jewish associations to be forbidden, and violations stringently punished. Translated into contemporary terms, Fries was protesting against an ambitious Jewish parallel society, which he thought should be dispelled by robust legal measures. Individual Jews would then have no choice but to assimilate into the predominant culture of the Christian majority or, in Fries's words, effect "cultural rapprochement with us."[21]

JEWS BETWEEN REVOLUTION AND REACTION

The sporadic anti-Jewish violence that took place in southern Germany during the politically uneasy period between 1830 and 1848 has always attracted considerable attention.[22] Yet few people mention the fact that where Jews most feared for their lives was in the heavily Polish sections of the Prussian region of Posen. The great Russian Jewish linguistic researcher Ignaz Bernstein reported that during one bid for Polish independence in the town of Miroslaw, Polish revolutionaries attacked Jews. "I wasn't any better off than the other local Jews," he wrote. "My wares, clothing, etc., were stolen, and our lives were threatened. I saved my wife and child by taking them to my friend Müller." Müller rescued mother and child by spiriting them away to the safe, German-dominated part of Posen. Bernstein tried to salvage some valuables from his house and grain-selling business, but Polish insurgents maintained control of the town for a whole week. Bernstein and his brother spent their nights cowering together in a small room, fearing the worst.

The local district administrator in Posen also recorded "varied acts of violence" carried out by insurgents against Jews.[23] Eventually, on their second attempt, troops loyal to the Prussian government succeeded in putting down the Polish national revolutionaries and saving the area's Jewish population. Events like this one helped establish a German-Jewish alliance against Poles that held until the Weimar Republic.

In both Germany and Eastern Europe, then, anti-Semitism was part and parcel of movements for freedom and democracy—and also of the striving of the disadvantaged for social and political emancipation. How can we understand this phenomenon? A national community, with its ideas of a popular spirit, blood relations, and common history, promised a modicum of security in a world that was changing at an unprecedented pace. The Industrial Revolution and the rise of the market economy had destroyed old certainties overnight. The masses, still largely agricultural, were being forced into the cities, where they lost their traditional networks of social support.

For most of these people, individual liberty meant loss and fear, and it fostered a desire for new forms of collective security. This was the backdrop against which the Romanian revolutionary Nicolas Balescu proclaimed in 1848: "For me, the question of ethnic solidarity is more important than the question of freedom. A people can use freedom only when it's able to survive as a nation. Freedom can be easily regained, if it is lost, but not ethnic identity." Romanian ethnicity had to be defined and defended against Hungarians, Russians, Ukrainians, Bulgarians, Turks, Germans, and Jews, and Balescu wasn't the only one who was willing to sacrifice the idea of freedom for such a cause.[24]

The history of the German national anthem illustrates the ambivalence at the heart of German nationalism. "Unity and justice and freedom" are the first words of the song as it is sung today. But when Heinrich Hoffmann von Fallersleben originally composed the anthem in 1848, it began with the exclamation *"Deutschland, Deutschland über alles, über alles in der Welt"* ("Germany, Germany above everything, above everything in the world"). These lines were used by the revolutionaries of 1848, and they were primarily inward-focused, a wish for an end to the territorial feudalism of many small hereditary German monarchies and for the establishment of a national republic.

But in the summer of 1881, students who founded a superregional association of extreme anti-Semitic fraternities appropriated Fallersleben's anthem as their own and howled it at a ceremony atop Kyffhäuser Mountain, "the most German of all German mountains," as they would later inform the kaiser, bursting with sycophantic pride. In 1891, an anti-Semitic movement that had coalesced around the librarian Otto Boeckel would plaster the words "Deutschland, Deutschland über alles" as a slogan on the front page of their newspaper, the *Reichsherold*. By that time, Ludwig Bamberger, a German revolutionary of the 1848 school, was forced to acknowledge that the song he and his fellow exiles in Paris had sung so often had become a kind of "anti-Semitic 'Marseillaise.' "[25]

Read as a social-historical document, Fallersleben's verses shed light on the extremism of nationally inspired German democrats. The anthem is the absolute antithesis of the "Marseillaise." In the French national anthem, people take up arms to battle for freedom and overcome tyranny with revolution. The German national anthem, by contrast, is a sentimental paean to community as embodied in German song, German women, German wine, German loyalty, and the German fatherland—the national corset that was binding in both senses, at once constraining and supportive, giving people a sense of unity and collective security.

When he wasn't articulating national pathos, Fallersleben wrote bizarre children's songs ("A little man stands in the forest, all still and silent") and crassly anti-Semitic poems. One set of verses, dating from 1840, is entitled "Emancipation." It begins by addressing "Israel": "You stole from under our feet / Our German fatherland." Fallersleben then descends into the crassest sort of Jew baiting: "You are instructed by this God / In usury, lying, and swindles." At the end, "Israel" is informed that Jews will be welcome among German democrats and revolutionaries only if they renounce Judaism: "If you do not leave this God / Germany will never open her ears to you / If you do not hate your enslavement / Never will you pass through freedom's gate."[26] German patriots lacked the courage to dismantle outmoded social structures, directly challenge regional feudal autocrats, or question the religious divide between Protestants and Catholics. Instead, their automatic response to problems was to blame a few tens of thousands of Jews, who supposedly possessed sufficient power to sweep a whole fatherland from under the cozy house slippers of men like Fallersleben, Jahn, Fries, Arndt, and their hordes of fraternity-brother and gymnastics-obsessed followers.

Such timidity stands in marked contrast to the behavior of the national revolutionaries' enemy, the reactionary Austrian prince Clemens von Metternich. In 1814 and 1815, while Jahn was inciting his followers with sermons full of national arrogance and hatred of foreigners and Jews, Metternich as Austrian chancellor was defending Jewish emancipation.[27] The early German nationalists may have understood their cause as a new departure, but Metternich was determined to suppress what he regarded as "the Teutonism of universities and gymnasts." We today have little sympathy with his motivations for trying to preserve the social and political status quo of the monarchic age. Nonetheless, in retrospect, Metternich must be credited with recognizing the harm that the vanguard of German populism and their many non-German imitators would do in the name of "national self-determination." Metternich predicted that a Germany unified by nationalist revolutionaries "could no longer be restrained, and would treat the world to spectacles far worse than even those of which France was capable in its most megalomaniacal revolutionary periods." He warned against the "pedantic" malcontents decked out in black, red, and gold and the "powerful riffraff" of older fraternity brothers. "God save Germany from a general revolution," he proclaimed. "Its reach would grow beyond all calculation."[28]

The prognoses of the coolly calculating master of political power games greatly resemble the nightmare scenarios envisioned by a man who fled Restoration Germany for Parisian exile: the German Jewish poet Heinrich Heine. Heine, too, clearly saw the danger lurking within Janus-faced German democratic nationalism. Heine despised what he called "the jingoistic champions of nationality, our nationalists, so-called patriots, whose heads are full only of race, blood, and similar idiocies." The appeal of these "so-called ultra-Germans" and "obscure fools," Heine wrote, could be traced back to powerful formulas with which one could excite a mob: "The words *fatherland*, *Germany*, *faith of our fathers*, etc., always electrify the muddled minds of the masses far more than the words *humanity*, *cosmopolitanism*, *reason*, and *truth*!"[29]

In tones similar to Metternich's, Heine also argued against Ludwig Börne, his fellow German Jew and political exile, who advocated a democratic revolution. Whoever incited Germans toward revolution, Heine warned, was planting seeds "that sooner or later will bring forth the most terrible fruits." On another occasion, Heine similarly cautioned that Germany would stage "a play, compared to which the French Revolution will seem like a harmless idyll."[30] In 1823, Heine explained why he supported revolution and popular rule in England and Italy while remaining mistrustful of German revolutionaries like Arndt or Jahn. "The arbitrary and inconsequential reason," Heine remarked sarcastically, "is that victory for them would mean that a thousand Jewish throats, and the best ones at that, would be slit."[31] Insofar as the archconservative Metternich hindered what Heine feared would be inevitable nationalist violence, the poet even had words of praise for the man who had exiled him: "Metternich never posed as a demagogue to cover up the fear in his heart, he never sang the songs of Arndt while drinking wheat beer, he never did gymnastics in the park, and he never mouthed holier-than-thou pieties."[32]

The point here is not to glorify Metternich but to underscore that merely advocating democracy did not preclude an individual from also being a bigot. German advocates of liberty and democracy, cloaking themselves in the flag of nationalism, were among those who originally blazed the paths that would eventually lead to catastrophe. They promulgated the German nation as a unit based on mythic origin, religion, and language. They elevated the value of national particularity, of an ethnically defined popular identity, above that of universal human rights. As a result, in the name of national unity, they excluded others.

Among the Germans who were shut out of the new national community was Ludwig Bamberger. A journalist and an early leader of the national revolutionary cause, Bamberger was a delegate to the Frankfurt Assembly and took part in the 1849 uprising in the Bavarian part of Rhineland-Palatinate, which saw revolutionaries briefly seize power. After that rebellion was quashed, he fled and was sentenced to death in absentia in his home city, Mainz. Moving from London to Amsterdam, then Antwerp and Paris, he became a successful banker. When amnesty was declared for former revolutionaries in 1866, Bamberger returned to Germany and enjoyed considerable influence in Bismarck's early liberal years. Overcoming a number of special interests, he succeeded in establishing the Reichsbank as the German national bank and the mark as the country's single currency and lost influence only in 1876, after Bismarck's turn away from liberalism.

Back in 1863, while still in exile, Bamberger and his wife snuck into Germany on one occasion. Between Gotha and Dresden, participants in a gymnastics festival poured into their train. "It was the first time since 1849 that I encountered beer- and wine-drinking German humanity in such masses," Bamberger recalled, "and the fact that we were crammed together in a wagon on a sultry August afternoon didn't make the experience any more charming." After describing the noise and shouting, the sweat and smoke of the gymnasts, Bamberger went on to talk about Germany in general, citing the final chapter in *The Prince*, where Machiavelli advises Italy on how to defend itself against the barbarians beyond its northern borders. Instead of worrying about barbarians outside the gates, Bamberger wrote, Germany should face the task of repelling "the barbarians within our fatherland."

According to Bamberger, the problem of internal barbarism could not be countered with "patience and sauerkraut." The only solution was for the German public sphere to combat every instance of crude hatred and injustice "with the vigor and persistence of an educated nation." Only then, Bamberger proclaimed, "will we have the right to say: We are one people and one land." Bamberger finished writing his memoirs in 1899, the year of his death. Their tone is weary. They are the remembrances of a man who, despite having been a Reichstag deputy, had personally suffered under the new brand of German enmity toward Jews. In a Reichstag session on June 14, 1882, for example, his former ally Bismarck had mocked him as a "*sujet mixte*."[33]

Börne, who was a generation older than Bamberger, excused the anti-Jewishness of the fraternity and gymnastics movement as a crutch helping revolutionary German nationalism to take its first steps. "I forgive the German people its hatred of Jews," Börne wrote, "because it is still a young people. Germans are like children who need to brace themselves on a bench to stand upright on their own. Germans need to cling to restrictions on freedom so that they may one day be able to do without those restrictions. If the German people had to do without prejudices, they would fall over a hundred times every day."[34] According to Börne's logic, the specific anti-Jewish hostility of the German people stemmed from their own relative helplessness, which he hoped they would soon grow out of. But to extend Börne's metaphor, the unsteady Germans never progressed beyond the status of an immature, aggressive bully who would go on to terrorize Europe in general and European Jews in particular.

With its various territorial associations and marked regional specificity, Germany seemed predestined to become a federal republic. In the nineteenth century, however, federalism would have entailed paying at least lip service to old monarchic authorities. Therefore, German nationalists focused on the creation of a unified central state as one of their main demands. Economic liberals called for unified weights, measures, and currency and for an end to import duties on goods transported between different German territories. Political liberals squandered their energy in searching for a unified folk spirit, an idea that would bind together the various local cultures. All these movements lost sight of what was most important: a commitment to individual liberty and a state conducive to openness and free-mindedness.

Even after the demise of the Wilhelmine system in 1918, article 2 of the ensuing Weimar Constitution—"the territory of the empire consists of the territories of the German states"—still stressed Germany's diversity. Jewish immigrants from Eastern Europe were officially given Bavarian or Saxon, rather than German, citizenship; when Albert Einstein was expatriated in 1934, it was as a Prussian, not a German. It wasn't until February 5, 1934, that Nazi interior minister Wilhelm Frick succeeded in establishing "German" as a designation of nationality on people's passports, and not until March 12, 1938—when Hitler presided over the fusion of Austria and Germany into the Greater German Empire—that the nationalist dream of a completely unified German state was realized, albeit in the form of a nightmare. Three days after the *Anschluss*, on Vienna's Heldenplatz (Heroes' Square), Hitler declared to frenetic cheering: "As leader and imperial chancellor of the German nation and the German Empire, I announce to history my homeland's entrance into the German Empire." A short time later, he used an appearance in Frankfurt to present himself as the man who had finally accomplished what the National Assembly had set out to do all the way back in 1848: "The work for which our forefathers fought and shed their blood ninety years ago can now be considered completed."[35]

Even Karl Renner, a leading Austrian Social Democrat, greeted the fusion of Austria and Germany into Greater Germany as the fulfillment of a historical dream. On April 10, 1938, a month after German troops had entered Austria, a popular referendum was held in which an overwhelming majority of Austrians sanctioned what amounted to their own annexation. Renner had served from 1918 to 1920 as the first state chancellor of the new Austrian Republic. Nonetheless, on April 2, 1938, he declared in the *Neues Wiener Tagblatt*: "I would have to deny my entire past as a theoretical trailblazer of nations' right to self-determination and as a German statesman if I did not welcome with a joyful heart the great historical deed of the reunification of the German nation. . . . As a Social Democrat and as an advocate of national self-determination . . . I will be voting yes."[36]

3

ANTI-SEMITISM AS A
POLITICAL FORCE

THE JEWISH QUESTION

Throughout the nineteenth century, there was constant discussion in German society about the proper status of Jews. The "Jewish question," or *Judenfrage*, was argued about in newspapers and pamphlets and debated at length in parliaments and government bureaucracies. Initially, around 1800, the Jewish question had carried positive connotations, at least among liberals: addressing the status of Jews was a way to make society more fair and rational. In the last few decades of the century, those connotations turned negative and the Jewish question was redefined as an issue of whether Jews enjoyed *too many* privileges.

This reversal was motivated by the fact that Gentile Germans were suddenly compelled to face what we might call, somewhat polemically, Jewish challenges. Bit by bit over the course of the 1800s, artisans, court-appointed merchants, owners of medium-sized farms, pastors, civil servants, and other respected figures had lost influence. The remaining trade guilds devolved into selfish monopolies that put the brakes on economic development; Berlin artisans, for instance, sought to use legal trickery to preserve their traditional privileges. Despite their efforts, the old social center was gradually replaced by a new middle class of lawyers, doctors, managers, publishers, brewers, stock brokers, theater directors, and department store owners. Their ranks contained a disproportionate number of Jews. Social status and prosperity were, in the main, no longer inherited but rather could be earned.

Life in rural market communities and country towns, once so steady, was increasingly sucked into the whirlpool of progress. Rural Germans now had to confront challenges like property taxes and mechanization. Impoverished and anxious about their livelihoods, great numbers of them moved to the cities, often with some reluctance. In 1871, only one German in twenty lived in a city with a population of 100,000 or more. By 1933, that figure would be one in three.

The population statistics for Berlin offer a vivid testimony to this mass urbanization. In 1813, the city had just 165,000 inhabitants; by 1875, that number rose to 970,000, and it would hit 4,000,000 in 1925. Such a massive inflow meant that for a number of decades the Christian majority in the city was largely made up of former farmers and agricultural laborers. At the same time, it was Jews who were in the forefront of the urbanization trend. Between 1811 and 1875, as Berlin's Christian population grew sixfold, its Jewish population multiplied by fourteen. As a result, the proportion of Jews within Berlin's overall population rose from 1.7 to 4.7 percent. (It would hold steady until 1925 before beginning to decline.)[1]

The explosive growth of German cities forced people to change the way they lived. Christian farming and artisan families who relocated to the city often needed two or three decades to adjust to their new environment and its faster pace of life. At the same time, representatives of German Christianity were preaching ever more insistently that people should cleave to the values of their forefathers. Almost as if to mock the fact that simple people had no option but to move from villages to cities, live among strangers, accelerate their everyday routines, and become flexible and quick-witted, the General

Assembly of German Catholics in Breslau in 1879 proclaimed: "It is the duty of Catholic boys and maidens to avoid acquaintances with people of other beliefs that could produce mixed marriages."[2] The reference was to Protestants.

Jews took a far more relaxed attitude toward migrating and creating new lives for themselves; they had been forced often enough in the past to move or even flee from one place to another. What's more, Jews were familiar with urban life. Many had been living in cities for quite some time, and new arrivals could count on help from relatives. The Social Democratic theorist Karl Kautsky characterized Jews as "the exaggerated type of the city dweller," ironically arguing that if one wanted to classify them as a race, then the species was *Homo urbanus*. Jews had trod as pioneers down paths that most people in industrialized nations, whether they wanted to or not, would also have to follow.[3]

The traditional immobility of German Christians, their attachment to house and hearth, forest and field, was compelled to yield to modern hyperactivity. Mortgages opened up the possibility of liquefying property that had been in families for generations. Money became divorced in mysterious ways from work people did with their hands, and it knew neither local nor state boundaries. The "rule of money," or the new "financial feudalism," as it was called, became the order of the day.[4] And Germans associated all of this with Jews, who were seen as embodying the terrifying forces of change that threatened to turn life upside down. Their less flexible adversaries accused Jews of destroying the bonds of sacred traditions, of sacrificing the spiritual and human profundity of the Christian West on the altars of mammon and mass production. Jewishness thus became synonymous with the hoarding of material wealth instead of good old-fashioned hard work. From one corner of Germany to the other, anti-Semites bellowed: "Jewish wealth is based on exploitation and usury, German wealth on honest labor."[5]

The greater ease with which the Jewish population adapted to the pressures of industrial capitalism drove home the difference between

Jews and Gentiles with painful clarity. By the latter part of the nineteenth century, most anti-Semitism had nothing to do with religion—or
with racial concerns, which would come later. Instead, it was focused
on social difference. The Christian majority, only too conscious that
they needed to move up the social ladder, became obsessed with how
quickly Jews were bettering themselves. Prominent anti-Semites of
the period exploited precisely this sort of resentment, founding anti-
Semitic organizations and political parties and issuing a seemingly
endless series of hateful pamphlets aimed at mobilizing the masses
against the Jewish minority. In 1880, anti-Semite Adolf Stoecker
warned the Prussian house of representatives that "Jewishness and
progress go together." One could "break the yoke of Jews," Stoecker
argued, only "if one renounced progress" and clung to tradition.[6]

It was in this period that German anti-Semitism became better
organized and much rawer in tone—developments that roughly par-
alleled Christians' discovery that they had fallen behind in their effort
to push their way into the new middle classes. Ironically, the anti-
Semites used the tools of modernity, such as mass communication
and democratic political parties, to advance profoundly antimodern
aims. The aggressive potential of this social movement was curtailed
by the authoritarian power of the Wilhelmine Empire under Kaiser
Wilhelm II, but it would emerge in full force after Germany's defeat
in World War I and the establishment of Weimar democracy.

It was not only destructive progress that Jews brought with them,
according to their opponents, but also social strife. In 1874, anti-
Semite Constantin Frantz argued that the ascendant Jewish plutoc-
racy had created the restless proletariat and therefore the "battle
between 'poor' and 'rich.'" As a result, he said, the middle class, which
by nature was harmonious, was being dragged down and the entirety
of society polarized. "Here the golden calf is promoted, and there the
red flag is raised," Frantz complained. Once "mammon"—a code
word for Jews—had destroyed the moral constraints that Christianity

imposed upon the masses, Frantz continued, the destitute would begin "to fall upon the rich and divide their ill-gotten gains among themselves." He envisioned what would follow: "And wouldn't it be a just form of Nemesis, if the plundering of the masses were primarily directed against those who contributed most to robbing them of their Christian faith and who possessed the greatest wealth without earning it through constructive labor, so that they really do deserve the least moral respect?"

From this barbed rhetorical question, Frantz turned to socialist Jews. They, he (and later Hitler) fantasized, were secretly allied with wealthy Jews, and their task was simply to distract the proletarians from their true calling, the establishment of a Christian, economically balanced social contract. But this situation would not last forever, Frantz prophesied, since the currents in society ran "in a direction precisely opposite to Jewish domination." In the not-too-distant future, Frantz predicted, Germans would have to open their eyes, and "the pseudo-Germanism of national liberalism would be deservedly dismissed." If that did not happen, the German Empire would soon become "a subsidiary of the Jewish nation."[7]

Wilhelm Marr, the man who founded the German League of Anti-Semites in 1879 and coined the term *anti-Semitism*, devoted his life to combating such nightmare scenarios. Like most of his contemporary and future allies, Marr focused his political agitation on "the social predominance of Semitism." Whether speaking in Vienna, Munich, or Heilbronn, he never failed to emphasize the disproportionate percentages of Jewish high school graduates and lawyers, and at the end of his crudely polemical pamphlets there was always a line about how Christians in one city or another were now less able to "provide their families with higher education." From that he concluded, like many other Jew haters before him, that Germany's Gentile citizens would soon be reduced "to the lowest forms of labor."

Marr is considered the father of racial anti-Semitism, but his writings reveal him to be above all someone who attacked people who had achieved what he himself had failed to do: rise in society. Marr promoted his writings as "a cry of pain from someone kept down," insisting that the real problem was not Jew baiting but German baiting, which broke out every time "a non-Jewish element dares to call attention to itself." "We are no longer equal to the challenge of this foreign tribe," he whined in the name of justice and equal opportunity, contrasting "agile Israel" with "thick-skinned German indolence" and "mushrooming Jewish talent" with "the ethical seriousness" of German Christians.[8] Constantin Frantz said much the same things, albeit in a slightly more elevated tone: "Thanks to the keenness of his eye, his skill in intellectual reflection, and his ability to coldly calculate, the Jew is in a far better position than the average Christian."[9]

As noted, Jewish Germans were indeed disproportionately represented in the bourgeoisie, and many Christians felt inferior to them and resented their success. As Marr's contemporary Walter Pohlmann noted, anti-Semitism was one of the weapons that the old order could use against the new to "defend passivity and lack of talent against greater industry and cleverness." It was a battle of "darkness against light—a light that was too bright for and thus unbearable to stupid eyes."[10]

PROGRESS, CRISIS, ANTILIBERALISM

In the first half of the nineteenth century, economic and political development in Germany proceeded at a leisurely pace, but it took off in the early 1870s. The mobilization of both people and the economy in Bismarck's wars, the unification of Germany in 1871, the economic and currency union between the various German states, new technological inventions, and French reparations payments following the Franco-Prussian War of 1870–71 gave a sudden, dramatic boost to German industry. In 1872, forty-nine new banks were founded in Prussia alone, along with sixty-one construction companies, sixty-five mining firms, twenty-two cement and brickmaking factories, fifteen chemical plants, and twelve rail companies. And the drive to establish new business continued into the first few months of 1873, with twenty-two more new banks, forty-five mining companies, twenty-two construction firms, and ten brickmaking establishments founded by the end of April. All told, between 1871 and 1873, German entrepreneurs built as many blast furnaces and established as many ironworks and machine plants as in the previous seventy years.

Investors were lured by promises of dividends up to 20 percent. Everyone was making money and eager to exploit the new possibilities. Within the space of a few years, wages had risen by 25 to 30 percent, and workers succeeded in getting the number of hours in the work week significantly reduced. "From 1871 to 1873," journalist and economist Max Wirth later recalled, "the upper aristocracy and the privy counselors were just as interested in easy profits as coachmen and servants. There was no difference between bank managers and secretaries or between men and women. People everywhere—on the stock exchange and in their homes, in hotels and bars, in political associations and singing clubs—were all involved in speculation."[11]

The good times did not last long, with the boom of 1870 followed by a devastating economic crisis in 1873. The crash was worldwide: it began in Austria-Hungary, spread to the German Empire, Switzerland, and Italy, and then moved on to hammer the United States, England, and Russia. Turkey, Egypt, and a number of South American states went bankrupt, while in the United States, eighty-three railroad companies declared insolvency. The Germans felt the downturn particularly severely. It had been preceded by the first great economic expansion Germany had ever known, which had led to euphoric celebrations of progress. Now, it seemed Germans were being presented with a hefty bill for the party.

In the months before the crash in September 1873, most government officials, leading economists, bank directors, and journalists ignored the signs of the approaching crisis. Everyone had bathed in the prosperity. So people were all the more eager to place the blame elsewhere when the crash became impossible to overlook: the culprits, they said, were Jewish robber barons. In truth, since Jews on average had more experience with the modern economy, it seems reasonable to assume that their investments were somewhat less likely to end in disaster than the quick-money schemes of the masses of Gentiles who had tried their hand in the stock markets.

As sociologist Jakob Lestschinsky later put it, the country's rapid industrialization made "backward and politically divided Germany into one of the most modern and important capitalist countries in the world." But many individuals perceived the process as extremely threatening—and it did not go unnoticed that Jews played a key role in it. A dangerous gap opened between technical and economic progress, on the one hand, and political and intellectual ability, on the other. In Lestschinsky's words, "the cultural base of the popular masses was too narrow for the rapidly developed capitalistic superstructure."[12]

The empire built on blood and iron lacked sufficient forces of integration. The rapid changes in people's lives cried out to be balanced by a sense of security that would come from a broadly accepted national identity, but that goal proved a problem. The name of the new state, the German Empire, referred back to the old transnational Holy Roman Empire of the German Nation. The Imperial Constitution of 1871 guaranteed what were, for the time, very modern voting rights, in terms of equality and secrecy, but the emperor's rule was still based on divine authority. The emperor was responsible for appointing and firing the German chancellor and all permanent civil servants. This power arrangement did not project, either internally or externally, the sort of self-confidence needed to soothe the uncertainties inevitably produced by large-scale industrialization. From the perspective of Bismarck, conditioned as he was by power politics, all that the new empire required was "the biggest possible army, a military commander, a guiding hand, enough money, and that's it."[13]

It was this historical situation, the end of the first phase of German turbo-capitalism, that saw the rise of organized anti-Semitism. From its very inception, anti-Semitism was directed against liberal economic policies and capitalism in general, and against finance capital and stock exchanges in particular.

Further reasons for the new forms of organized anti-Semitism that appeared in the late 1870s can be found in the government's anti-Catholic cultural campaigns early in the decade and in Bismarck's gradual turn against liberalism. These were interrelated phenomena. By cooperating politically with nationalist liberals, Bismarck had sought to establish a secular, bureaucratic state. As a result, against the will of Catholic functionaries, he had to institute public offices to carry out secular marriage ceremonies and supervise education, redefining the core of the state's sovereign responsibilities. In 1872, Pope Pius IX went so far as to characterize this shift as an attack by (liberal) Jews on Christianity. In the years that followed, a significant segment of the Catholic press in Germany moved decisively into the anti-Jewish camp.

Then, between 1876 and 1879, Bismarck reoriented his domestic policy, targeting the very liberals who had allied with him in his cultural battle against Catholics. At the same time, he took aim at socialists: their political organization, the Social Democratic Party (SPD), was essentially banned for a time. Henceforth, Bismarck's decisions played to conservative factions within the Reichstag, while his anti-Catholic campaign was wound down with some halfhearted compromises. Supported by conservatives, the German chancellor gradually introduced protective levies, tax privileges, and subsidies benefiting large-scale agrarians and steel barons. He sold this new protectionism to the public as an attempt at supporting "national labor." In 1878, Bismarck, himself a major landowner, informed the newly appointed Prussian finance minister, Arthur Hobrecht, about how he would deal with liberal parliamentarians in the future: "University graduates who have no trade, property, skill with commerce and industry, who live from honoraria and credit, will have to submit in the coming years to the economic demands of the productive parts of the population or forfeit their seats in parliament."[14]

It was in this context that historian Heinrich von Treitschke opened what became known as the Berlin Anti-Semitism debate. The discussion commenced with the 1879 publication of Treitschke's article "Our Prospects" in the prestigious journal *Preussische Jahrbücher*, which he also edited. The historian explicitly addressed his text to the sons of the rapidly declining artisan and merchant class, who were the first in their families to attend university. This was a group of people fearful for their future. Acting as a mouthpiece for these extremely discontented Christian students, Treitschke raised the idea that "in recent times a dangerous spirit of arrogance has been awakened in Jewish circles." Treitschke demanded that Jews show more "tolerance and humility," writing: "The instincts of the masses have recognized in Jews a pressing danger, a deeply troubling source of damage to our new German life." The most knowledgeable Germans, Treitschke proclaimed, were calling out with one voice: "The Jews are our misfortune!"

In his characteristically pompous, if polished, style, Treitschke also raged against "overeducated ignorance," "softheaded philanthropy," and "the coddling and babying of criminals." He called for a politics of steadfast morality and unrelenting state sanctions against the increasing "barbarization" of the masses. He also advocated for the "strengthening of imperial authority," an end to parliamentary bickering, and "true solidarity between the crown and the people."[15] Treitschke's polemic, issued on behalf of national collectivism and a powerful state, was aimed against liberalism. Since Jews tended to be liberals, that was all the more reason for them to be pilloried in the piece.

The background of Treitschke's attack was political. Treitschke was a member of the National Liberal faction in the Reichstag, and after some of his colleagues refused to follow Bismarck's new protectionist line the group was riven by division. A minority, led by the German Jewish deputies Ludwig Bamberger and Eduard Lasker, were unwilling to support protective levies and tax breaks that would benefit large landowners and the coal and steel industry. They felt compelled to leave the party and form a splinter group. The majority, however, followed Bismarck's lead, and Treitschke was one of Bismark's most ardent supporters. Bamberger warned that the debate was not just about this or that protective levy but "a matter of life or death for the free, peaceful, modern development" of Germany. For Bamberger, the conflict pitted two completely different types of economic thinking against each another: "the collectivist versus the individualist."[16]

Until 1876, Bismarck had depended on support from the National Liberal Party, and National Liberal Jewish German deputies and their constituencies were part of the chancellor's parliamentary majority. When he turned his back on liberalism, Bismarck consciously encouraged a split between freethinking politicians. To Germany's lasting detriment, he destroyed the nascent and thus still relatively weak individual liberty movement and helped national, state-organized collectivism achieve its great breakthrough. He thus also indirectly helped German anti-Semitism grow in the fifty years to come. The Iron Chancellor's change of political orientation was a far more significant factor in this historical turn than his rare (though frequently cited) anti-Jewish statements.

Many nineteenth-century Germans argued for the rights of Jews and opposed anti-Semitism. Their efforts and courage are often forgotten today, overshadowed by the later genocide. The public no longer remembers that Bismarck, as Reich chancellor, aggressively promoted the legal equality of Jews in Romania, Bulgaria, and Serbia at the Congress of Berlin in 1878. He "would not rest until he had the word of every individual representative," Bismarck proclaimed, to promote "the equality of faiths in as earnest and compulsory fashion as the world has ever seen."[17] Likewise, historians today seldom mention the demonstrative interventions on behalf of Jews undertaken by Kaiser Friedrich III, who in November 1879 described the "current anti-Semitic agitations" as a point of "humiliation and shame for Germany."[18] In December 1890, an official in the Grand

Duchy of Hesse-Darmstadt ordered that anti-Semites be placed under close surveillance and that immediate and vigorous action be taken "against such illegal activities as disturbing the peace as well as all insults to Israelites."[19]

Indeed, when anti-Semites publicly petitioned Bismarck in 1880 to revoke measures aimed at Jewish equality, their open hostility called forth an immediate reaction. Historian Theodor Mommsen warned of a potential "civil war between a (Christian) majority and a (Jewish) minority," and on November 14 of that year, in the German capital's most important conservative newspaper, seventy-five influential Berliners published a statement condemning the anti-Jewish agitation. The authors included Mommsen and his fellow historian Johann Gustav Droysen, Mayor Max von Forckenbeck, venerable city magistrate August Gesenius, doctor and medical researcher Rudolf Virchow, and industrialist Werner Siemens, as well as a number of leading politicians, professors, and lawyers. Their statement did not pull any punches. It rejected the "race hatred" that had recently appeared "like a contagious disease . . . in the most shameful manner." In the name of law and human honor, the authors demanded that "all Germans be equal in their rights and duties. Ensuring this equality is the responsibility not just of official tribunals but of the conscience of every individual citizen." The authors warned about the dangers of the new breed of anti-Semites and the consequences of stirring up the passions of the populace: "Even if the leaders of this movement of envy and resentment preach their message in the abstract, the masses will not fail to perceive practical consequences from this sort of talk." Calls were already audible, the authors complained, for special extraordinary laws directed against Jews, and they asked: "How long can it be until the mob joins in the cry?"[20]

Wilhelmine society was by no means entirely anti-Semitic. In fact, its leading minds thanked Providence, to quote Mommsen, for alloying the somewhat brittle "German metal with a percent of Israel." Likewise, the young Thomas Mann praised "the indispensable stimulus for

European culture that is Jewishness," especially as Germany "so bitterly needed" it.[21]

MORE EQUALITY, PLEASE!

Treitschke's "Our Prospects" polemic characterized Jewish immigrants
to Germany from Eastern Europe as "an invasion of young, ambitious
trouser salesmen" who aimed to see their "children and grandchildren
dominate Germany's financial markets and newspapers." The nationalist historian pilloried the "scornfulness of the busy hordes of third-
rate Semitic talents" and their "obdurate contempt" for Christian
Germans, noting "how tightly this swarm kept to itself." The holder
of four professorships in his lifetime, Treitschke worked himself into
a veritable frenzy over "the new Jewish nature," whose tendencies and
attributes included "vulgar contempt," "addiction to scorn," "facile
cleverness and agility," "insistent presumption," and "offensive self-
overestimation." All of these qualities, Treitschke claimed, worked to
the detriment of the Christian majority, with its "humble piety" and
"old-fashioned, good-humored love of work." If Jews continued to
insist on their separate identity and refused to be integrated into the
German (which, to Treitschke, meant Protestant) culture of the nation,
the historian threatened that "the only answer would be for them to
emigrate and found a Jewish state somewhere abroad."[22]

The hostility toward Jews that Treitschke displayed in his 1879
article was symptomatic of Germany as whole. Treitschke had previously advanced some of these sentiments in less polemic form in 1870,
while he was a professor in Heidelberg, but they hadn't found much
resonance.[23] Ten years later, the time was ripe for such ideas. There
was the economic and social turbulence of Wilhelmine Germany, for
one thing, and, for another, the special circumstances and excitement
in the German capital, where the number of Jews—and particularly well-to-do Jews—was rising. Jew haters argued that emancipation had gone too far, that it had led not just to legal equality but to

significant privileges for Jews, which should be rolled back as soon as possible.

On November 20 and 22, 1880, at the request of liberal-minded representative Albert Hänel, the Prussian parliament took its turn debating the Jewish question. Concerned by a petition to the government demanding limits on Jewish immigration and restrictions on the trades that Jews were allowed to practice—a petition signed by more than 220,000 Gentile Germans—Hänel demanded to know what the government was planning to do to combat such efforts to strip Jewish citizens of certain rights. The Ministry of State under Bismarck answered Hänel with a cool but clear declaration that it did not intend to change the laws concerning freedom of religion.

During the debate, another liberal-minded deputy, the physician Rudolf Virchow, dismissed as utter nonsense the idea of a Jewish race with inherent special characteristics, which was beginning to take hold among some anti-Semites. Racial thinking, Virchow argued, was motivated "primarily by envy" of Jews' success in working their way up in the world. Virchow took particular exception to a recently published pamphlet entitled *Modern Jewry in Germany and in Berlin in Particular*, written by the court pastor and Prussian parliamentary representative Adolf Stoecker. Stoecker had complained that Jews were disproportionately forcing their way into institutions of higher learning: "In and of itself, such a drive toward social privilege and higher education would deserve the highest admiration. But for us it means the most intense sort of struggle for survival. If Israel continues to grow in this direction, we will be in completely over our heads." Virchow read this passage out loud and then turned to Stoecker: "Every possible form of free development will be ruled out, and there will no way to keep the peace, if you go so far as to blame a father for sending his children to better schools."[24] The National Liberal deputy Arthur Hobrecht put forth similar arguments, tracing "a good portion of the ugly envy" of Jews back to a "lamentable lack of self-confidence and energy."

As if to provide an example of such jealousy, the conservative deputy Jordan von Kröcher replied by criticizing "the massive intellectual superiority" of the National Liberal Party, which counted a number of Jews among its ranks. Kröcher castigated Berlin as "a metropolis of the intelligentsia" that lorded its advantages over the honest provinces, with their supposedly dimwitted populations. Julius Bachem, who represented Catholic moderates, fretted that "a Jewish progressive terrorism" could be felt in Berlin, Breslau, and Frankfurt am Main. He also dismissed Berlin's widely read humor magazines as the "unworthy essence of the reformist Jewish spirit in its worst sense." He accused Jews of possessing "an excessive gall" and listed impudence, flippancy, and cynicism as the central qualities of the "disbelieving reformist Jewish press."[25]

During the course of this ever more heated debate, the liberal-minded representative Albert Traeger picked up on the label that Stoecker and his allies often applied to themselves: the neologism "Christian-social." Unlike the Social Democrats of the SPD, Traeger argued, the "Christian-social" faction did not focus "on the genuine misery of the truly destitute, poor, and miserable" but rather on those who felt they were "not well enough situated." Traeger argued that "this is simply a matter of envy being whipped up, the envy of those who possess less of those who possess more. The jealousy of the incompetent is being used as a weapon against those with greater abilities."[26]

The Catholic deputy who spoke after Traeger, Ludwig Windthorst, said that he opposed making the "extraordinarily difficult question of our Jewish fellow citizens" into an explosive public issue. Windthorst cautioned: "I think tossing this into the general spotlight is, in view of the moods that prevail among the broad masses, both awkward and extremely worrisome."[27] But Windthorst spoke in his own name only, not for the Catholic Center Party, of which he was the head. And his fellow party member Bachem immediately went on the offensive, blaming Jews' desire for social advancement for the general rise in anti-Semitism, particularly in economically underdeveloped parts of Europe—Russia, the Danube River nations, and the backward areas within the German Empire. Jewish ambition, Bachem blustered, was prompting a "monstrous transference of liquid and nonliquid assets to the benefit of Jews."[28] A few days before the debate, the Berlin correspondent of the *London Times* had written that Germans were hateful and envious because they were incompetent businessmen whereas Jews weren't, and that analysis proved prescient.[29]

German anti-Semites combined a class-oriented, sociological view of Jewishness with issues of pressing concern to working people. Stoecker attacked Jews for "speculating on the stock market" and "dancing a witches' dance around the golden calf." The court pastor claimed that Jews were to blame when workers were driven to "the existential brink" and lost their livings. He called the pressure that Jews purportedly exerted on the world of German business "one of the reasons for the dramatic worsening of the social question."[30] As a consequence, he believed that those who were being pushed to the margins by big-time Jewish capitalism would join forces: "Isolation and atomization have put us in our current position, so we are seeking an organization in which workers again feel like a band of brothers who stick together."[31]

Wilhelm Marr also defined the Jewish question as a social one. He understood anti-Semitism as an answer to "abstract [read: Jewish] theories of freedom, which would more accurately be called [theories of] impudence."[32] But confrontations between Jews and their detractors did not always remain theoretical or purely verbal. On New Year's Eve 1880, groups of frenzied youngsters went through the streets of Berlin hollering "Jews out!" They physically blocked Jews from entering cafés, beat up passersby, broke windows, and caused "other forms of senseless destruction." "This all happened," according to a 1909 history of the German labor movement, "in the name of defending German idealism against Jewish materialism and protecting honest German labor against Jewish exploitation."[33]

Just as Hitler would do later on, Stoecker offered his followers the prospect of a social benefits program. He called for laws limiting the workweek, progressive income and inheritance taxes, taxes on stock market profits and luxury items, a ban on child labor, and the introduction of a social security system and state-owned enterprises. "The Christian Social Workers' Party," Stoecker's party manifesto stated, "pursues the goals of narrowing the gap between rich and poor and of increasing economic security."[34] In January and February 1881, Stoecker spoke at mass rallies attended by up to three thousand people. The titles of his speeches were "Artisanship Past and Present," "The Sins of the Negative Press," "The Jewish Question," and "Compulsory Accident Insurance." Bismarck observed that Stoecker's speeches were aimed at exploiting the envy and rapacity of the non-propertied masses against the property-owning class.[35]

Beginning in 1889, the anti-Semitic German Social Party expanded on the basic ideas of Stoecker's earlier Christian Social Workers' Party, taking over all of its demands and insisting on direct elections in Prussia with secret ballots so that disgruntled groups in the wider society could vent their dissatisfaction. At some point in the future, the party envisioned the parliamentary system's yielding to a state order organized along the lines of trades, seeing harmonious collective interest groups as the key to establishing permanent economic security. The German Social Party wanted to see Christian artisans, merchants, and farmers protected from the unfettered free market, domestic and foreign competition, false advertising, extortionately high interest rates, swindles, middlemen, and "fluctuations in grain prices due to speculation in the commodities market." It insisted that the "discrepancies between the rule of those with property and those dependent on property, or 'capital' and 'labor,' " be made central to the political agenda. This, the party stated, was crucial to maintaining domestic stability. Anti-Semitic measures were always one of the first steps toward this social ideal: "We demand limits on all of those liberties benefiting Jewry because they drain the blood from and do great damage to productive, honest working Germans."[36]

For all their vehemence, the various anti-Semitic parties in the Wilhelmine era, such as the Christian Social Party and the German Social Party, did not come together in a single, unified, potent movement. Groups came and went, never progressing beyond regional significance, while their leaders attacked one another as charlatans and blowhards. More significant in the medium-to-long term were the numerous trade organizations that excluded Jews. They included the Imperial German Association of the Middle Class, the Farmers' League, and the association of Nationalist Legal Clerks, as well as student fraternities. These were joined by both older and more recent anti-Semitic groups, such as the German League (Deutschbund), the Wagner and Gobineau Clubs, the Reich Hammer League (Reichs-hammerbund), and the Pan-German League, under chairman Hein-rich Class.

The manifestos of the German Social Party and the Pan-German League laid the foundations for much of the ideology of the later National Socialist German Workers' Party. In 1912, Class put forth the following demands: "Resident Jews are to be subject to laws on foreigners, and all Jewish immigration is to be discontinued. A Jew is defined as anyone who belonged to the Jewish faith on January 18, 1871, as well as anyone descending from such people, regardless of whether only one parent may have been Jewish. In addition, Jews are to be excluded from public offices and military services and prohib-ited from directing or working for German newspapers and public banks. Property ownership and mortgages are prohibited. In return for the protection they enjoy as foreigners, they are to be taxed dou-bly." As a justification for his demands, Class cited the advantages that Jews enjoyed in their education and talent, which enabled them to get ahead more quickly than Christians. "The masses were very slow to get started," Class wrote. "Indeed, you can say that whole segments of society have yet to catch up."[37]

Like the leaders of all the other anti-Semitic associations, the Prot-estant pastor Stoecker interpreted the Jewish question not as a reli-gious or racial conflict but rather as "an issue of social concern." His attacks were directed not against traditional Jews and their beliefs but against modern, secular Jews. One of their cardinal sins, in Stoecker's eyes, was being too clever, and he resented their "ominous" drive to better their social status. With a mixture of admiration and contempt,

Stoecker noted that "even poor Jews sacrifice everything they possess to give their children a good education." Instead of doing this, Stoecker suggested, they should stop trying to "maintain their distance from manual labor" and should become, like Gentile Germans, "tailors and shoemakers, factory workers and domestic servants." If the social situation did not change, the pastor warned, Jews would "increasingly become employers while Christians would labor and be exploited in their service." The daily newspaper *Germania*, which was loosely affiliated with the Catholic Center Party, published similar polemics: "The progress of Jewry in the last decades in terms of intellectual and financial power is nothing short of horrendous. It's unprecedented in ancient, medieval, and modern history. The means that Jews have for putting other peoples under their intellectual and financial yoke are ever expanding!" The journalist who wrote this article blamed what he saw as a negative trend on the desire of young Jews to attend university. Even Jewish orphanages, he complained, "almost exclusively produce merchants and university students, while Christian orphans, because they lack the necessary means, can only become artisans, physical laborers, servants, and the like."[38]

My maternal great-great-grandfather was a Prussian royal guardsman named Friedrich-Wilhelm Kosnik (1837–1910). He grew up in a poor religious household in which his mother encouraged him to read the Bible in its entirety at least twice a year. In 1861, Kosnik held watch over the coffin of the deceased Prussian king Friedrich Wilhelm IV. In 1863, he was deployed, together with sixty thousand other soldiers, on Prussia's eastern border to cut off the escape routes of Polish revolutionaries who were rebelling against Russian rule. Kosnik enjoyed telling stories of his military service. After he was discharged, he joined the rail service and worked his way up from train conductor to stationmaster third class. His son Friedrich, the only one of his male children to survive to adulthood, rose to become a midlevel school administrator. In an autobiographical sketch, Friedrich wrote that his father had been one of the best pupils at his grammar school and had always regretted "not being able to study at university." Still, immediately upon completing his education, Friedrich-Wilhelm Kosnik did become the scribe of a town called Schlawe. The final and highest rung on his career ladder was master of a train station on the outskirts of Leipzig. It was in that city that he joined the anti-Semitic Reichshammerbund and made the acquaintance of the group's leader, Theodor Fritsch.[39]

As an active Reichshammerbund member, my great-great-grandfather occasionally gave speeches to the association, but there's no record of what he said. His son, however, praised his talents as a public speaker. Kosnik would have been talking to people from modest circumstances similar to his own, and it's likely that he echoed the sorts of sentiments Fritsch published in his pamphlets—for instance, calls for "respect and protection for the economically weak who can simultaneously be the mentally and morally strong." Fritsch demanded that the state guarantee "a proper distribution of prosperity and the flourishing of the whole." In Fritsch's eyes, that entailed breaking Jewish dominance and slowing the pace of Jewish economic progress: "The whole mechanism of enrichment, put in the service of unfettered addiction to profit, has not increased the health, security, and happiness of individual human beings." Fritsch's attacks were calculated to appeal to millions of confused and uprooted people who had moved from the rural periphery to Germany's industrial centers. "In the big cities," Fritsch wrote, "Jews and Jewish sensibilities rule, and a person accustomed to nature feels like an alien, a clueless child, who falls into one Jewish trap after the next."[40]

Today, people speak of Fritsch with justified revulsion, but we should not forget that he was also the pioneer of the modern urban gardening movement and a proponent of ecologically sound city infrastructures. Many of the ideas in his 1896 book *The City of the Future*, which was heavily influenced by English models, were adopted by twentieth-century urban reformers. They included allotment gardens for the working class, children's playgrounds in spacious and sunny courtyards, sunlit school buildings, circle lines in public transportation, radial street layouts, and separate industrial and residential areas. Fritsch's overarching urban concept was based on communal ownership of property, a system where people would receive freeholds without mortgages or interest. As a city planner, Fritsch wanted to prevent "native soil"—which he regarded as the ground for a happy existence—from becoming "a playing field for recklessness and frivolity and addiction to profit seeking."[41] And to him, profit was synonymous with Jews.

In 1912, sociologist Werner Sombart described the hateful views of men like Fritsch, Stoecker, and Marr as "social anti-Semitism." It was the product of competition-driven envy, although the jealousy was directed only against competitors named Kohn and not ones called Müller. Sombart estimated that Jews in turn-of-the-century Berlin rose up the social ladder three to four times faster than Gentiles. A few decades before Sombart, Stoecker had arrived at roughly the same calculation. According to the 1867 Berlin census, Jews represented 4 percent of the city's population but 30 percent of households that hired tutors for their children. Thirty-five years before World War I, and seventy years before Hitler, Christian Social anti-Semites had framed the Jewish question as one of whether Christians were being disadvantaged—as an issue, so to speak, of a "fairness gap." "A half million Jewish citizens are occupying positions of importance in our society that greatly exceed their actual numbers," Stoecker thundered in a parliamentary speech in 1880. "Equipped with a strong capital base, as well as great talent, this part of the population is exerting destructive pressure on our public life." It is no surprise that the manifesto "Modern Jewry," which Stoecker wrote for his Christian Social Workers' Party, prominently featured a slogan common to all modern anti-Semites: "A bit more equality, please!"[42]

4

THE MAINSTREAM'S
DANGEROUS INDIFFERENCE

SOCIAL DEMOCRACY AND ANTI-SEMITISM

The rise of a social anti-Semitism rooted in the Gentile Germans' envy of their Jewish fellow citizens was accompanied by the increasing dominance of collective modes of thought. The tendency to prioritize the native collective over the rights of individuals made it more difficult for leaders within the social-democratic and liberal movements to recognize the danger of anti-Semitism and to combat it effectively. The anxiety that the German majority felt about the disproportionately successful Jewish minority produced not only hatred on the social fringes but also a dangerous indifference within the social mainstream to attacks on Jews.

This tolerance of anti-Semitic attacks was evident even within the Social Democratic Party (SPD), although ever since the party's founding in 1863 Jewish members and functionaries had been prominent in the organization. One particularly important leader was the Berlin textiles entrepreneur Paul Singer, who was elected to the Reichstag by convincing margins in 1884 and 1887. In 1885, his fellow party members chose him as their parliamentary chairman, and in 1890 he was made party cochairman. Singer held the latter office until his death in 1911 and was known for his powerful voice and eloquence.

One incident in particular illustrates the strong support that Singer enjoyed among the proletariat in the German capital. Singer was speaking at a large-scale workers' meeting when suddenly a delicate voice called down from the upper rows of the auditorium: "Hurray for Jewish Paul!" According to one account, the audience took up the cry: "Hundreds, thousands chanted 'Jewish Paul, Jewish Paul!' Singer stood at his lectern, at first amazed and speechless, then deeply moved as he registered his listeners' tribute. The workers at the meeting refused to calm down. They stormed the stage, lifted Singer in their arms, and carried him triumphantly out of the building and into the streets." When Singer died, at the age of sixty-seven, workers turned his funeral into a mass demonstration that began early in the morning and didn't end until late at night. "No powerful leader on earth could have been given a better send-off," a Berlin newspaper declared.[1]

Despite the respect given to leaders such as Singer, anti-Semitism held sway among some within the SPD. In January 1881, the party newspaper *The Social Democrat* published a bizarre editorial that would set the tone for later social-democratic analyses of anti-Semitism. "In the empire of piety before God and pious virtue, more and more people are complaining about society's being 'Jewified,'" wrote the author. He went on to complain that the Jewish German banker Gerson von Bleichröder had received an aristocratic title, that "everything is now for sale and Jewified," and that "in fact bargaining has become the basic principle of the German Empire." Consequently, he said, anti-Semites of the era were due a measure of understanding: "We could interpret it as a sign of gradual improvement that resistance to the spirit of greedy haggling is being voiced, if it were not directed solely against the small-time hagglers. The way things are, though, people are attacking only circumcised Jews [i.e., Jewish converts to Christianity], while the Jews that pull the strings are glorified and celebrated."[2]

In 1882, Paul Mehring, who would become one of the most prominent SPD members, published a pamphlet vigorously defending Heinrich von Treitschke. The author of a biography of Karl Marx and the publisher of the works of Marx and Engels, Mehring praised the historian for depicting the negative effects of Jewish emancipation in "the only worthy fashion" and "with manly courage." He also condemned the cries that went up "whenever a frank word against Jews became audible." He accused the various liberal parties of "unscrupulously" exploiting recent anti-Jewish violence in the eastern German region of Pomerania. As a Pomeranian resident, Mehring argued that "in many a town the foolishness first came about because so much was made of the subject." He did not mention the fact that Gentiles in the town of Neustettin had burned down a synagogue. Instead, he held up Treitschke's continual anti-Jewish provocations as "a moral and social clearing of the air."

Mehring dismissed most, if not all, of Treitschke's adversaries as "pathetic opinion terrorists," while promoting the historian as a courageous fighter against moral corruption: "Who would deny that a long list of asocial and amoral Jewish practices are no longer spreading as furiously in our national life as they were two years ago?" Mehring did see a danger of anti-Semitism's "unchaining the beast." The Jewish question, he wrote, evoked the three most powerful sources of human hatred: conflicts of religion, race, and social class. But to combat this danger, Mehring argued, "extremely frank and determined discussions" would have to commence about how to oppose which forms of Jewish evil.[3]

Mehring joined the SPD in 1891 and quickly rose to become one of its most important intellectual representatives. As the editor in chief of the party's theoretical journal and a popular newspaper in Leipzig, as well as, for a time, the director of the party academy, Mehring had enormous influence. In later years, he voted against Germany's entering World War I; months before his death in 1919, he also helped found the German Communist Party, the KPD, together with Karl Liebknecht and Rosa Luxemburg. Yet he consistently maintained the opinion, advanced in his defense of Treitschke, that there was a crucial Jewish problem that had to be addressed. Over time, he merely revised the targets of his attacks, taking to task the few remaining genuine liberal politicians for being "philo-Semites"—as if somehow his main enemies were not Jews but those who unduly befriended Jews.

Mehring was fond of personifying philo-Semitism, accusing it of speaking with a forked tongue and concealing its true intentions or "claiming to defend Jews while it protected capitalism through thick and thin." Thus, Mehring argued, it was part of "the same order of enemy of class-conscious workers" as anti-Semitism. At the same time, Mehring continued to play down and ignore anti-Jewish violence: "In speaking of the brutalities that anti-Semites commit against Jews more in word than in deed, we should not overlook the brutalities that philo-Semitism commits more in deed than in word against anyone who believes in socialism, whether he be Jew or Turk, Christian or heathen."

Though it hid behind various masks, Mehring said, the fundamental Jewish identity celebrated a "religion of practical egotism." As he put it, "global and religious Jewry today is in fact born of bourgeois life and receives its final education in the monetary system." Mehring praised anti-Semites for realizing that capitalist exploitation was at work among the philo-Semitic adherents of cosmopolitan economic freedom, who, he claimed, "have pulled the wool over our eyes for years." With reference to Marx, he repeatedly announced that "society would be emancipated from Jewry" as soon as the historical advantage of Jews—their penny-pinching business sense—was "removed" by social revolution.[4] In 1933, National Socialism would invert this proclamation: Hitler and others promised that as soon as the National Socialist revolution had removed Jewry, economic exploitation would be overcome and a socially just utopia would be nigh.

Mehring went one step further in his 1902 introduction to Marx's essay "On the Jewish Question." There he wrote of "Jewry as a class" that, as the result of the modern economic system, had accrued far too much power "not to push at the constraints that hemmed in its practical dominance." Mehring accused Jewry, in another personification, of only pretending to support democracy while in reality "tending to betray democracy and liberalism, if they threaten its own rule." Jews, Mehring claimed, suddenly mutated into "hissing reactionaries" whenever "the consequences of addressing the common good ran contrary to a specific Jewish interest."[5]

Mehring's repeated attacks were not the only examples of anti-Semitism in the German Social Democratic tradition. The popular humor magazine *The Real Jacob*, for example, often contained caricatures of capitalists with stereotypically Jewish features. On the other hand, such attempts at humor, like Mehring's obsessive hostility, remained the exceptions to the rule. Indeed, thousands of SPD functionaries and opinion makers felt a duty to combat Jew baiting and refused to bolster their anticapitalist agitation with anti-Jewish resentment.

A more significant problem was that the SPD leaders became entangled in their own theory-heavy ideology when it came to the issue of anti-Semitism. Social Democrats interpreted the special role played by Jews in trade and modern innovation as a result of the bourgeois capitalist order that was to be overthrown with social revolution. Sociologically, they saw anti-Semitism "as part of class warfare, . . . a product of the desperate struggle of doomed social strata."[6] It was thus regarded as a middle-class phenomenon that had little relevance to a workers' party. Early Social Democrats assumed that the ruling classes encouraged anti-Jewish hatred to distract the working masses from the goal of their struggle and weaken them through division. Leaving aside such theories, almost all leading Social Democrats treated the Jewish issue as a religious and therefore private matter that had no place in programmatic party declarations.

Social Democratic leaders saw early on how class ideology could be transformed into racism, but they misinterpreted what was happening. Beginning in the 1880s, they mistook the adherents of anti-Semitic national-socialist movements for believers who had been led astray but who would sooner or later return to the fold and fight for the one true cause. The common saying "anti-Semitism is the social-ism of fools" was one expression of this attitude. No one knows who coined the saying, but it was used constantly by the SPD leadership. Party leaders also distinguished between anti-Semitic "mob thinkers" and ordinary men on the street prone to occasional outbursts of anti-Semitism. According to orthodox social-democratic opinion, the resentments of the latter category revealed a "high degree of social dis-satisfaction" that was being temporarily diverted into "false channels" but that would ultimately "outlast the whole anti-Semitism con" and benefit the SPD. This way of thinking was apparent as early as 1881, in the social-democratic response to the anti-Jewish pogroms in Russia. "Once unleashed," wrote one SPD leader, "popular dissatisfaction will not stop with the Jew, but end in an uprising against the tsar."

Social Democratic leader August Bebel engaged in a similar line of reasoning in his speech "Social Democracy and Anti-Semitism" of November 1893. The previous June, despite restrictive election rules, anti-Semitic parties had surprisingly won 16 of 397 voting districts in the parliamentary election. This unsavory stirring up of hatred, Bebel argued, was a reaction to social problems—but since the right-wing parties offered no real solution, anti-Semitic circles could be fertile ground for social-democratic teachings. The SPD, Bebel concluded, would reap the harvest and gain new members.

Bebel delivered his speech at the SPD's annual convention. At the same event, the SPD adopted the official position that anti-Semites were battling a by-product of capitalism, "Jewish exploitation," and would eventually be forced to realize that "not just the Jewish capital-ist but the whole capitalist class is their enemy." In the Social Demo-cratic magazine *Vorwärts* (*Forward*), readers were told: "As culturally repellent as anti-Semitism may be, it is involuntarily a promoter of culture. It is, in the full sense of the word, fertilizer for social democ-racy." In another article, Franz Mehring argued that anti-Semitism would teach the economically deprived "a very useful primary course in social democracy" and that nationalism and socialism would soon make common cause against the "accumulating sins" of bourgeois liberalism. Implicitly, Mehring recommended supporting the anti-Semite Paul Förster ("an intellectually capable and personally honorable man") against his liberal challenger in an upcoming run-off election. Mehring posed a rhetorical question: "Can the SPD support brutal and naked capitalism and its political expression—liberalism—against anti-Semitism, which in its own way envisions social revolution?"

In late 1893, the Austrian socialist Heinrich Braun offered a comparable analysis of anti-Jewish groups in Germany. He, too, regarded anti-Semitism as a political current in which "a radical anticapitalist tendency is trying, with increasingly clarity and purpose, to assert itself." To emphasize his point, he cited conservative German chancellor Leo von Caprivi, who had called anti-Semites "an early crop produced by the social-democratic movement." But Braun went even further, romanticizing anti-Semites into political awakeners serving the cause of social democracy by "seizing levels of society not yet ripe for social-democratic propaganda and shaking them out of their lethargy." Braun argued: "The importance of the sociopolitical work done today by anti-Semitism cannot be underestimated from the perspective of a revolutionary development of society. It has overcome the centuries-old ignorance of the peasantry and turned this most lethargic group in the population into a passionate movement. Its propaganda is reaching small-time artisans, low-level bureaucrats, and other groups to which the Social Democratic movement has little access." Anti-Semitism, Braun concluded, would "most likely, according to the law, so to speak, of social gravitation, feed into the larger and more powerful Social Democratic movement."[7] Those born later knew that Braun was on the wrong track. Germans did not follow a putative law of social democratic gravitation but rather of national-social gravitation.

NAUMANN'S NATIONAL SOCIALISM

Liberalism's lack of vitality is an often underestimated reason Germany went down the path it did in the nineteenth and twentieth centuries. In the final quarter of the nineteenth century, liberalism was squeezed between conservatism, the Christian Social movement, and socialism. Even the German word for liberalism, *Freisinn* (free-mindedness), fell into disuse. Collectivism of both social and national varieties prevailed over the idea of personal liberty, and many of the politicians who had come together under the liberal flag went along with the spirit of the times, betraying the ideal of free-mindedness and helping hasten the transition to the national-socialist politics of power.

Friedrich Naumann typified the internal weakness of German liberalism. Born in 1860, the son of a Protestant pastor, Naumann studied theology and became a pastor himself before turning to politics in 1894. Initially active in Stoecker's Christian Social Party, he soon left it because he disagreed with its focus on anti-Semitism. In 1897 he founded the National Socialist Association and published his political manifesto, "The National Socialist Catechism: Declaration of Principles of the National Socialist Association." That organization would later merge with other leftist liberal groups to form the Progressive People's Party. With only brief interruptions, Naumann served as a deputy to parliament from 1906 until his death in 1919. A year before he died, Naumann cofounded yet another political party, the German Democratic Party (DDP). It combined nationalist and socialist positions with a few depleted remnants of liberalism. Together with the Social Democrats and the Catholic Center Party, the DDP was part of the main centrist coalition that wielded power throughout most of the Weimar Republic. Because of this, Naumann is known as one of the fathers of Weimar democracy. His "National Socialist Catechism" is rarely mentioned.

Naumann's catechism contains a political program in the form of 268 questions and answers. Here are some of the more intriguing entries:

> *Why do you call yourselves national-socialist?* Because we're convinced the national and social belong together.

What is the national? It is the drive of Germans to extend their influence around the globe.

What is the social? It is the drive of the working masses to extend their influence among the people.

Is it likely that the influence of the working masses will increase? It is not only likely but certain, since the size of the working population and its education are constantly increasing.

So we can expect large-scale wars in the future? Indeed. Very large-scale ones. England, Russia, and China are the three great powers that will inevitably butt heads.

Can we Germans not be neutral in future great conflicts? We can if we want our people to become extinct.

Why is international socialism a lost cause? Because the cultural levels of various peoples greatly differ and the progress of one people depends on the decline of another.

Could we not extend the influence of all cultured peoples? No. The market is not big enough for all these peoples. The market grows more slowly than the expansion desired by cultured peoples. The fight for the global market is a fight for survival.

Wouldn't it be better to expand the market within one's own nation? That should happen wherever possible, but it won't change the fact that we will need increasing amounts of grain, petroleum, cotton, and other necessities from abroad if we want to survive.

What is the state? The state is the embodiment of the life of the people in the form of laws and administration. It is not an institution of one ruling class, although it is misused as such.

Can we reduce the economic dependency of the masses? Yes, this is the goal of social reform. The success of reform depends on whether the body of the people as a whole flourishes.

Why does social reform depend on the flourishing of the body of the people? Because no new economic classes can arise within a people in decline, as we can see in Spain and Italy.

Does social reform have good prospects in Germany? Yes, insofar as it is pursued in conjunction with the expansion of the power of the German people.

Why must the working masses be nationalist? For reasons of self-preservation.

What kind of politics does that entail? A politics of external power and internal reform.

What is the task of a confident and stable foreign policy? The expansion of German economic power and the German intellect.

What are the basic principles of Germany-first politics? It needs to be determined whether we are prepared for a major battle against the world's leading sea-trading power, England, if we want to expand our economic influence. And it remains to be seen whether, given this enmity toward England, our old animosity with France might not decrease and whether our political friendship with Russia is necessary.

What consequences will such a foreign policy have? It will require looking at our means for doing battle to see if they are adequate for a conflict with England.

What are you demanding with regard to the fleet? An appropriate strengthening of the German navy.

Do Germany's current colonies meet your demands? No, but it's better than having no colonies, and the ones we have need to be kept.

What kind of colonies should we be striving for? Colonies in mild climates where it's possible for Germans to settle.

How can we acquire such colonies? Through peace treaties after successful wars.

What is the main conflict in cities? The one between property owners and tenants.

Whose side are you on? The tenants'.

Is there a Jewish question? Yes.

In what form? The Israelites are a separate ethnic group from Germans.

Are there other foreign ethnic groups in Germany? Wends [Western Slavs], Lithuanians, Poles, Danes, and French.

Can a state be created with only German citizens? That is completely impossible.

Is it possible to strip the Jews alone of their citizenship? No, but even if it were possible, it would be unfortunate.

How so? The collective power of Jewry would turn against the state. There is nothing less prudent than turning an influential minority against the state without stripping them of their power.

Isn't the conflict between Germans and Israelites understandable given how different they are? It is understandable and can be overcome as a social conflict only when the Israelites adopt German and Christian ways of thinking.

To what extent is the social question a Jewish question? It is only in specific regions and professions. The solution is not political anti-Semitism but economic rules.

Would it not be advisable to close Germany's eastern border to non-German elements? If it is possible to reduce migration from east to west with state means, we will definitely support it.

What sort of spirit should rule in the German Empire? A just, free, German, Christian spirit.

Will you enlist the cooperation of the Israelites? We would like to, providing they think in national-socialist terms and are not hostile toward Christianity.

To what are you most fundamentally committed? National socialism on a Christian basis.[8]

Naumann's "Catechism" of 1897 eradicated the last visible remnants of individualistic freethinking from the ideology of political liberalism. In their stead, the talk was of state and military activism, colonial adventures, state-run social programs, and the desirability of keeping Germany free from "foreign" influences, whether "Israelites" or Eastern European immigrants. Later, in his book *Central Europe*, published just after the start of World War I, Naumann amplified his theory with concrete details. He interpreted bloody trench warfare as a battle for an imperial and socialistic future and argued that Germany, once it had won the war, should annex foreign territory and establish spheres of influence. Naumann saw the wartime socialism of Kaiser Wilhelm II's government as a model for the state of the future, in which "organs of state, syndicates of entrepreneurs, and labor unions are mere organs within a communal form of life."

Naumann glorified the war as the "creator of a Central European soul." Whereas in his "Catechism" he had focused on Great Britain as the enemy, he now rejected any possibility of Germany's peacefully coexisting with Russia and France either and demanded that Germany acquire territory for economic expansion in Eastern and Southeastern Europe. "As long as the sun still shines," he wrote, "we have to maintain the idea of joining the ranks of the world's top economic powers. That includes the incorporation of the other Central European states and nations." Severe economic pressure was to be applied to create a new empire between the Baltic and Black Seas. Existing states would be reconstructed as well-functioning members.

Naumann placed special emphasis on a diligent, unionized, and disciplined German workforce: "German workers, united with enlightened entrepreneurs, syndicate directors, privy councils and officers, are hardly the most charming or amusing company imaginable. But they do represent the most effective, dependable, and lasting sort of human machinery. The living machine of the people continues to function whether the individual lives or dies. It is impersonal, or superpersonal. It may have its friction and breakdowns, but as a whole it is something that could never have existed in the past. It is our character, as it has coalesced in history." And over the course of World War I, the author noted with approval that "state and national socialism has been growing on all sides."[9]

Thirteen years after the publication of Naumann's *Central Europe*,

Hitler wrote his *Second Book*, which he refrained from publishing for tactical reasons. It discussed German foreign policy and a future Europe under German domination. Hitler lifted many of the central ideas from Naumann, adding a number of digressions on racial theory, the future of the automobile, and the rise of the United States as a world power.[10]

On the one hand, Naumann moved German liberalism to the right by propagating German imperialism. On the other hand, he repositioned it to the left by deemphasizing personal and economic freedom in favor of national-socialist collectivism. It would be unfair to call Naumann a predecessor of Hitler's, and he was certainly no anti-Semite. But he did bring together socialistic, imperialistic, and nationalistic ideas into a coherent line of thinking that ultimately would meld into the ideology of the NSDAP.

In 1930, Naumann's German Democratic Party (the successor to the Progressive People's Party) incorporated the anti-Semitic People's National Reich Association and renamed itself the German State Party. After parliamentary elections in March 1933, the party had five deputies, including Theodor Heuss, later the first president of the postwar Federal Republic of Germany. All five of them voted for the Enabling Act of March 24, 1933, which gave Hitler dictatorial powers. One of them, Reinhold Meier (who would later become state premier of Baden-Württemberg), explained why he had ignored his reservations and approved the measure to end German democracy: "In light of our lofty national goals, we feel committed to the view expounded today by Imperial Chancellor Hitler."[11]

═ 5 ═

WAR, DEFEAT, AND JEW HATRED

THE 1916 JEWISH CENSUS

The Central Association of German Citizens of the Jewish Faith was established in 1893 as a reaction to growing anti-Semitism. Its founding purpose was to help Jewish Germans "vigorously defend their equality as citizens and members of society as well as support them in their committed maintenance of a German mind-set." This formulation was directed against both German jingoism and Zionism. Zionism took on organized forms at the turn of the century, but it did not resonate much among German Jews, whose leaders were quick to intervene when young people were captivated by the idea. The chairman of the city council of Königsberg (today's Kaliningrad), for instance, saw to it that the Zionist sporting club Makkabi was not allowed to use a public gymnasium. The grandfather of philosopher Hannah Arendt attacked the young Makkabi members as anti-German agitators. And commenting on the idea of resurrecting the state of Israel in Palestine, the geographer Alfred Philippson wryly remarked:

"Where there's water, people die of malaria. Where there's no water, they starve because nothing grows."

Many prominent German Jews reprimanded their younger Zionist coreligionists while maintaining some sympathy for their ideas. For instance, the Central Association's lawyer, Ludwig Holländer, proclaimed: "German Jews are stepchildren, and stepchildren must always be on their best behavior."[1] But with their craving for action and deeds, young Jewish nationalists weren't terribly interested in the admonitions of their elders. Those who preached restraint, they felt, failed to recognize a real and present danger, acted against the interests of their own people, and were squandering valuable time. Inspired by romanticized socialism, the athletics movement of young Gentile Germans, and utopian visions of a Jewish state, Jewish nationalists set about reviving "Jewish popular culture." They accused the typical assimilated Jew of "cutting the ties connecting himself with his forefathers and betraying an eminently important Jewish duty, the duty of blood."[2]

The vast majority of German Jews, however, stood behind the kaiser and the empire, and a great many German Jewish poets composed odes to Germany's aspirations to world power. At the start of the Franco-Prussian War, Berthold Auerbach wrote a poem entitled "In Alsace Across the Rhine, There Lives a Brother of Mine," which staked a patriotic German claim to French territory. Later, Robert Lindner wrote a popular song promoting German naval might. During World War I, Ernst Lissauer wrote anti-British verses: "We have but one common hatred, we love together, we hate together, and we have but one common enemy." Kaiser Wilhelm II awarded Lissauer the Red Eagle Order for his work, and German soldiers at the front developed a special ritual around Lissauer's verses. When two soldiers met, one would say "May God punish England," and the other would reply: "May he punish it."

In 1914, liberal politician Paul Nathan celebrated the seventy million Germans of "all parties . . . Catholics, Protestants, and Jews" who pursued the common goal "of waging the fight forced

upon us to protect Germany from political and economic destruction."
The following year, Jewish German physician Magnus Hirschfeld
praised German orderliness, determination in battle, and the "glori-
ous edifice of the new German Empire." Twenty-year-old Nachum
Goldmann, who would found the World Jewish Congress in 1936,
likewise lauded Germany and its "spirit of militarism" as the "bearer
of modern civilization." Many German Jews bought war bonds, and
they served loyally in the German military. In 1918, the head rabbi in
Strasbourg, a native of Alsace, resigned his post rather than have to
greet French troops as they arrived to retake authority over the region.[3]

Many German Jews hoped that the war would finally make them
full members of German society. This vision remained unfulfilled. In
the summer of 1916, the parliamentary deputy Matthias Erzberger of
the Catholic Center Party—with the support of the National Liberals
and even some Social Democrats—petitioned the Reichstag to commission a census aimed at determining the following: "How many people
of Jewish extraction are serving at the front? How many behind the
lines? How many in military administrations? How many Jews have
been complained about or deemed unfit for military service?" This
strange statistical exercise was prompted by anonymous denunciations
of Jews' alleged unwillingness to fight for Germany, and the Army
Supreme Command reacted positively to the demands. On November
1, 1916, amid an atmosphere of calumny and suspicion, the Prussian
minister of war commissioned a survey of Jews' readiness to fight. Statistics were collected about the numbers of dead and wounded and
whether soldiers were stationed at the front lines or toward the rear.

The Jewish German community was shocked and insulted by the
survey. The Central Association wrote that it could not believe
that such a census had been ordered "amid this holy battle." In fact,
the survey mostly showed that Jews made up as high a percentage of
German soldiers as the Christian majority, relative to their proportion of the population. Casualties, too, were proportional. After pressure from the Central Association, which was concerned about some
misleading exceptions to that overall pattern, the results of the survey

were not made public, but the campaign to discredit Jews as cowardly shirkers of national duty continued.

The details of the situation were quite ambiguous and complex. Many Jews saw wartime service as something they in particular owed to their homeland and as a down payment on a better future. Yet in addition to the basic anti-Semitic thrust of testing Jews' enthusiasm as soldiers, the census distorted the facts in ways that obscured Jewish German patriotism. Germany's Jewish population was disproportionately urban and had lower birthrates than average. Moreover, many young Jews had converted to Christianity, so Jews were on average older than Gentiles. They thus had fewer young men who qualified for military service. In addition, before the war, Jews were prohibited from becoming officers, even though they were comparatively well educated. A disproportionate number of them therefore became military doctors, pursers, depot managers, translators, and supply organizers rather than frontline commanders. All these factors explained why relatively high numbers of Jewish soldiers served behind the lines.

At the same time, Jews who had served in the German military prior to World War I were far less likely to get promoted than their Gentile comrades. Of recruits with some form of higher education, only 2.9 percent of Protestants and 2.1 percent of Catholics remained common foot soldiers, compared with 45.8 percent of Jews.[4] Because Jews were so rarely promoted, disproportionately high numbers of them fought as common soldiers at the front—and they conspicuously displayed their courage and patriotism.

In 1921, the novelist Jakob Wassermann described how he was treated by his Gentile commanders in the military: "Although I applied all my honor and all my strength to doing my duty as a soldier and measuring up to the performance that was demanded, I didn't succeed in getting the recognition of my superiors." Wassermann sensed that the officers were contemptuous of him and his kind, and he noted "the clear tendency to treat satisfactory performances as a given while holding up the unsatisfactory ones for public pillory." He continued: "There was no pretense of different segments of society coming together; human qualities were completely disregarded; imagination or any originality of expression awakened immediate resentment; getting promoted beyond a certain level was out of the question; and all of that was because one's category of religious faith bore the designation Jew."[5]

My grandfather the German philologist and reserve army lieutenant Wolfgang Aly (1881–1962) was no doubt the sort of superior who angered Wassermann. His memoirs of World War I, which were based on his wartime correspondence, give us an impression of the sort of talk that prompted the Jewish census. Of a major under whom he served in the summer of 1916, he wrote: "He drank, and that made him unpredictable. He was a real connoisseur and demanded delicacies at the front, the names of which I hardly knew. And he was in the pockets of Jews. Private Kohn (a banker from Mannheim) ruled over the staff, making sure that more and more Jews were assigned to buying supplies. With rage, I witnessed the quantities of food that were being removed from our starving homeland. Within the staff, people laughed at the fact that I had a wife and five children to provide for. Every time the heavily laden Kohn returned from the home front, there was a big party." In autumn 1917, Wolfgang Aly wrote about the first strikes among German munitions workers: "It is typical of the situation as a whole that during a period of calm and successful work at the front, there is talk for the first time of an 'internal struggle,' i.e., in the homeland, in which Jews are also mentioned."[6]

At the general meeting of the Central Association on February 4, 1917, the census was the main topic of discussion. Reporting on the survey was the deputy chairman, the liberal politician and honorary citizen of Berlin Privy Councillor Oskar Cassel. He had succeeded in wringing from the newly appointed Prussian minister of war a declaration that the census had revealed nothing negative about the patriotism of Jews. In his own statement, Cassel reasserted that "despite everything we, as free German men and as pious and faith-bound

Jews, will continue to do our duty for the duration of this sacred struggle. . . . May we be rewarded in peacetime with freedom and full unity among all Germans." He went on to quote the German national anthem, for which he earned thunderous applause. Three resolutions were proposed decrying the census as deeply insulting, but the overwhelming majority of those in attendance rejected them, deeming them to be "no longer necessary."[7]

Nonetheless, an unarticulated undertone of disappointment ran throughout the discussions at the meeting. The recognition that assimilated Jews hoped to gain, which many had thought was at hand, remained an unfulfilled wish. Jews in other countries at war also had to put up with anti-Semitic obstacles, but as banker and politician Carl Melchior remarked, "in no other country is the agitation against Jewish soldiers as intense as in Germany."[8] Here it would be remiss not to mention Friedrich Naumann again. In his 1915 book *Central Europe*, he hailed Jewish bravery and insisted that after the war "mutual" social antagonisms should be laid to rest, since integration in the trenches was "worth every bit as much politically as baptism ceremonies."[9]

For the instigators of the census, the survey yielded the devastating insight that Jews—who had proven to be more suited to modernity in so many respects—were now also showing themselves to be the equals of Christian Germans as soldiers. Nonetheless, the study's misleading data about the relatively high numbers of Jews serving away from the front could be used to stir up further hatred. In the end, Germany's future foreign minister Walther Rathenau was right when he predicted in 1916: "The more Jews fall in the war, the more their enemies will use that fact as proof that Jews all sat safely behind the front lines exploiting people with exorbitant prices."[10]

WARTIME SOCIALISM, DEFEAT, CHAOS

Prior to 1914, the SPD officially promoted the idea of proletarian internationalism in contrast to nationalism. In reality, the party had already compromised this stance. Tacitly, all the major socialist parties were pursuing national aims. The constant tension between the revolutionary party devoted to social transformation and the more reformist trade union movement reflected the fact that the working masses were less interested in revolution per se than in social advancement and guarantees with respect to their standard of living. There were many ways to achieve those ends in the twentieth century, but few of them conformed to what revolutionary theorists considered the proper paths of history.

The much-heralded idea of socialist internationalism went up in smoke in the early days of August 1914. Everywhere in Europe, proletarian and bourgeois soldiers were marching enthusiastically, side by side, to face common national enemies. Together they would wage a bitter war for four and a half years. The imperial German government did not have to arrest Social Democratic leaders, as it had once envisioned doing. Indeed, in 1914 Kaiser Wilhelm proclaimed: "I no longer know any parties, only Germans." As a concrete manifestation of that statement, the words "For the German populace" were inscribed on the facade of the Reichstag in 1916. Conversely, Social Democratic deputies voted nearly unanimously to approve lines of credit to finance the war. Their class comrades from France, Belgium, and Britain likewise joined forces with their respective bourgeois governments and produced highly nationalist propaganda about "Jerries" or "Huns." In every European country Social Democrats invoked concepts of higher truth and superior culture to justify waging war against the enemy.

Proletarian internationalism is dead, long live wartime socialism— that was the rallying cry, and this way of thinking survived beyond the war, both in Germany and elsewhere. In 1931, German economist Wilhelm Röpke was still complaining about steadily increasing economic protectionism among the nations of Europe. "One cannot draw attention often enough," Röpke wrote, "to this unfortunate product of nationalism and collectivism, two unsettling tendencies that were dramatically encouraged by the war."[11]

The Social Democratic deputy Paul Lensch was an example of

what Röpke was talking about. In 1917, in a book entitled *Three Years of World Revolution*, Lensch positively celebrated the world war.[12] He argued that Bismarck's break with liberalism in 1879 had pushed the Iron Chancellor "into the role of a revolutionary" and paved the way, in terms of historical development, for "a higher, more mature form of economy." Lensch added: "We came to the realization that within today's global revolution Germany represents the revolutionary, and its great enemy England the counterrevolutionary side." Lensch's justification for this argument was that "English individualism" promoted a weak concept of state authority and a strong sense of personal liberty, while Germany enjoyed "the more mature principle of society focusing on social organization or socialization."

The national socialism advocated by the SPD since the start of World War I was expressed in statements like "The state has undergone a socialization process, and social democracy a process of nationalization." It was Germany's "historical mission" to go down this entwined path of double collectivism—as well as to pursue the war that Lensch styled as a fundamental social revolution. The ultimate aim was not liberty and maximum freedom of personal development but the "freedom of security" offered by collective discipline and strict organization.[13]

Thus, during World War I, the ethnically conceived people gradually and tacitly came to replace the proletariat as the focus of the Social Democratic desires for social revolution. Lenin himself used the German wartime economy as a model for Communist economic development in Russia, and there was considerable justification for doing so. For Lensch, Germany's wartime economy was "a small preview of the forces that a totally organized society would someday be able to produce."[14]

World War I destroyed the old governmental and social structures of Central and Eastern Europe, ultimately leading to starvation and defeat, chaos and misery, close-mindedness and hatred. Some two million young German men fell in the conflict, around a quarter of them in the final months of fighting. Millions more Germans were left crippled, widowed, or fatherless. As a result of the British naval blockade, 500,000 Germans died of malnutrition: in 1917, the average city dweller was given only 1,400 calories of food per day on which to survive. "Standing in long lines for groceries in the city rendered demoralized people frantic, defiant, and above all angry at the rich, who were feeding themselves far better 'through the back door,'" wrote historian Friedrich Meinecke.[15] Hundreds of thousands died young of tuberculosis, influenza, and sheer exhaustion. Children showed symptoms of malnutrition and rickets. Demobilized soldiers and desperate, starving women stumbled zombielike through daily routines that had suddenly become arduous.

Germans' suffering was in vain. What was the point of living, some asked themselves, if all had been for naught?[16] Housewives had come close to starvation, and the middle and upper classes lost major portions of their wealth as a result of the now worthless war bonds they had purchased out of a sense of patriotic duty. The Imperial German Army had been defeated. There were no celebrations that would have helped compensate for and overcome the horrors of the front and the psychological damage done to the eleven million soldiers who returned home. The trauma of having experienced artillery barrages, poison gas alarms, splintering grenades, and the deaths of their comrades gnawed at their psyches. "We young men who have been through war have a lot to work through ourselves," wrote Joseph Goebbels in his 1929 novel *Michael*. "The fact that so and so has lost an arm is not half as bad as the internal wounds we bear from war and destruction."[17]

My father, born in 1912, repeatedly spoke of how horrible it was for him and his siblings when his own father returned home defeated from the war. In his recollections, the household life they had previously led with their mother, grandmother, and southern German maid had been pleasant. Now that was over. Artillery officer Wolfgang Aly had served as a battalion leader on the western front; with their long-range howitzers, he and his men had achieved "fantastic" results, "firing off a hundred rounds in a single night." But they were also targets for deeply entrenched French units, in much-contested stretches of the front near Verdun and elsewhere. During a two-week home leave he was given in July 1917 after narrowly surviving a gas attack, my grandfather, then thirty-six years old, noted: "For the first time, I was absolutely done in. I couldn't bear the noise the children made and could only allow myself to be tended to."

Four months before the end of the war, my grandmother, then thirty-five, one of the emaciated German women, wrote: "Wolfgang is so shattered that he falls asleep on the bench he's sitting on." And of her own condition, she recorded: "My nerves are worse than ever. Pray to God with me that I don't bring misfortune down upon my family." After the war, she could see what patriotism had blinded her to for the previous four years: "How terribly we're doing! Who knows whether our children will bear the scars for the rest of their lives."[18] Shortly thereafter, her oldest child contracted tuberculosis. Despite expensive treatments in Davos, Switzerland, he died a few years later.

For four and a half years, the Germans had driven themselves to the brink of exhaustion fighting enemies whose economic resources extended nearly across the globe. Moreover, Germany had to provide financial and material support to its economically weak ally, the Austro-Hungarian Empire, and was forced to redeploy troops badly needed in the West to the southern and eastern fronts. German troops had given their all and fought honorably. For example, immediately after the Battle of Tannenberg, in which Germany inflicted a massive defeat on the Russian Imperial Army, German general Paul von Hindenburg had ordered his officers and soldiers to "forget that the captured adversary was a former enemy." Indeed, as Hindenburg later recalled, the fury of battle was "transformed with surprising speed into solicitous sympathy."[19] Hindenburg ordered that German and Russian soldiers who died at Tannenberg and the subsequent battles in Masuria be buried together in a joint ceremony; many of these common cemeteries still exist today. It was a humane gesture, motivated by traditional military values that would soon be lost in the age of ideological warfare.

World War I didn't come to an end simultaneously on all its fronts. The Central Powers forced Russia to capitulate in early 1918, while they in turn were defeated by the Entente in the West in November of that year. The cease-fire and the armistice agreements unleashed extreme social forces in all the countries concerned and led to a series of border conflicts and civil wars. The defeated nations of Russia, Romania, Austria, Hungary, and Germany lacked internal solidity and flexibility. The winners of World War I, by contrast, were Western democracies with liberally organized societies and state structures. Confident peoples get over defeats with relative ease, as France did in 1813–15 and 1870. The situation is different with a people divided by internal rifts. "Defeat was unbearable for Germany because it was and remained as senseless as the war itself," wrote German sociologist Helmuth Plessner in 1936. "At the end of an evolution that promised national consolidation and, however belated, political maturity, Germany was drawn into a battle against a world order, when it had no alternative order of its own."[20] Still bitter and angry, most Germans were of no mind to accept that their sacrifices had been pointless. Instead, they retreated into resentment, feeling that their government, which became a democracy on November 9, 1918, was treating them with "boundless ingratitude."[21]

FROM CEASE-FIRE TO DICTATED PEACE

The Treaty of Versailles, which the German delegation was forced to sign in the summer of 1919 under the threat of renewed hostilities, was viewed in Germany as insult added to injury. Naturally, what the outraged Germans overlooked was that they had demanded comparably draconian territorial concessions and reparation payments after emerging victorious in the Franco-Prussian War of 1870–71, even though that conflict, with its 120,000 French and German casualties, had been relatively minor. Moreover, in 1918, Germany had dictated terms of peace to the nascent Soviet Union that were far harsher than those in the Treaty of Versailles.

Nonetheless, there were other ways in which the victors humiliated their former foes in 1919, and these provoked collective resistance and inadvertently strengthened the old, reactionary elites in Germany. In a number of regards, the Versailles treaty violated the armistice agreement of November 1918, to which Germany had agreed. That agreement had been based on Woodrow Wilson's Fourteen Points speech, which promised diplomatic openness, freedom of navigation of the seas, the removal of economic barriers, the reduction of national armaments, and the impartial adjustment of all colonial claims. The Treaty of Versailles—together with the mandatory administration of the Saar region of Germany and the status of the Free City of Danzig (Gdansk)—negated all these principles.[22]

Germans particularly took umbrage at article 231 of the treaty, which reversed the Wilsonian principle of a "peace without victory." The clause blamed Germany exclusively for World War I, justifying demands for reparations. Unlike in the case of previous peace treaties, reparations were to be made because of moral culpability, not just military defeat. In formulating the newly moralistic language, French and British statesmen had yielded to demands of their respective populations that Germany had to be made to pay. Seventeen million people had died in World War I. The masses in the Western European democracies demanded revenge and left pragmatic negotiators with little room to maneuver.[23]

The article assigning sole blame for the war to Germany united most Germans in a blanket denial of any responsibility. It allowed the Nazi Party, a short time later, to proclaim: "Germany's innocence in the world war, as can be documented, has been proved in every respect."[24] The extraordinary amount demanded in reparations also led to an unfortunate psychological response by allowing Germans to deny any responsibility for the rampant inflation, mass unemployment, and economic crises of the Weimar Republic. Instead, German

economic woes were blamed entirely on foreign influence and sometimes on a global Jewish conspiracy.

The ink had hardly dried on the treaty in 1919 before the victors
revised it to make the document less punitive. The Entente gave up
demands for the extradition of war criminals, and the British government decided not to take the treaty too literally. As of 1920, economic
circumstances forced the victors to extend deadlines for reparations
payments, a concession that also raised the amount of interest Germany was compelled to pay.[25] Many Germans had the feeling that
they were being indefinitely subjugated, since they were denied the
possibility of repaying their debts ahead of schedule, as France had
proudly done after the Franco-Prussian War. That early repayment
had reduced interest charges and had been crucial to France's ability
to overcome the shame of defeat and restore a sense of national pride.

Beginning in 1929, when the burden of reparations payments combined with the Great Depression to wreak economic havoc, Nazi propaganda condemning the "shameful peace" drove masses of voters into
Hitler's waiting arms. Theodor Heuss, who would later become the
German president, remarked in 1931—not without justification—that
"the cradle of the National Socialist movement was Versailles and not
Munich."[26] In the months after he was named German chancellor in
1933, Hitler regularly declared paragraphs of the Versailles treaty null
and void. He did so with great glee, basking in public approval that
went far beyond the Nazi Party rank and file. The victors in World War I
tolerated this bellicosity until 1939, in part because they no longer
believed in the wisdom of a treaty that had been concluded in the spirit
of revenge. A bad conscience encouraged appeasement.

The clauses within the Versailles treaty that violated Wilson's
Fourteen Points reinforced old hatreds and created new ones. Above
all, they prevented Germans from seeing that the agreement did con-
tain a series of justifiable propositions. There was no alternative to

the founding of a Polish nation-state, which required Germany to cede territory primarily occupied by people of Polish descent. Moreover, because World War I had been waged largely in Belgium and northern France, it was reasonable to expect Germany to contribute to the reconstruction of those areas. It was also logical for Germany to give back Alsace-Lorraine, which it had seized from France in the Franco-Prussian War. And it made sense for Germany to refund the six billion gold marks it had demanded in occupation costs from Belgium and to return the property, machinery, and transport equipment it had commandeered.

The main problems lay elsewhere. The Versailles treaty blocked European economic recovery, prevented Germany from repairing war damage, and choked off any new optimism—to the detriment of the victors as well as the defeated. Economist John Maynard Keynes, who represented the British Treasury as part of his country's delegations, had warned of such negative consequences while the agreement was still being negotiated. In fact, he left the negotiations in protest, saying that the treaty would drive Germany and Europe into economic and political ruin. In the fall of 1919, he published a scathing critique directed against the victorious nations as well as Austria and Hungary. He accused the former Entente allies of virtually enslaving a generation of Germans, yielding to crass self-interest at the cost of humiliating millions and stealing from the pockets of an entire populace. Keynes's criticism was aimed at France in particular, but it fell on deaf ears. It wasn't until August 1932 that President Herbert Hoover would characterize the Treaty of Versailles as a "poisoned" wellspring of "political instability." A short time earlier, André Tardieu, who served multiple terms as French prime minister and foreign minister, called the agreement a useless work, divorced from reality.[27] But such insights came too late.

Keynes had already recognized the truth in 1919. He predicted that the imposed peace settlement would quickly lead to a massive devaluation of the German currency. He even specified the economic laws and political consequences that would yield hyperinflation by

1923, remarking: "There is no subtler, no surer means of overturning the existing basis of society than to debauch the currency." Keynes also noted that "if prices are continually rising, every trader who has purchased for stock or owns property and plant inevitably makes profits." Such an inflationary process automatically gave rise to the stereotype of the "profiteer" hated both by the middle classes and the proletariat. "By combining a popular hatred of the class of entrepreneurs with the blow already given to social security by the violent and arbitrary disturbance of contract and of the established equilibrium of wealth which is the inevitable result of inflation," Keynes concluded, "these Governments are fast rendering impossible a continuance of the social and economic order of the nineteenth century. But they have no plan for replacing it."

Inflation permanently altered people's moral outlook. It undermined the two most important pillars of bourgeois-capitalist society: respect for property and trust in the monetary system. On October 1, 1923, the exchange rate between the dollar and mark stood at 1 to 240 million. By November 1, it was 1 to 130 billion. Nine days later, when Hitler and his henchmen attempted the Beer Hall Putsch in Munich, the exchange rate had exceeded 1 to 500 billion. It is easy to understand how belief in progress based on the production of goods and the circulation of money could be superseded in this environment by an idea that put purportedly primeval forces of human existence at the center of politics. Mammon's apparent disdain for human suffering led philosopher Ernst Jünger to call for a "true" revolution in the Nazi *Völkischer Beobachter* newspaper. "Blood and not money will be the moving force," Jünger wrote. "It will allow for the freedom of the whole after the sacrifice of the individual. It will throw up waves that will reach the limits closing in on us. It will purge all the substances that harm us."[28]

The currency devaluation brought international trade to a standstill, drove the nations of Europe into economic isolation, and encouraged desperation and paralysis in Germany itself. From Keynes's perspective, the economies of the Continent had been severely rocked, while the character of the peace settlement had hobbled the natural forces of economic life. With great prescience, Keynes warned: "An inefficient, unemployed, disorganized Europe faces us, torn by internal strife and international hate, fighting, starving, pillaging, and lying." Keynes also saw the dangers of a Germany that was kept down, economically paralyzed and politically entrapped: "If we aim deliberately at the impoverishment of Central Europe, vengeance, I dare predict, will not limp. Nothing can then delay for very long that final civil war between the forces of Reaction and the despairing convulsions of Revolution, before which the horrors of the late German war will fade into nothing, and which will destroy, whoever is victor, the civilization and the progress of our generation."

Paragraphs 240 and 241 of the Treaty of Versailles obliged Germany to obey the instructions of a special committee of the victorious Entente nations. De facto, the young Weimar Republic was forced into foreign receivership. For one of the German negotiators in Paris, this meant that Germany "would remain for decades to come shorn of all rights, and deprived, to a far greater extent than any people in the days of absolutism, of any independence of action, of any individual aspiration in its economic or even in its ethical progress." The negotiator, whom Keynes cited, added that German democracy would be "annihilated at the very moment when the German people was about to build it up after a severe struggle."[29]

At first the victors did not specify the amount of reparations Germany would have to pay. When they finally did set a figure in 1921, the sum was an astonishing 138 billion gold marks plus interest over a period of fifty years. In the spirit of a wise bankruptcy administrator trying to keep Europe functioning economically, Keynes suggested in early 1922 that reparations be reduced to 28 billion marks, an 80 percent cut, and that one billion of that be used to alleviate the particular misery in Poland and Austria. Those ideas were ignored. Keynes was trying to ensure that Germany would not be saddled with a debt that was impossible to repay and that would be considered unjust.

Instead, Keynes pleaded, Germans should be encouraged to work hard to wipe the slate clean.[30]

Keynes's warnings went unheard. Germany's government tried its best to meet payment deadlines, but just as Keynes had prophesied in 1919, the German currency was rocked by the double burden of the nation's own wartime debts and reparations. In January 1923, France and Belgium occupied the industrial Ruhr region on the pretense of securing deliveries of coal that Germany had failed to make. In fact, only a small portion of the deliveries had been delayed—and that because inflation had partially paralyzed the German economy. The occupation provoked a nationalistic German underground movement, replete with terrorist attacks. When occupation forces executed Albert Leo Schlageter, who had used explosives in several acts of sabotage, his death made him into a martyr and reinforced Germans' active and passive resistance. Paris began offering support to separatists in the Rhine region, on Germany's border with France and Belgium, and the German government feared the country could fall apart. The French-Belgian military adventure in the Rhine permanently discredited the Treaty of Versailles. Henceforth democratic parties, statesmen, and private citizens who were willing to pursue a negotiated solution were pilloried as "fulfillment politicians"—traitors selling out German interests to the French by fulfilling the terms of the Versailles treaty.

The irony is that Germany's prospects for making the transition to a democratic republic were not all that bad. On January 19, 1919, a free and fair election yielded 163 seats in parliament for the SPD, making it the largest party, and centrist parties earned a massive majority of 327 out of a total of 421 parliamentary seats. An election for the Prussian parliament seven days later produced similar results. Germans were expressing a clear preference for democracy and republican moderation. The newly created Weimar Republic survived the attempted far-right Kapp-Lüttwitz putsch in 1920 as well as Communist-organized mass unrest that cost more than a thousand people their lives. Government leaders were quick to address the chaos and tried to rein in antidemocratic forces within the German military. The Weimar Republic was shaken by the assassinations of Finance Minister Matthias Ersberger and Foreign Minister Walther Rathenau in 1921 and 1922, and it was further burdened by the perceived humiliation of the peace treaty—even though the government of Kaiser Wilhelm II, who had quickly abdicated, bore responsibility for the German defeat. Still, the Weimar Republic did manage to deal, more or less, with difficult situations.

France's occupation of the Ruhr, though, undermined the authority of the tenuous government without achieving any of Paris's economic aims. The blast furnaces of Lorraine remained inactive, since occupation actually hindered supplies of German coal from reaching France. The French satiric magazine Le Rire ran a caricature of a shivering French general, wrapped in a fur coat on the Rhine, reporting back to Paris: "Everything under control here. The only thing we lack is coal. Please send some as quickly as possible."[31]

Despite such inauspicious circumstances, the leaders of the Weimar Republic succeeded in renewing and reforming Germany. They created a centralized financial administration and a unified corpus of tax legislation for the first time in German history; even Bismarck hadn't been able to do that. After the period of hyperinflation, they stabilized the mark. They expanded the educational system, improved opportunities for working-class children, and built hundreds of housing projects thanks to a tax on property owners. Many of these homes are today listed as World Cultural Heritage sites. Thousands of Jews were allowed to join the upper ranks of the civil service, which removed one of the last barriers to full Jewish equality, and illegal immigrants were naturalized in droves. In cities like Heidelberg, Cologne, Berlin, and Leipzig, committed democrats served as majors, police chiefs, and judges. In 1925, Berlin prohibited the construction of any more of the grim and often unsanitary dwellings to the rear of

buildings' internal courtyards. City leaders planned and realized garden communities, established public beaches and swimming pools,
founded new schools, electric plants, and waterworks, created two
major parks, and expanded the public transportation system at a rate
never seen before or afterward.

It is wrong to view the Weimar Republic as a system that was
incapable of action and doomed from the outset. The problem was
precisely the opposite. The achievements of the Weimar Republic
encouraged upward social mobility. Its success awakened expectations of a better life to come—expectations that the system was ultimately, due to pressure from within and without, unable to fulfill.

RACIAL WAR INSTEAD OF CLASS STRUGGLE

The republican revolution in Germany on November 9, 1918, had
come after a military defeat in which masses of people had refused to
obey orders. It did not emanate from a positive political vision about
Germany's future that was supported by a majority of the population. Large numbers of demobilized, unemployed soldiers, continuing
food shortages, waves of refugees from territory Germany had been
forced to cede in the peace treaty, left-wing and right-wing putsch
attempts, and national rivalries on the German Empire's eastern borders all contributed to the rise of paramilitary-style political parties,
replete with marching, uniforms, banners, visions of the evil enemy,
and unquestioning loyalty to leaders. Regardless of their specific ideologies, all these parties and associations of young men shared a
similar military outlook. "In war, the masses learn to disregard the
value of human life and to ruthlessly sacrifice individuals as means to
an end," left-wing Social Democrat Curt Geyer wrote in 1923, adding
that violence had become a favored solution to political disagreements. That was the danger he saw in the radicalization of Germany's
working classes.[32]

Millions of men had been released from the military, with its emphasis on commands and obedience, into the liberal Weimar Republic.

They now lacked orientation, tending to fluctuate in their alle-
giances and "to run from one party to the next," as Social Democrat
Karl Kautsky put it in spring 1920. They might start with the SPD
only to move on to parties even further to the left or to the far right.
"Now we face the danger," Kautsky warned, "that they will surren-
der to anti-Semitism or despair of politics altogether."

Such fears motivated Kautsky to publish a new edition of his
book *Race and Jewishness*. He had brought out the first edition in the
fall of 1914 in the hope that a satisfactory end to the war would bring
an end to debates about the "Jewish question" among civilized
peoples. The tone of Kautsky's foreword to the 1920 edition was quite
pessimistic. There, he wrote that it was more "important than ever to
make the proletariat critical of and immune to" nationalism and
racial hatred.[33] Kautsky was particularly worried that vacillations by
the restless masses at the heart of the new republic could leave the
state incapable of action. A bit later, Curt Geyer wrote a book about
how quickly left-wing radicalism could swing over to the right of the
political spectrum. In it he described how in the early 1920s miners
from the town of Mansfeld had been radicalized and had taken up
arms. But they also quickly "turned toward German nationalist organizations." Regardless of which political direction the revolutionarily
unchained masses directed their aggression, a lack of moral scruples
and a lust for rebellion and political adventurism remained.[34]

The novelist Jakob Wassermann was another figure worried about
popular hatred toward Jews. Wassermann had grown up in a shel-
tered environment as the son of an economically struggling toymaker
in southern Germany. It was only during his period of military service
just before World War I that he became acquainted with the anti-
Semitism of many young Germans from the lower classes. "For the
first time I encountered the slow-witted, rigid, almost speechless
hate that had penetrated the populace," Wassermann wrote in 1921.
"The label 'anti-Semitism' hardly begins to define the character, the
source, the depth, or the aim." Wassermann was far more taken aback
and hurt by the malicious behavior of common soldiers than by the

resentful behavior of his superior officers. (Literary sociologist Leo Löwenthal would use similar terms to describe his impressions of a military regiment in the town of Hanau in the final year of World War I: "There I become personally acquainted with the dull-witted, anti-intellectual anti-Semitism of the sons of workers and farmers.") Wassermann drew attention to elements of "clerical obdurateness, the rancor of the disadvantaged and betrayed, and uncertainty, lies, and lack of scruples." He saw low self-esteem as the root of the hostility: "There is something specifically German about this. . . . This is a German hatred." Twelve years before the Third Reich, Wassermann warned: "Unfortunately, it is open season on today's Jew—in terms of public sentiment, if not legally."[35]

Recent research into local German history has shown that Hitler was one of the restless young men Kautsky and Geyer described. Photographic and film evidence document that on February 26, 1919, the future Führer attended the funeral procession for Bavarian state premier Kurt Eisner, who had been murdered by a right-wing nationalist. Hitler thus paid his last respects to a socialist from a Jewish family: Eisner had been elected the leader of a council of workers, farmers, and soldiers on November 7, 1918, at a mass rally in Munich and had promptly proclaimed the "Bavarian Soviet Republic." In the tumultuous months that followed Eisner's murder, the revolutionary Bavarian government deployed the soldier Hitler as a sentry to guard the city's main train station, an assignment reserved for people considered especially loyal. Hitler's comrades soon elected him company liaison and, in early April 1919, deputy counsel in a regiment that was incorporated into the "Red Army."

On May 3, 1919, the Bavarian Soviet Republic was toppled by a force of regular army members and paramilitary bands of decommissioned former soldiers, or *Freikorps*. Fifteen months later, the relatively obscure agitator Adolf Hitler spoke in the main hall of Munich's Hofbräuhaus on the topic "Why Are We Anti-Semites?" He proclaimed his intention to eradicate finance capital and warmly praised the socialism of the working masses and of salt-of-the-earth, machinery- and factory-oriented industrialism. At the end of his address, Hitler posed a question to himself: "How can you as a socialist be an anti-Semite? Are you not ashamed?" His answer: "A time will come when we will ask: How can you as a socialist *not* be an anti-Semite? A time will come when it will be obvious that socialism can be realized only in conjunction with nationalism and anti-Semitism. The three concepts are inseparably connected."[36]

In 1919, the young philosopher Ernst Bloch was living in Munich, where he experienced firsthand the rise and fall of the Bavarian Soviet Republic. Five years later he wrote a short but very precise analysis entitled "Hitler's Force." He had no way of knowing that Hitler had been a defender of the Bavarian experiment in practical communism. Nonetheless, Bloch seemed to sense the connection: "After the high point was over, the same people who darkened the streets with count-less processions during Eisner's funeral called for socialists to be cru-cified and hounded their leaders into their graves. From one day to the next, the Soviet stars were swapped for swastikas on their ban-ners. From one day to the next, the popular court, the revolutionary tribunal that Eisner had created, placed revolutionary Eugen Leviné in front of the firing squad." Bloch attributed the shift in part to the "organized proletariat," which by no means consisted solely of impov-erished workers and rabble but included, and indeed was led by, intellectuals, university students, and journalists. The ringleaders had figured out how to exploit the spectacle of marches, parades, and noisy public events. They gave the rabble, Bloch sneered, "its homo-geneous head."

In his sketch of the developments leading to Hitler's Beer Hall Putsch of November 9, 1923, Bloch emphasized Hitler's rhetorical power, the mythological aspects of the Nazis' platform, and anti-Semitism as key to the Führer's popular appeal among younger people. "One should not underestimate the enemy," Bloch wrote. "One should determine what is a psychological fact for so many people and what appeals to them. Without doubt there are many parallels here with left-wing radicalism in a demagogic and formal sense, if not in terms of content. Such parallels made it easier . . . for the Bavarian rabble to switch flags." On both the left and right, Bloch asserted, "young people are called to defend themselves, the capitalist, parliamentary state is rejected, and demands for dictatorship are made." Both left and right preserved "forms of command and obedience," and both held up the "virtue of decisiveness" in contrast to the "cowardice of the bourgeoisie, that eternally chattering class." As Bloch put it, "the genus of Hitler and his ilk is above all revolutionary in character."[37]

Author Wilhelm Michel, who wrote for Carl von Ossietsky's left-wing magazine *Weltbühne* ("World Stage"), regarded national and cultural insecurity as "especially crucial for understanding German anti-Semitism." He concluded: "Our hatred of Jews is commensurate with our lack of popular stature and national consolidation. Our hatred of Jews is commensurate with our dependence on foreigners, our amorphousness, our poor self-image and the general disorder of all our values. Hatred for Jews is a measure of how far we remain separated from our own being." In Michel's estimation, during the chaos of the immediate postwar years, more and more Germans reacted "brutishly, stupidly, uncertainly, and ineffectively"—in a "confession of national impotence and abjection"—to their less than ideal situation.[38]

Amid the imperial pomp of Wilhelmine Germany, and particularly during the first phase of World War I, when Germans seemed headed toward victory, this sort of anti-Semitism had remained below the surface. After the German defeat in 1918, it emerged with significant force. Michel characterized Germans as barbarians who sought to take out their frustration at being defeated by a superior tribe on the next best victim they could find: "The war is lost. The fear is gone. A tiny, shabby bit of misery squats disconsolately atop the ruins of

Wilhelmine Germany. There's not even any proper beer. . . . The tribe is growing restless and is arming itself. Defeat must be avenged. The perpetrator is beyond reach. The tribe, disillusioned, is starving. It needs action. Collective butchery is one of the best intoxicants. The tribe fans out. It finds the interloper, the Jew. The tribe dances around him, screeching with delight at having found a tangible, identifiable object for the orgy of violence that will compensate for its disillusionment. The tribe circles around the Jew, passing him from fist to fist, and the cudgels are lifted to smite him down. Hooray, it's almost like 1914."[39]

The political platform of the Nazi Party was rooted in two nineteenth-century ideas with revolutionary connotations that could easily be combined with anti-Semitism. One was the concept of the ethnically homogeneous nation; the other was the idea of social equality. The Nazis promised the lower classes of ethnic Germans greater social acknowledgment and better opportunities for social advancement. In the "Ten Commandments for Every National Socialist," published in 1929, Joseph Goebbels wrote: "Germany's enemies are your enemies—hate them with all your heart. Every ethnic comrade [*Volksgenosse*], no matter how poor, is a piece of Germany—love him as you do yourself."[40]

In the first part of its twenty-five-point program of 1920, Hitler's party adopted some of the demands that had been made by Christian Social anti-Semites in the late imperial periods in both Germany and Austria. These included insisting that only "native" Germans could be citizens of Germany and excluding Jews from the national community. The second part of the program contained anticapitalist promises of the sort one could have also found in reasonably moderate Social Democratic and trade union circles, including the eradication of non-labor-derived income, the alleviation of "interest slavery," the nationalization of listed companies, profit-sharing arrangements for workers at large companies, the communalization of large retail stores, the noncompensated seizure of land for public purposes, measures to prevent real estate speculation, the expansion of old-age benefits, and better job protection for mothers-to-be and young workers. The authors of the document also wrote: "Personal enrichment during the war must be seen as a crime against the people. Therefore, we demand that all wartime profits be confiscated without exception."

In the third, sketchier, but no less crucial part of their program, the National Socialist Party emphasized the importance of internal unity and privilege for all ethnic Germans. To that end, the NSDAP proposed creating a strong central authority, stopping immigration by non-Germans, and requiring the state "to ensure the ability of ethnic German citizens to live and work." The Nazis' demands in this regard did not distinguish among Germans of various classes and Christian denominations. Hitler insisted on religious neutrality where Christianity was concerned. "I place great value on our party's closing the gap that divides our people," Hitler said at a 1928 conference. "Protestants and Catholics must come together without exception."[41] That sentiment corresponded to point 24 of the Nazi program, entitled "Positive Christianity." It reaffirmed Germans' freedom to choose their own religions as long as their choices did not violate the "morals or mores of the Germanic race."

The party program characterized the historical German shortcoming of internal discord and denominational rivalry—symbolized by the fact that German speakers had butchered other German speakers during the Thirty Years' War—as an expression of the "materialistic Jewish spirit." Germans had internalized this materialistic spirit as they might an infection, the Nazi program said, but they desperately needed to overcome it. Of course, people who are fighting off an infection are also encouraged to make sure that they are not reinfected by some external germ. Point 4 of the program thus explicitly linked the internal reconciliation of Germans with the exclusion of Jews. It read: "Only ethnic comrades can become citizens. And only someone who is of German blood, regardless of denomination, can be an ethnic comrade. Therefore, no Jew can become a citizen."

The guiding idea of the program was that of the *Volk* as an organic unity, an interwoven collective that was naturally resilient, like "a tree, a coral reef, or a swarm of bees." Continuing the metaphor, the program stated that the individual was "merely an example of species, a building block, when society was analyzed."[42] The individual would wither and die without the collective. Similarly, the Nazis proclaimed that only a people pulsing with the same blood and a unified will would be able to face the challenges of the times. Popular and ethnic collectivist theory, for which its inventors and propagandists coined the neologism *völkisch* (folkish), defined the individual as defenseless, incapable of surviving on his own without the whole. It also promoted the totality of state, people, and race, a sixty-million-headed embodiment of Pan-Germany.

Recent experiences encouraged thoughts and emotions of this kind. They included the camaraderie of the regiment, the communally suffered mass slaughter of World War I, the dictated peace (which assigned to the Germans a collective responsibility for the conflict), and the ever more refined and rapid American-style rationalization of companies and government administrations during the Weimar Republic. All these experiences conformed to the "swarm of bees" rhetoric. For millions of Germans, community, even that born of desperate circumstances, was a welcome replacement for splintered traditional families and for the lost belief in spiritual and secular authorities. Clinging together promised to provide safety and reassuring warmth—provided, of course, that the community was properly led.

The idea of the *Volk* as a natural, growing organism was reflected in point 16 of the Nazi program, in which the party announced its fight against those forces that exercised "a corrosive influence on the life of our people [*Volksleben*]."[43] Such forces included political partisanship and parliamentary posturing and speechifying. Those associated with such abuses were excoriated in Nazi jargon as defeatist scaremongers, know-it-alls, vermin, parasites, interlopers, and traitors. Until well into the modern age, Christians had spread legends about Jews poisoning town wells, intentionally spreading the plague, and murdering Christian babies. Now, in the twentieth century, anti-Semites asserted that, wherever Jews were active, they stirred up popular unrest and sowed discord. This flexible stereotype could be used to interpret a variety of unsettling events—major conflicts of interest, market competition, bank failures, inflation, foreign and civil wars, and revolutions—as Jewish machinations. The notion of the divisive Jew allowed Germans to avoid taking responsibility for problems they themselves had caused. It was not military defeat and poor politics that had weakened German fortitude. The damage had been done by an internal enemy, the Jews, and in particularly perfidious fashion.

The corollary conceit to the stereotype of the divisive Jew was the promise that national solidarity would finally become reality. This idea played on the popular belief that the German nation had broken apart too often and had thus squandered historical opportunities. A stab-in-the-back legend arose, which held that in the final days of the war and during the ensuing peace negotiations Germany had been betrayed from within its own ranks. Traitorous "fulfillment politicians," so the legend ran, had completely undermined selflessly fighting German soldiers. Such images merged seamlessly with the phantasms of alien Jewish forces that had dissolved Germans' natural will to unity. There were two main versions of this obsessive Nazi self-deception. In one, the "Jew" was an "assimilator," hardly distinguishable from Gentile Germans and thus all the more perilous; in the other, the "Eastern Jew" appeared as an outsider, unwilling to integrate and happy to live in a murky parallel society. Yet regardless of which image of Jews was used, Nazi propagandists depicted them as inherently harmful to the German people. Both sorts of Jew were considered selfish, unpatriotic, and deeply implicated in international anti-German conspiracies.

Ethnic collectivist propaganda developed further stereotypes of the plutocratic and the Bolshevist Jew. Whereas the former was allegedly bent on destroying the German middle classes and enslaving farmers and workers to the needs of big capital, the latter dreamed of a global Communist revolution that would spell the end of morals, religion, public decency, and legitimately acquired property. Nazis favored these relatively novel images, though they were not averse to drawing on the litany of traditional Christian anti-Jewish stereotypes as well. In his "Why Are We Anti-Semites?" speech, Hitler concluded by proclaiming: "We want to prevent Germany from suffering a death by crucifixion!"[44] In those days, Hitler's was a local movement, but word of his anti-Semitic agitation spread as far north as Hamburg. There, in January 1923, banker Max Warburg wrote to industrialist and politician Hugo Stinnes: "The reports of the atmosphere in Bavaria make me afraid that, on top of Germany's other humiliations, our poor country will devolve into a nation of pogroms."[45]

6

WEAK MASSES, STRONG RACE

THE PATHOLOGICAL IMPOTENCE OF THE DULL-MINDED

Even in the early nineteenth century, people like Goethe had little good to say about grumbling, coarsely behaved nationalist romantics of the Arndt or Jahn variety. By contrast, Germany's greatest author enjoyed the witty company of intelligent Jews. "As a rule they are more keenly curious and apt to contribute than any German nationalist," Goethe wrote. "Their ability to understand things quickly and analyze them in depth, as well as their native wit, makes them a much more receptive audience than you can find among the real and true Germans with their slow and dull minds."[1]

In 1831, Gabriel Riesser wrote of discrimination against German Jews: "Only a knavish people can take pleasure in the further subjugation of a minority. Only an impotent, cowardly nation can seek in the subordination of the few a means of ramping up their own self-confidence and a way of trying to spur themselves out of their pathological impotence."[2] In 1880, Ludwig Bamberger described politically organized social anti-Semitism as the result of "an emotion that does not know itself." Forty-eight years later, the Viennese writer and Zionist Heinrich York-Steiner interpreted "the perennially strong anti-Semitic sensibilities" of Germans as the consequence of "political and national weakness." By 1932, York-Steiner was making the point even more forcefully: "German anti-Semitism is not the result of some disproportionate popular sentiment. It is rather the reaction to the unconscious sense that one's identity is uncertain and weak. German popular identity is the most tenuous of all the large nations of Europe." Historian and sociologist Eva Reichmann-Jungmann analyzed the situation in similar terms in 1929, when she described the weak German national sense of self as a perennial obstacle that had caused a great deal of suffering for German Jews.[3]

Around the same time, historian Arthur Rosenberg was also reassessing the popular echo that had greeted Treitschke's anti-Jewish polemics in 1880. Rosenberg interpreted Treitschke-inspired academic anti-Semitism as the "ideological framework" of Christian students and scholars who resented their lack of superior status in Wilhelmine society. Trained to be subservient and without a clear social framework, Rosenberg argued, they had no idea what they should do with their new bourgeois freedoms. Heinrich Mann painted a nearly identical picture in his 1914 novel *Man of Straw*. Shortly before his first exam in a law course, the antihero Diederich Hessling runs into an intellectually more accomplished former school classmate, Wolfgang Buck, the son of a mixed Jewish-Gentile marriage. Hardly do the two say good-bye before Diederich cries out as if bitten by a tarantula: "Those are our worst enemies! The ones with the fancy so-called education who want to tamper with everything we Germans consider sacred! A Jewish upstart like that should be happy that we tolerate him among us. He should be learning his Pandects [code of law] instead of opening his big mouth. I spit on his artsy old books!"[4]

Christian university students envied the rosy career prospects of their Jewish peers. In an attempt to "defend their social position," to follow Rosenberg's analysis, they retreated back into anachronistic fantasies about Germanic superiority. Since their actual achievements remained modest, they elevated German ethnicity into a kind of aristocracy to which their Jewish peers could not belong. To quote historian Konrad Jarausch, Christian students were scared and frustrated by the "imminent overcrowding" in their future professions and the "overrepresentation of Jewish students" in coveted departments like medicine and law.

This was the atmosphere in which a variety of student organizations founded the nationalist and anti-Semitic League of German Student Organizations in 1881. That summer, the delegates met on Kyffhäusser Mountain with all its mythic national significance. The empty jingoism of their bellowed slogans was commensurate with their failure as individuals, and it was no accident that those in attendance particularly applauded one sentence from the opening speech: "The vast majority of students have come round to the realization that an effective containment and a courageous and practical battle against the negative and harmful aspects of Jewry, which lacks its own fatherland, is needed in order to save ours."[5]

Twelve years later, in 1893, August Bebel delivered a keynote speech at the annual SPD party conference in Cologne. The speech was entitled "Social Democracy and Anti-Semitism," and it addressed the anti-Jewish agitation at German universities. The students, Bebel explained, came primarily from the class of small tradesmen and artisans that was now faced with economic extinction. Worried about their futures, they were fleeing to university in the hopes of getting "some governmental position or other."[6] In a humorously intended passage, Bebel went on to describe students who had been raised with little respect for education and whose chief concern was to be taken care of, students who "passed their time in bars, at fencing competitions, or at other locales that I will refrain from mentioning." In contrast to the "so-called Germanic students," Bebel praised Jewish students' "great stamina, persistence, and sobriety"—both in their demeanor and in their avoidance of alcohol. "They most often do better than their Germanic fellow students on exams," Bebel reported, while the latter "seek to make up for what they lack in knowledge and character through sheer attitude." Such Germanic students became followers of anti-Semitism because they saw Jews as superior competitors.[7]

Sociologist Werner Sombart was even more frank than Bebel (or, later, Rosenberg) in identifying the difference between stubborn adherence to the past, on the one hand, and quick-witted flexibility, on the other, as the real cause of the intellectual gap between Gentile and Jewish students. Sombart found in 1912 that on average "Jews are quite a lot more clever and industrious than we are," and he used this insight to justify prohibiting Jews for the most part from holding academic chairs. As far as science was concerned, Sombart admitted, it was regrettable that most of the time if there were two candidates, the "stupider one," and not the Jew, was chosen. Nonetheless, Sombart supported protective restrictions because otherwise "all university lectureships and professorships would be held by Jews or Jewish converts to Christianity."[8]

Sombart's remark about Jewish converts refers to the fact that, as was only logical, Jewish intellectual superiority did not automatically cease when Jews converted to Christianity. And it shows how the logic of racial anti-Semitism could creep into the discourse of a serious thinker, though Sombart himself was no racist. In 1912, he dismissed what he sarcastically called the "Aryan theory and all these other 'theories' of a 'noble race' struggling to preserve its culture." He explicitly rejected the assumption that Jews had specific racial characteristics, arguing that "the standards of proof of our 'racial theoreticians,' . . . like all of their opinions, are drawn out of thin air and remain unsullied by any of the usual scientific rigor." Valuing sociological facts over speculation, Sombart concluded that Jewish social influence would grow all the faster "the less adroit and more sluggish and divorced from economic reality the majority population becomes."

Sombart did later embrace some anti-Semitic ideas. In his 1934 book *German Socialism*, he deemed the Nazi regime a legal form of state, recommending that Jews be stripped of their rights. He warned: "In order to liberate us from the Jewish intellect, which should be a main task of the German people and above all of socialism, it is not enough to shut out all the Jews." Instead, Sombart insisted that the entire "institutional culture should be reconfigured so that it can no longer serve as a bulwark of the 'Jewish intellect.'"[9]

In 1902, the philosopher Friedrich Paulsen had advanced arguments similar to Sombart's 1912 proposal for barring Jews from occupying too many academic chairs. "If the learned careers were subjected to open competition in the same ruthless fashion as other economic careers," Paulsen contended, "they would in time fall overwhelmingly, if not monopolistically, into the hands of the Jewish populace with its superior wealth, energy, and persistence." Because such a situation would be perceived as foreign dominance, Paulsen thought, it was legitimate to put some "restrictive pressure to bear to prevent an overabundance of Jews in the learned professions . . . as hard as that might be on particular individuals."[10]

It was hardly rare for "stupider" Gentile professors to slander the work of their Jewish colleagues. For example, in 1916, the economist Gustav Schmoller reviewed a work by the private lecturer Hugo Preuss, whom he described as "one of the most gifted new teachers of governmental law." But he introduced Preuss to his readers with the following words: "He has become one of the leaders of the Berlin communal freethinking movement, which, based as it is socially within circles of Semitic millionaires, now more or less dominates our capital city." Schmoller went on to speculate as to why Jews like Preuss were such "orthodox democrats." "I cannot escape the notion—as industrious and admirable as they are—that their political outlook and judgment are excessively informed by a single idea," Schmoller wrote. "In their circles there is such superiority of intelligence, character, and talent that they consider it unjust and harmful to state and society that their tightly knit community does not yet dominate the university, the military, and the top echelons of the civil service as it does the city of Berlin and its administration." Given this putative arrogance, Schmoller found it proper to admit only small numbers of Jews to the higher ranks of the military or the civil service. Otherwise, Schmoller feared, "they would swiftly develop into an intolerant dictator of the state and its administration." By the end of his harangue, Schmoller had worked himself into a rage: "How many cases have proven the truth of the prophecy that once you admit the first Jewish full professor, you'll have five of them or more in ten years' time!"[11]

Historian Dietrich Schäfer was a disciple of Treitschke's and the successor to his chair at the University of Berlin. In 1908, he wrote an evaluation for the local Ministry of Education in the state of Baden. It was aimed at preventing social philosopher Georg Simmel, the son of Jewish converts in Berlin, from being given an academic chair at the University of Heidelberg. Simmel is considered one of the founders of modern sociology, and in contrast to those of Schäfer, his works are still read around the world today. Schäfer's evaluation of the man began: "I do not know and did not want to ask whether Prof. Simmel has been baptized. He's an Israelite through and through, in his external appearance, his demeanor, and the character of his intellect." Schäfer accused Simmel of possessing a "pseudointellectual manner" combined with a lack of talent for "seriously coherent thought."

Schäfer's evaluation was shot through with willful myopia and sexual jealousy: "He speaks very slowly, in drips and drabs, and without offering much content, but what he says is concise, well-rounded, and polished. Those qualities are greatly valued by certain circles of listeners in Berlin. He often concludes his remarks with aperçus, and not accidentally his primary audience has an extremely high contingent of women, even by Berlin standards. The Oriental world too— people who have flooded to and settled in Berlin from the eastern countries semester after semester—is also well represented. His whole manner speaks to their basic orientation and taste. There's not a lot that's positive to be gleaned from his lectures, but people do get a momentary prick of excitement and intellectual enjoyment. Moreover, considering how these circles stick together, the Jewish, half-Jewish, or philo-Semitic lecturer will always find fertile soil at a university at which thousands of comparable listeners are available."[12] Simmel did not get the professorship.

In 1910, in honor of the hundredth anniversary of the University of Berlin, the Prussian Ministry of Education commissioned historian Max Lenz to write a four-volume chronicle of the institution's past. He devoted one section to the career of legal scholar Eduard Gans (1798–1839). Lenz introduced him as the son of the Berlin banker Abraham Isaak Gans, a man "of financial, if not moral, repute . . . with customers in the higher social circles," and noted that he had enjoyed a personal relationship with Prussian state secretary Karl August von Hardenberg. Lenz accused Eduard Gans of shirking the fight against Napoleon in 1813, even though Gans was only fifteen at the time: "Courage was not, according to statements by his friends, Gans's great strength—although perhaps he had his reasons for hiding behind the stove. In verbal confrontations, he was all the more skillful." For Lenz, Gans was "a wunderkind" but too "brash," and the historian recounted with relish how in 1819 Berlin students had refused to acknowledge the authority of "this beardless boy who had barely outgrown his toddler's shoes."

At the age of nineteen, Gans was already publishing polished and impassioned essays. Lenz viewed him as the epitome of what was bad about lawyers and described with no small sympathy how the legal faculty battled—in vain—to exclude this extraordinarily talented young man. Gans had had the presumption to ask for a teaching position, although, as Lenz pointed out with disgust, he had "neither experience nor official rank nor social position on his side." Instead, Lenz suggested, Gans was only so bold because he had "powerful backers." His difficulties obtaining a position convinced Gans to turn to the more liberal University of Heidelberg, but there, Lenz reported, the professors also "had no desire to see a Jew as one of their colleagues." Gans was allowed only to complete his doctorate, after which he returned to Berlin. Back in the capital, the legal faculty accused him of "superficial striving for novel and spectacular discoveries" that were "utterly misguided and without scientific merit."[13] In 1825,

Gans converted to Protestantism, and at the age of twenty-seven he was granted an extraordinary academic chair, without, as Lenz resentfully noted, "being required to go through the intermediary stage of a private lectureship." Lenz himself had needed almost twenty years of hard work to achieve an ordinary academic chair, and even after he became the dean of the University of Berlin in 1911, his dry-as-dust style drew negative comparisons with that of the eloquent Treitschke.

Max Lenz was one of my great-great-uncles and yet another "proud German" whose anxieties about competition led him to be resentful of Jews.[14] His family history also illustrates how progressive attitudes among Gentiles often gave way to national chauvinism. For centuries, Max Lenz's forefathers had been blacksmiths. His grandfather Carl, a master coppersmith, became a businessman who owned a ship company and served in the local government of the town of Kolberg. His father, Gustav (1818–1888), was drawn "irresistibly" to academia. He studied law and philosophy in Berlin under none other than Hegel and Eduard Gans himself.

By his own admission Gustav Lenz did not think much of religion, and in 1848 he was an enthusiastic supporter of the cause of German democracy and liberty. Those views probably cost him a permanent appointment to the Prussian civil service after he had clerked for a judge at a regional superior court. Instead, Gustav became a practicing lawyer and a writer in the town of Greifswald. In 1854, he wrote an essay entitled "On the Historical Development of the Law," in which he vigorously argued, in the spirit of his teacher Eduard Gans, that Germany should adopt liberal Roman law. He also criticized the ideologues and defenders of Christian German jingoism as dull and "grotesque" pedants who merely tossed around "desiccated" abstractions and who had withdrawn from modern society into a "ghostly facsimile" of the past. The goal of Gustav Lenz's treatise was to cause "a collision of minds . . . in the oppressive atmosphere of our days." A reviewer praised Lenz's "innovative and vigorous, if sometimes exaggerated and injurious, language."[15] Later in life, Gustav Lenz would become a royal counselor of justice and a supporter of Bismarck. In the end, as our family chronicle notes with relief, he had "found a way to make peace with the new state."

Max Lenz's sister Anna is also worthy of attention. In 1874, at the age of twenty, she married the historian Bernhard Erdmannsdörffer, who was twenty-one years her senior. She bore him five children. That same year, thanks to the influence of his friend Treitschke, Erdmannsdörffer was appointed professor in Heidelberg, while Treitschke himself moved to Berlin. Two of Anna's letters from that time demonstrate the role played by the Jewish question in Christian marriages—and elucidate what Dietrich Schäfer meant in his evaluation when he wrote that Simmel had the women of Berlin lying at his feet.

In July 1879, Anna wrote to her mother back in Greifswald: "Fascinated reading Hensel's *The Mendelssohn Family*. Bernhard with an aversion to everything Jewish. I only need to mention it, and he teases me that I'm talking like a Jew. No matter. I find it interesting. Likable, intelligent people who wrote the most charming letters." In 1881, she ended a letter reporting on a serious fight with him by remarking: "Sometimes my darling spouse could use a bit of the nature, the tender attentiveness of a Jewish husband. He is a true German in the sense of the old Germanic tribes, in which the men lay about on bearskins while the women worked."

Near the end of his life, a melancholy Gustav Lenz began to regret the career opportunities that his early liberalism had cost him. In an attempt to cheer him up, his son-in-law Bernhard Erdmannsdörffer listed the old man's life achievements: "The founding of five good German family lines, whose head and patriarch you are. And not one drop of Semitic blood—that, too, is something."[16]

Most Christians, staid and obedient as they were, were easily enraged by the "lively, brash, and frivolous humor of the Jewish genius" and by the Jews' "bizarrely flexible, sarcastic, skeptical, and undisciplined intellect," to quote Sombart and York-Steiner.[17] Karl Kautsky concurred when he commented that Jewish intellectual qualities were the "stumbling block" for racist theoreticians. In his 1915 book *The Conquering Jew*, British historian John Foster Fraser also scoffed that German academics needed anti-Jewish discriminatory rules because the contest "between the sons of the North, with their blond hair and sluggish intellects, and these sons of the Orient, with their black eyes and alert minds, is an unequal one."[18]

In other words, to the extent that Germans belatedly began to climb the social ladder, they perceived their lack of education and mental agility as embarrassing shortcomings. Racist theories were an excellent way of concealing that embarrassment, as the following examples illustrate.

In 1890, a young man named Carl Müller was studying at the University of Leipzig. He was a member of the conservative dueling fraternity Dresdensia, and in a short polemic entitled "Jewry within German Student Culture" he bitterly complained that a professor of the Hebrew faith had been appointed dean of a German university.[19] For Müller, that was a sign of a serious "illness, the growing presence of Jews in power." Two characteristics of his Jewish fellow students particularly provoked his ire. One was that they stood up for their coreligionists "devotedly." The second was that "there are far fewer failures among Jewish students than among Germans." The reason, according to Müller, was that Jews were more diligent and ambitious in their studies: "Like all money-hungry people, the Chinese or the Greeks, for instance, Jews are moderate eaters. A Jewish law student talks more about the law than he has to when he enjoys a small glass of beer! He's always going on about something, and that impresses others. His mind is quick to comprehend, but his understanding never runs deep. Why should it? The way such a student is, he'll get through his exams in the time prescribed, and Germany will be enriched by one more Jewish candidate for a senior civil service position." Jews, as Müller stressed in every second sentence, were interested only in money, and that's why he ended his polemic with this appeal to his Christian peers: "Stand up to the Jewish students with pride in your superiority!"[20]

In 1922, the editor in chief of *Deutsches Volkstum* ("German Folkhood") magazine, Wilhelm Stapel, published a book entitled simply *Anti-Semitism*. It was aimed, one might say, at the well-heeled middleclass Jew hater. Stapel justified his endeavor by writing that when he saw his own kind "being seriously disoriented by a foreign entity, no matter how intellectually excellent and superior," he had the right to defend himself. A few years later, Julius Goldstein—a Jewish philosophy professor whose appointment had been contested by anti-Semites—mocked Stapel's confession of intellectual inferiority as an example of the sort of aggression that sprang from weakness. "How lacking in backbone is the German 'kind,'" Goldstein asked, "if it can be so easily undermined?" Such eloquence from Jews enraged Stapel. In 1932, he fumed: "There would be no such thing as anti-Semitism if Jews were capable of keeping their mouths shut. They're capable of anything except keeping their mouths shut." By contrast, Stapel praised the taciturn German manner, crediting it with "grace," "nobility," "distinction," and "depth."[21]

In August 1924, a delegate to the Bavarian parliament, Ottmar Rutz, complained that the government of the southern German state contained too many Jews, as did the faculties of Bavarian universities. This unfortunate situation, Rutz objected, was always justified by the idea that Jews were a "gifted race"—which he said was a sign that people in positions of influence "did not recognize the core problem." Rutz demanded a Christian monopoly on state jobs, arguing that the converse of the "gifted race" logic was the "native exclusion" one. "We must remember," Rutz said, "that every Jewish professor and every Jewish civil servant keeps down a descendant of the German people. This sort of exclusion is what's really at stake. It's not a matter of insulting or attacking one or another descendant of the Jewish people. This has nothing to do with all of that, and nor do my petitions. This is solely about productively promoting the descendants of the German people and protecting them from exclusion."[22] Rutz was a lawyer who practiced in Munich and sat in parliament as part of the "folkish" fraction, a stand-in organization for the Nazi Party, which was banned at the time following the unsuccessful Beer Hall Putsch of 1923.

Occasionally Jews turned the tables and made fun of the simple-mindedness of the Germanic race's self-appointed defenders. In a poetic parody entitled "Old Germanics," for instance, journalist Kurt Tucholsky uses the figure of a drunken, slow-witted member of the fraternity "Teutonic Strength," a perpetual university student who is depicted singing a drinking song: "Germany must be / Entirely free of Jews. / And we must drink ourselves silly / While others pay their dues. / He who laughs at us is dead wrong / We'll graduate by 1940—that's not so long."[23] Tucholsky's poem was published in 1925.

A story heard by Jewish philosopher Rudolf Schottlaender in 1936 and subsequently passed on by him runs in a similar vein. A Jew and his wife, to make ends meet, rent out two rooms in their house to a working-class Gentile family. The children of the Gentile family attend the same school as the children of an SS man who lives across the street, but they always get better grades. "No wonder," sneers the SS man's wife to her neighbor. "It's no big trick when you're living with Jews."[24]

Ethnic ideologies, Zionist Fritz Bernstein argued in 1926, have the advantage of being "primitive." The idea of one's superiority cannot be disproven. Thus it allows people to "excuse themselves for their timidity, maintain the pretense that they don't know their own strength, and disguise any awareness of their vulnerability." If a Gentile German student was unable to come up with brilliant performances in business or law, then at least his larger group, his race, was capable of excellence. It was enough to be a Teuton. "He wasn't a Jew and that was the positive thing about him," Thomas Mann has a minor character in *The Magic Mountain* proclaim.[25]

Insofar as Jews were better at education, work, and earning money, they could be collectively defamed as coldhearted, calculating, rootless materialists, as members of a group that presumed to drag the most cherished values of the nation and the Christian religion through the muck. Jews were alleged to do this, depending on the situation, in know-it-all, nitpicking, arrogant, brazen, destructive, or cynical fashion.[26] The often contradictory language of racism, as many contemporaries noted, served to conceal both Gentile envy of others' success and the corresponding doubts about their own prospects. In 1920, the Association for Defense against Anti-Semitism published a pamphlet entitled *The ABCs of Defense*, which stated: "All the racial theoreticians' rhetoric about worldviews and the rest of their ideological talk is aimed entirely at concealing the economic basis on which anti-Semitism is truly built."[27]

In his 1931 book *Hitler's Way*, political scientist and future president of the Federal Republic of Germany Theodor Heuss concluded that the Nazi doctrine of race was the end product of an "astonishing inferiority complex" that deified Aryans in the interest of concealing a psychological deficit. The Belgian social psychologist Hendrik de Man, who lived in Frankfurt and himself had an ambiguous relationship with Nazism, described the exaggerated nationalism of Hitler's followers to a "discrimination complex, . . . a psychological release valve for feelings of social inferiority, . . . and a compensatory mechanism par excellence for a threatened collective sense of self-worth." When Hitler came to power, political philosopher Erich Voegelin asked how it could be that "a minority so tiny as to be virtually invisible"— again, Jews represented only 1 percent of the total population—could attract such hatred. Voegelin found the answer in "a feeling of inferiority on the part of Germans."[28]

Writing in exile in 1937, Thomas Mann characterized Nazi-style anti-Semitism as a by-product of "weakness, foolishness, and injustice." In Mann's eyes, the ideology served the need "to seek and to find a guilty party for the suffering, the transitional miseries, and the critical doubts of the age." It also addressed the desire of Gentile Germans to "feel a little stronger, better, and even more genteel" in comparison with Jews. Ostentatious displays of arrogance, Mann concluded, grew out of "social and ethnic feelings of inferiority." "Thick-headed provincialism," Mann wrote, "poisoned the atmosphere and made the word *international* an insult."[29]

Heuss drew attention to the legend, repeated in *Mein Kampf*, that the ancient Jews were in a far superior position to "the clumsy but almost boundlessly honest Aryans"—and that the former tried to subjugate the Germanic tribes in Central Europe. Even Hitler conceded: "The intellectual characteristics of Jews have been schooled over the course of millennia. The Jew today is considered 'clever' and was so, in a sense, throughout history." Nonetheless, Hitler consoled his supporters, Jews lacked the "cultural potency" of Germanic idealism.[30]

In his 1928 manuscript on foreign policy, Hitler wrote of the danger of the so-called Hebrews' uprooting "popular [*völkisch*] intelligence" with their "wits, cleverness, deception, perfidy, and dissimulation."[31] In summer 1941, the commander of the Wehrmacht's 22nd Infantry Division, Count Hans von Sponeck, ordered his men to separate—that is, to kill—all Jewish POWs from the Red Army. "Capturing them is especially important," Sponeck reasoned, "since they usually speak several languages and are more intelligent than the mass of other prisoners." A bit later, Hitler justified his policy of having Jews eliminated with the argument that they possessed a "racial core that has such a devastating effect when blood gets mixed that it completely unsettles people."[32]

PROGNOSES: MOSCOW, VIENNA, MUNICH

The early twentieth century saw the rise of utopian societies that although initially pursued in the name of equality and togetherness soon turned violent. Many writers greeted these social experiments with euphoria; others prophesied the worst. Three works in particular appear to me to be especially revealing about the era's desires for social homogeneity and/or racial purity and about the development of a morality that allowed for the destruction of dissidents. Perhaps the best known today is Yevgeny Zamyatin's novel *We*, written in Moscow in 1920, which deals with the Bolshevik Revolution and its dreams of making all members of society absolutely equal. The other two are Hugo Bettauer's novel *The City without Jews*, written in Vienna in 1922, and Siegfried Lichtenstaedter's story "The Jewish Marshal," composed in Munich in 1926.

Zamyatin's parable depicts the triumph of a form of egalitarianism that seeks to eradicate all difference, destroying individual human characteristics and indeed individual human beings in the name of justice and equality. In strident language, the author, an engineer by trade, presents a picture of a society in which every detail is socially engineered, in which individual liberty is demonized and the collective elevated to the level of a divinity. Zamyatin had actively supported the Bolshevik Revolution, but he quickly became disillusioned with the practical consequences. *We* was published in England and France in 1924 and 1925. It wouldn't appear in the Soviet Union until 1988.[33]

In Zamyatin's totalitarian state, human beings are designated by numbers and made to wear uniforms. The protagonist of the novel is called D-503. Private property, nicotine and alcohol, and feelings like envy are unheard of; love, passion, and amorous jealousy are all considered threats to the community. A central government office regulates exactly how much sexual contact members of society, or "numbers," may have with one another—and that contact is kept as emotionally cool as possible. The society's national holiday is known as Unanimity Day. On that day, a figure called the Benefactor is unanimously reelected to lead the all-regulating One State that arose after a cataclysmic war two hundred years in the past wiped out most of the earth's population. The homogeneous populace live in identical glass-walled square houses, almost entirely free of any sort of excitement or tension. On Unanimity Day, everyone cheers: "Hail to the One

State, Hail to the Benefactor, Hail to the Numbers!" As the novel opens, the society is planning to send a rocket called *Integral* into space to colonize other planets.

Despite this degree of conformity, the state needs to remain vigilant about its weaker constituents, who are susceptible to the elemental temptations of freedom and thus represent an acute danger to the happiness of the masses. To preserve the public welfare, the Benefactor has his secret police, the Bureau of Guardians, keep tabs on all the people on the street. They do this with the help of ultrathin membranes, strung up across the streets, that are capable of recording the quietest of sounds.

Numbers who are found to have succumbed to freedom's temptations lose their right to be "building blocks" of the One State and are sentenced to death. The executions are carried out by the "Benefactor's Machine," a 100,000-volt mechanism located on the central square of the state. After the execution, nothing remains of victims except "a small puddle of chemically pure water, . . . nothing more than the dissociation of material, the splitting of the atoms of the human body." The Benefactor celebrates this eradication of dissidents as a ritual and communally approved act of purification for the greater good.

Occasionally, dissidents are not vaporized but preserved in formaldehyde so that scientists can study them. The aim is to better protect society against the virus of individualism and one day to learn how to eradicate the few surviving remnants of the human soul.

City without Jews, subtitled *A Novel for the Day after Tomorrow*, was published in 1922 by the pulp-fiction Viennese publishing house Gloriette. It sold 250,000 copies, and was made into a film two years after its publication. Its author, Hugo Bettauer, was a Jewish convert to Christianity, a prolific writer who wrote four novels in 1922 alone. He was also an advocate of sexual freedom and the publisher of the successful weekly magazine *He and She*, which mixed lifestyle advice with eroticism.

In Bettauer's novel, as in real life in 1922, Vienna is in the throes of rampant inflation and crisis. The people elect a would-be political savior, Dr. Karl Schwertfeger, from the Christian Social Party. This figure was an obvious reference to Dr. Karl Lueger, the anti-Semitic mayor of Vienna from 1897 to 1910. Lueger forcibly modernized the city and protected the interests of the poor and the Christian middle classes while railing against the Jews. Hitler would later recall Lueger riding around the city in an open carriage to the cheers of the Viennese. The number of Jews cited in Bettauer's novel, 500,000, corresponds to the number living in Germany at the time; in Austria, the Jewish population numbered only around 200,000. And in the first half of the novel, all of those half-million Jews are expelled from the city.

The narrative starts with a crowd scene in which all of Vienna seems to have taken to the streets: "the bourgeois and the workers, fine ladies and common women, adolescents and old men, young girls, small children, invalids in wheelchairs." It is a warm day in June, and everyone is milling around, sweating in the sun and shouting about politics. There are repeated cries of "Jews out!" and "Long live Dr. Karl Schwertfeger, long live Austria's liberator!" Slowly, a black government vehicle makes its way through the crowd. Schwertfeger gets out of the car. Like Lueger and later Hitler, he is a man who has remained single and lives to serve the nation. He ascends the staircase of the Austrian parliament and enters the chamber where he will speak in defense of the long-planned "Law on the Expulsion of Non-Aryans from Austria."

The proposed law gives all Jews six months to get their finances in order and quit the country. Those who defy the law by secretly remaining in Austria or taking more than the allowed sums of money with them are to be subject to the death penalty. "Descendants of Jews," defined as the children of mixed marriages, are likewise required to emigrate, as are Jewish converts to Christianity. After a bit of debate, the rule is waived for "descendants," provided that the parents have not "married again with Jews." The law explicitly rules out exceptions for elderly or ill Jews or for "Jews who have rendered special services to the country." Otherwise, Schwertfeger observes, Jewish money and influence would continue to spread night and day: "No, there are no exceptions, no protection, no pity, and no closing our eyes!"

The savior Schwertfeger has but a single argument for the necessity of his law. He describes Gentile Austrians as members of a "naïve, true-hearted, good," but rather slow-developing mountain people, who are "no match" for Jews. This is the reason he sounds the alarm: "The Jews among us cannot tolerate such tranquil evolution. . . . Who is driving the automobiles? Who is splurging in nightclubs? Who is filling the coffee houses and the expensive restaurants? Who is draping his wife with jewels and pearls? The Jew!" Schwertfeger also has an answer for how the Jews could have gotten so much further ahead in Austria than the Gentiles: "With their uncanny sharpness of mind, their cosmopolitan sensibility divorced from tradition, their catlike flexibility, their instantaneous intellectual grasp of things, and all the skills they have honed in millennia of subjugation, they have overwhelmed us. They have become our masters and have seized control of our entire economic, intellectual, and cultural life." Schwertfeger's speech earns him thunderous applause.

When he is finished, the only Zionist deputy of parliament, the engineer Minkus Wassertrilling, gets his turn to speak. He welcomes the law because, as he says, "half of those expelled will gather under the Zionist banner" and leave for Israel. After Wassertrilling's speech, as a precautionary measure, some thugs arrive to remove certain deputies from the parliament building, and the law is approved unanimously. The remaining formalities are quickly dispensed with, and people celebrate until deep in the night.

The following week, Aryan writers are gearing up for the end to their long period as wallflowers on the Austrian literary scene. Their long, boring plays have "slumbered in their desk drawers," and their leaden philosophical tracts, which took them years to write, have gathered dust in publishers' warehouses. Now these very same authors can look forward to the prospect of future success. Conversely, the gifted Jewish poet Max Seider takes his life "so as not to let his tired, sensitive soul freeze to death in a foreign land." Jewish journalists and editors for the major papers move to London and found a weekly entitled *In Exile*. Vienna's prostitutes are in mourning as their clientele now consists of the city's notoriously tightfisted Gentiles, who like it quick and cheap and never indulge in more extended and costly pleasures. Voluptuous Juno with her husky voice has little time for Baron So-and-So from the Foreign Office, but she's full of praise for Herschmann from the Anglobank. Ever since he was a customer, she says, "I've been absolutely mad for Israelites."

The trains loaded with Jews begin pulling out of the stations ahead of schedule, and curious onlookers are sometimes subject to outbreaks of sympathy. Schwertfeger reacts by ordering trains to depart only at night and to use the switching yards on the outskirts of the city. With the deportations having been rendered almost invisible, Aryan Austrians are able to celebrate their good fortune more openly. The Jewish exodus, they expect, will "make groceries cheaper and allow wealth to be distributed more equitably." A character named Wilhelm Habietnik, formerly a salesman in the ladies' department of a luxury fashion shop, buys the building with the help of credit from a neighborhood bank. Similar stories take place across the city.

Lower-class men and women, conscious of the injustice of what's going on, occasionally scratch their heads at such developments, but they drown their misgivings in alcohol. And the promise of future advantages helps ease people's moral qualms: "Even within circles of organized, social-democratic laborers, there is great satisfaction at the departure of the Jews. What particularly lifts the mood is that there suddenly is no longer any competition for apartments. In Vienna alone, forty thousand apartments that used to belong to Jews have come free since the beginning of July."[34]

Surprisingly, Bettauer's story has a happy ending: the Jews are eventually allowed to return to the city, because without them its economic and intellectual life has ground to a halt. That is the plot of the second half of the novel. But it is the novel's first half, the story of the expulsion, that proved darkly prophetic. Sixteen years after *The City without Jews* was published, all of the details described there—and far worse ones—would become reality: the singling out in law of Jews and half-breeds, the expropriation of Jewish property, the advantages enjoyed by Gentiles looking for apartments, the sinecures doled out to historians for their weighty, unreadable tomes, and the lack of exceptions when it came to the deportations. Hitler did, in fact, clear out forty thousand apartments that had been rented or owned by Viennese Jews. To great public approval, German and Austrian government officials stripped Jews of their worldly goods, drove them abroad, and loaded those who remained into cattle cars for concentration camps in Eastern Europe. To avoid burdening the consciences of ordinary Viennese, the deportation trains did indeed depart from remote switching yards. A total of 48,593 people ultimately left Vienna in this fashion. Only 2,098 of them survived.

As early as 1900, Siegfried Lichtenstaedter had refined the art of political prognosis, which he called historical prediction or the historiography of the future. The circumstances of his life as a Jew acutely attuned him to the hypocrisy of Christian humanism and allowed him to see through nationalistic arrogance and policies that were cloaked in moral rhetoric but really served to advance Germany's imperial interests. Of course, he got details wrong here and there, but nonetheless he was able to anticipate basic historical trends, identify obscure harbingers of what was to come, and extrapolate what they would mean in the future.

Lichtenstaedter studied Oriental languages and law at the University of Erlangen and the University of Leipzig. It's possible that he originally hoped to secure an academic position, although he may also have flirted with the notion of getting a job in Turkey. In any case, he had no success. In 1898, he obtained a high position in the Bavarian financial administration and became a royal counsel (later he was appointed a senior royal counsel). In many respects, his life resembled that of Franz Kafka. Lichtenstaedter never married and he spent his days working at an undistinguished job, while at night he wrote works diagnosing the pernicious social trends of his time and predicting what would come of them. He published most of these works under pseudonyms, as Ne'man or as Dr. Emin Mehemed Efendi. Lichtenstaedter's writings were laced with a Bavarian love of the ridiculous, and they were full of polished polemics and clever narrative conceits. His narrators could be a British journalist investigating an alleged Muslim lack of culture, an unscrupulous Russian government minister, an erotically obsessed French diplomat, or a German anti-Semite modeled on examples from everyday life in Munich.

After devoting much of his energy to assimilating into the Gentile mainstream, in the 1920s Lichtenstaedter began once more to play an active part in the Jewish community of the Bavarian capital. He was critical of Zionism, advising Jews to focus on "Jewish pride" and "Jewish singularity" rather than emigrating. But he soon altered his view. In 1935, he refrained from writing a book to be titled *Foolish Israel* because he deemed the times "so difficult and distressing for the German Jewish community . . . that they prohibit the self-indulgence of expressing scorn."[35] Starting in 1933, he began encouraging Jews to flee Germany—and not just for Palestine. If people were to survive, he argued, "the flow of emigrants should be diverted into as many riverbeds as possible." It was crucial not to stubbornly insist on impossible unrealistic destinations. "May God grant," he urged his readers in 1937, "that it's not too late!"[36]

More than three decades earlier, between 1901 and 1903, Lichtenstaedter had written his year-by-year fictional history of the future, *The New Empire: A Contribution to the History of the 20th Century.* For 1910, he predicted that Italian troops would land in Tripoli and that a major war would break out in the Balkans, the perennially unsettled corner of Europe, over Macedonian and Albanian independence. He also foresaw that Bulgaria and Greece would play a

leading role in a struggle with the Ottoman Empire, citing a ficti-
tious newspaper in Sophia that had issued a "fiery call . . . to evict
the Turkish enemy from the civilized halls of Europe." By January
12, 1910, the Greek parliament would indeed be speaking of "the
inalienable rights of their oppressed Hellenic brothers," as opposed
to the "barbarians" of the Ottoman Empire.[37]

For the year 1912, Lichtenstaedter invented a "horrific" blood-
bath meted out by Muslims on Armenians in the eastern Anatolian
city of Erzurum. As part of the backdrop, he described how the British and Russians supported Armenian nationalism, and he depicted
how the interests of various powers in parts of the Ottoman Empire
led them to stir up hatreds between the major groups there.

For 1939, Lichtenstaedter included in his history of the future a
newspaper article published in Vienna after Austria had been unified
with Germany. Dated June 23, 1939, the fictional piece is about "a
marvelous summer solstice celebration among German students"
near Vienna. The students, the article reports, are "suffused with feelings of ethnic German solidarity" to such an extent that they exclude
from their celebrations anyone who clings to "the outmoded, foreign,
Jewish, and effeminate ways of thinking." In the back garden of an
inn named German Lightning, revelers break out in indescribable
cheers at the singing of the latest German patriotic song, "When
Parasitic Peoples Threaten Us." It provokes smiles from a couple of
Czech and Slovenian onlookers, who are subsequently "punished in
appropriate fashion."

In a further fictional article written for October 2, 1939, the German government is shown reacting harshly to anti-German agitation
among the Slavic populations of Prague, Zagreb, and Ljubljana,
declaring that German patience is at an end and that punitive, war-
like actions are long overdue "to create lasting order and calm." Lichtenstaedter's fictional source points to the "most recent incidents of blood
spilling," committed by "an ignorant, mesmerized Slavic mob," as
the reason for the crackdown. "He who sows wind will reap a
storm," the German government is quoted as saying, while adding

that the punitive action will not damage Germany's friendly relations with Russia.

The second volume of Lichtenstaedter's *The New Empire* was similarly prescient. In those pages, on October 1, 1945, a Russian commissar arrives in Prague "to administer the liberated western Slavic countries." On January 1, 1946, he issues an "edict of tolerance" that stipulates that in the future Russian will be the language used for instruction in schools in those countries.[38]

In 1926, four years after Bettauer's *City without Jews*, Lichtenstaedter published a collection of everyday observations and farces entitled *Antisemitica: Aspects Humorous and Serious, True and False*. One of the anecdotes in the collection is called "If a Jewish Ancestor of Bismarck Is Discovered." Another describes a cultural history of the nineteenth and twentieth centuries that claims that Jews were to blame for the widespread alcoholism of the period. Jewish wholesalers brought wine to the market, the fictional argument goes, while Jewish bankers extended credit to brewers to make beer and Jewish businesses sold tankards, jugs, and mugs. And as if that weren't bad enough, Jewish furniture stores "most unscrupulously provided bars with the tables, benches, and chairs they required."[39]

In Lichtenstaedter's fictional world, this cultural history appears in 1999. Here, though, he missed the mark severely: it would take only twelve years before the ambitious young German historian Werner Conze, later one of the leading lights in his field in postwar West Germany, would recount that the name of the Führer had penetrated to even the most remote Byelorussian-settled villages in Poland, "above all thanks to his clear policies on the Jewish question, the effects of which the poor Byelorussian farmer feels on a daily basis." Conze specified what he meant: "What little the estate owner grants him, the Jew coaxes out of his pocket," so that a Byelorussian peasant can "only vegetate dully and miserably" and inevitably anesthetizes himself "with the schnapps of the village Hebrew."[40] No less austere an institution than the German Research Association supported Conze in his efforts to enrich the body of human knowledge with such valuable scientific insight.

The most cutting satire in Lichtenstaedter's *Antisemitica* is entitled "The Jewish Marshal."[41] It takes place in Anthropopolis, a city of 200,000 people, including 2,000 Jews. One day, the city needs a new marshal to enforce court-ordered repossessions (there is only one such position in the whole of Anthropopolis). For the first time a Jew is appointed, and popular unrest quickly follows. The business of repossession, some people complain, is now 100 percent in Jewish hands, even though Jews represent only 1 percent of the population. The constitution of Anthropopolis guarantees Jews equal rights, but now, as any idiot can figure out, they have seized "rights that are 100 times greater than that." It's even worse than that, say the city's mathematicians. They remind people that "the Aryan population has zero—zero!—representation and that the number one divided by zero is by no means equal to 100 but is in fact infinity." Seen from that perspective, Jews are "overprivileged in truly endless proportions," while Aryans are the victims of an unprecedented injustice.

For years, the man now appointed as marshal has been part of an informal group of people who get together to play cards. Suddenly, "in keeping with the spirit of the times," this small social circle becomes an official, state-sanctioned club. Encouraged by warnings from self-appointed guardians of ethnic identity at the newspaper *The Anthropopolitan Dawn*, the card enthusiasts begin to take their civil responsibilities seriously. In the first paragraph of the club's founding document, they insert a new phrase: "The Anthropopolitan Card Club pledges to play the game in the pure Anthopopolitanian spirit and in a manner worthy of the Aryan race." That unfortunately means that the Jewish marshal can no longer take part. The same thing happens to him at the Singing Club and with various sports teams, so that soon he has little social contact outside "the intimate circle of his coreligionists."

A short time later, a new opera, *The Dying Hercules*, is performed. The composer is the brother of the increasingly unpopular marshal, whose social standing isn't helped at all by having such an artsy relative. The opera house is half empty, and from some of the filled seats come sarcastic whispers: "Good God! Now Jerusalem is giving us an opera as well!" Some younger audience members take tambourines and other instruments and disrupt the performance, claiming to be protecting native art from "pretenders and swindlers." The music critic at the *Dawn* pans the opera, saying he is defending timeless principles against contemporary commercial philistinism. His review ends with the words: "The temple of art is not a retail store, and the realm of the aesthetic is not a stock exchange—take that to heart, Israel!"

The marshal's situation becomes more and more precarious, until one day the investigative reporter from the *Dawn* uncovers a sixty-year-old case of usury. He writes a detailed article that is featured prominently in the newspaper's weekend supplement. The case sounds extremely complex, but everyone with a bit of common sense can grasp the basics. The instance of usury involved the grandfather of the maternal uncle of the marshal's wife. And since the uncle—beneficiary of the shameless acts, exploiter of the people—contributed significantly to the wife's dowry when she and the marshal were married, the marshal himself has directly profited from the charging of cutthroat interest rates.

In an accompanying editorial, the journalist pulls no punches, saying that the people's "patience has come to an end." Unlike in the Bible, he warns, the sea will no longer part for the benefit of Israel and destroy its enemies. "In this day and age, the opposite may well happen," the journalist writes. "Israel could be rendered harmless and its enemies—or more accurately, its victims—could be saved. There are bodies of water other than the Red Sea. And there are rivers even in our Anthropopolitanian lands with enough water to render the entire people of Israel harmless." Soon, the Jewish community, wishing to forestall more anti-Semitism, officially requests that the marshal give up the post. A few days later, bowing to public pressure, he resigns.

Lichtenstaedter's allegory was published in 1926. A few years later, fiction would become reality. In the Nazi youth organizations and in the SS, thousands and thousands of people sang a catchy ditty with the lyrics: "See the Jews try to flee. / They even cross the deep Red Sea. / But the closing waves never cease. / And all the world at last has peace."[42]

Another piece of fiction of the period, Herbert Friedenthal's *Invisible Chain*, ended with the question that its author was forced to ask himself in Berlin in 1936: Should one stay or go? For Friedenthal, anti-Semitism was not something that could be outrun. Whether in Sydney or Tanganyika, the Jewish question was a traveling companion that could not be shaken off. "You carry it with you," Friedenthal wrote. "As long as you haven't answered it, it's always there, wherever you are." Palestine might offer a way out. But Kai, the hero of Friedenthal's novel, does not relish the idea of compulsory integration, the different climate, the threat of malaria, and the inevitable fighting with native Arabs and refuses to go down the Zionist route. His girlfriend, Miriam, is of a different mind, arguing: "I'm afraid that the few hundred thousand existences that save themselves by going to Palestine will one day be all that's left of the Jewish people."[43]

In 1938, the seventy-year-old Siegfried Lichtenstaedter did in fact visit Palestine. He was impressed with the progress Jews had made building settlements there, but he didn't want to be a burden to anyone and returned to Germany. In response to an ordinance of January 1, 1939, requiring Jews with first names of non-Jewish origin to be renamed Israel, he gave up his real name and adopted one that German authorities considered recognizably Jewish.[44] On June 6, 1942, Munich police deported him as part of a transport to the Theresienstadt concentration camp. Dr. Lichtenstaedter died there on December 6 of that year.

Both Lichtenstaedter in Germany and Bettauer in Austria clearly depicted popular anti-Semitism spreading in the early 1920s, well before the global recession that triggered further economic and political developments in both countries. Moreover, the anti-Semitism they described already contained all of the ingredients that would become elements of official German state policy after 1933. Both writers blamed its rise on the Christian population's mistrust of modernity, the constant demands of social aspirants for more "fairness," fear of Jewish entrepreneurial spirit, and the German majority's retreat into collectivism. Such collectivism was an attempt to create the social homogeneity that Zamyatin caricatured in *We*. In its radicalized form, striving for equality meant discriminating against, excluding, and ultimately exterminating all those who were different.

THE CONCEIT OF PURITY

The first German academic position in racial hygiene was established not by Hitler and his henchmen but by the deans of the University of Munich, in 1923. A scientist named Fritz Lenz occupied that chair. Four years later, in Berlin, academics founded the Kaiser Wilhelm Institute for Anthropology, Human Heredity, and Eugenics, under the directorship of Eugen Fischer. The institute was closed in 1945, and the attached society was renamed the Max Planck Society. Its most famous member was undoubtedly Josef Mengele.

The theoretical trappings of racial pseudoscience date back to the middle of the nineteenth century, when it began to evolve in various European countries in the gray area between biology, medicine, anthropology, and ethnology. In time, its adherents came to believe in an inherent difference in rank between human groups. Theories of this sort proved very attractive to many citizens of the European colonial powers and to many whites in the United States. If groups of people could be differentiated through supposedly empirical, biological rules, then it was possible to defend laws that denied basic human rights to "natives," "savages," and "niggers." In this respect, racial science served a clear purpose, legitimizing the discrimination that had long been the established practice toward enslaved and indentured non-Europeans.

Lacking any major colonies, the Wilhelmine Empire in Germany did not need racial science to this end. For that reason, Frenchman Arthur de Gobineau's four-volume *Essay on the Inequality of the Human Races* (1853–55)—which argued that the Caucasian race, and in particular its Germanic branches, had special creative abilities— took more than forty years to be translated into German. (An American edition appeared almost immediately, much to the delight of slave owners.) The first German edition of Gobineau's work was published only in 1897, and a second complete one did not follow until 1902. Even in its hesitant adoption of racist paradigms, the sluggish German nation demonstrated how far behind it was.[45]

On the other hand, since Germans were not particularly receptive to the idea of universal human rights—the concept played little role in public debates—they didn't need any fancy theoretical trappings to justify denying rights to certain groups. Soon enough, racist theories that had proved so successful in France, England, and the United States were adapted to meet German needs, directed specifically against minorities who were seen as threatening competition. Racial theorists in general emphasized the intellectual superiority and the general supremacy of their own people, and German racial science eventually also found adherents in other countries, although its political influence remained limited. Between 1925 and 1927, for instance, Hans F. K. Günther—soon to become one of the most ambitious racist thinkers in the Third Reich—presented a series of guest lectures at the State Institute for Racial Biology in Uppsala, Sweden.[46]

By the late nineteenth century, the belief in innate racial characteristics had become an unquestioned part of intellectual culture throughout the West. For a fairly absurd indication of how widespread such thought was, we need look no further than an official protest that Albania sent to other European governments in 1883 after the disputed region of Northern Epirus was awarded to Greece. The Albanian memorandum argued that Greeks and Albanians could not be expected to coexist under a common rule because "Greeks are a broad-skulled people while Albanians are a long-skulled one."[47]

Today such statements seem comical. But even the great German physician Rudolf Virchow took skull measurements in hope of finding differences between Aryans and non-Aryans. He focused on Hungarians, who were believed to have originally come from Central Asia, although to his credit he soon admitted that no significant differences existed between them and other groups. An anthropological examination of hair and eye color among 6.8 million German schoolchildren, 75,000 of whom were Jewish, also yielded no results that would have allowed Virchow to distinguish between a Germanic and a Jewish race. Virchow noted that 32 percent of Jewish children had light hair, and 46 percent had light eyes.[48] Still, ignoring scientific data like these, the English racial theorist Houston Stewart Chamberlain, the Germanophilic son-in-law and admirer of Richard Wagner, described the lengthened Germanic skull as typical of an "ever-active brain, tortured by longing."[49] Chamberlain also contrasted "the Aryan Germanic people of light" with the bugbear of the "everlastingly bestial" Jewish race.

Chamberlain's ever-active brain made racist thinking popular and acceptable in educated society. Kaiser Wilhelm II himself was completely taken by such Germanophilic nonsense, praising Chamberlain as a "brother-in-arms and ally in the fight of the Germanic people against Rome and Jerusalem." The German emperor made Chamberlain's main work, *The Foundations of the Nineteenth Century*, recommended reading for the Prussian officers corps and read aloud from the tome to his sons. In his 1922 memoirs, Wilhelm wrote that "Germandom in all its majesty was first revealed and propagated to the German people by Chamberlain"—although the former kaiser had to admit that such majesty, as Germany's breakdown in World War I showed, was no guarantee of perpetual success.[50] Twenty years later, Hitler would offer pretty much the same assessment in his political testament.

Early racial theory wasn't systematic, and it lacked a clear biological-political orientation. That changed just before World War I, when Eugen Fischer emerged as the leading scientific promoter of

German racial and genetic hygiene. In 1913, he published the first of his "bastard studies," an examination of the offspring of German and Dutch fathers and native women in the Rehoboth region of Africa, in what is today Namibia. Supported by the prestigious Humboldt Foundation at the Royal Prussian Academy of Sciences, and with typical German academic diligence, Fischer closely investigated 2,567 members of what he considered "a population of bastards."

Previously, anthropologists had been concerned with individuals—their facial expressions, demeanor, and social behavior, their fortunes and misadventures. Fischer's brand of anthropology, on the other hand, was a quantitative theory of types. Bodily measurements, lines of heredity and ancestry, and classifications and externally imposed calculations replaced personal observations. Results were analyzed to confirm categories of ethnicity, body type, and race. Fischer and his acolytes successfully promoted the new methodology, reducing their discipline to something like a human version of agrarian studies on breeding. Indeed, the goal of Fischer's new form of anthropology was an orderly form of human "production." Generalizing from the empirical data of his field research, he concluded that the normal "spiritual lives" and "intellectual qualities" of human beings were racially inherited and that the mixing of races ("bastardization") reduced the quality of human genetic material.

The final sentence of Fischer's first major study would go on to have particular influence on later biological politics—or, as he called it, "anthropobiology." After arguing that the new discipline should be dramatically expanded, Fischer wrote: "Only then can we, and indeed we must, push ahead with practical eugenics and racial hygiene."[51] Even while doing his research in South-West Africa, Fischer echoed Gobineau by proclaiming: "The future belongs to the study of race and the subsequent conservation of certain races."[52] From its very inception, then, German racial biology was a discipline that pressed for political and social change.

In 1920 and 1921, Fischer coauthored the two-volume *Human Heredity and Racial Hygiene* with Lenz and the director of the

Center for Breeding Research at the Kaiser Wilhelm Institute, Erwin Baur. It quickly became a standard reference work, known simply as Baur, Fischer, and Lenz and going through multiple editions until 1944. It was even translated into English and Swedish. In polite academic prose, this work made racist and geneticist resentment seem legitimate—covering it, as novelist Jakob Wassermann wrote, with a "splendid and virtuous coating of social and racial philosophizing."[53]

Baur, Fischer, and Lenz transformed vulgar prejudice into what seemed like scientific discoveries. The hook nose of the caricatured Jew became the genetically dominant convex nose of pseudo-science. Jews, Fischer determined, were a "pre-Asian" race, completely distant from European ones. "One can very well speak of typical racial characteristics for Jews and Germans and distinguish them clearly and precisely," he noted with satisfaction. The characteristics of "bastard populations"—descendants of mixed marriages between Jews and the people whom Fischer considered true Europeans—proved that Jewish characteristics such as "black hair" and "one or the other aspect of physiognomy" always emerged as dominant. In a subsequent passage, Lenz went into the genetic perils of Jewishness, citing statistics to suggest that Jews were more prone to going blind or deaf and that they suffered more often from diabetes and mental illness. Conversely, Lenz claimed, Nordic peoples were superior to all other races in their "determination and careful foresight . . . so that in terms of their intellectual gifts they are the pinnacle of humanity."

In the name of science, Fischer seconded the idea that "the introduction of the Nordic race to the peoples of Europe" was "undoubtedly" the reason the Continent produced so many excellent thinkers, inventors, and artists. Lenz found that Jews' genetic characteristics made them "less successful at controlling and exploiting nature than at controlling and exploiting people." Jews, for Lenz, were almost a "soulful race . . . thanks to an astonishing ability to insinuate themselves into the souls of others and make them bend to their will."[54]

In another passage, Baur endorsed the idea of human breeding, provided that "the breeder has a clearly defined goal in mind." After

1931, Baur enthusiastically promoted the Nazi cause and criticized as too lax a 1933 law permitting the compulsory sterilization of people with vaguely defined "genetic diseases." Baur's death in December 1933 prevented him from doing anything more to advance Hitler's cause. His name lived on, though: until its demise in 1990, Communist East Germany awarded an Erwin Baur medal for excellence in research into the breeding of plants.[55]

Fischer, for his part, effusively welcomed the "new age" heralded by "the people's chancellor," Hitler. In the summer of 1933, he recalled his own pioneering work in bringing about change: "Without the triumph of genetic science, there would be no doctrine of the eugenic, racially hygienic ethnic state.[56] In May 1933, upon becoming the dean of Berlin's university, Fischer removed hundreds of Jewish professors and students. A few months later, he applauded the law mandating the sterilization of the "genetically ill" and other measures aimed at expunging "ethnically foreign elements." In 1937, he was one of the authorities upon whose recommendation children born to German mothers and French occupying soldiers in the 1920s (the so-called Rhineland bastards) were sterilized, even though there was no law explicitly permitting such action.[57]

Fischer supported the persecution of Jews and Sinti and Roma and never tired of warning that the German people were threatened with extinction and that the race needed to be saved. To improve the German genetic pool, Fischer recommended that society follow the example of the livestock breeder, who sorted out inferior animals and brought them to the slaughterhouse. He constantly attacked the "narrow-minded middle classes" and "the world of Marxism" (that is, the Social Democrats), which had blinded the people to their most precious possession: their genetic heritage. Germany, he felt, had been saved just in the nick of time.

Hitler would adopt the pseudoscientific framework put forth by Fischer, albeit in cruder language, claiming that "blood mixing" usually led to "degeneration of the race" and the sort of "purulent herd in which the maggots of the international Jewish community flourish and cause the ultimate decay of the people." In *Mein Kampf*, Hitler demanded the creation of state institutions to preserve the purity of German blood and an end to "persistent racial corruption," that is, the intermarriage of Gentiles and Jews. He also called for "special race commissions" to monitor newly settled territories. The goal was to produce and encourage the development of "superior racial material" in the interest of pure-blooded Germans.[58] In 1933, Fischer proclaimed: "Today we are experiencing the passionate reinvigoration of millions through the words and deeds of one man, a leader who rescued a people."[59]

Racial theorists claimed that their teachings were based on empiric data and careful biological research. In fact, much of the racist theorizing in the 1920s was based on mere speculation, and the results of racial "research" were always disputable and sometimes simply invented.[60] This in itself is not significant: lots of scientific discoveries suffer the fate of being proven wrong at a later date. What *is* significant is that ever greater numbers of respected biologists, doctors, and anthropologists, as well as a growing scientifically minded portion of the general populace, thought that "genetic and racial hygiene" was a promising new discipline. Funds were made available to support it, and doctoral dissertations, academic working groups, research fellowships, university chairs, and prestigious publications series weren't long in following. Public interest, and the enthusiasm of young people particularly, helped the discipline to flourish.

Racist teachings that parroted the language of biology had repercussions throughout the humanities. Soon, biological notions of race were connected with the older idea of a specific German spirit, popularized by the Romantics. The German cultural soul, deeply rooted in popular soil and constantly reinvigorated with fresh sap, tempted a number of Weimar intellectuals into writing anti-Semitic texts. No matter how respectable and discreet their choice of words, the upshot of these evasively formulated documents was always that Germans

and Jews were divided by irreconcilable intellectual and cultural differences. Johann Plenge and Margarete Adam were two such intellectuals. Their examples show how anti-Semitic prejudice, even when
it took the seemingly harmless form of mere reservations about Jews,
could bind together Germans of diverse social backgrounds and
political outlooks.

Johann Plenge was a Social Democrat who taught government at
the University of Münster and had a knack for raising money. In the
immediate postwar years, students considered him an inspiring, icon-
oclastic lecturer. On November 17, 1919, Plenge addressed them with
the following words: "Gentlemen. For today's lecture we have chosen
a surprising topic, one that deviates somewhat from the norm: the
political worthiness of the Jews." Plenge explained that he was alter-
ing the syllabus because a Jewish student had complained about
Plenge's denigrating Judaism in a previous lecture. After reassuring
his audience that he himself was not Jewish, Plenge launched into a
rambling lecture about human incompatibility. He drew distinctions
between Christianity ("deeper and more meaningful"), Islam ("Negroid
characteristics"), and Judaism ("extrinsic") before proceeding to assert
that Judaism entailed more than religious belief. "Judaism," Plenge
explained, "is a congenital race," and that was why Jews displayed a
specific "sort of social behavior" that attracted criticism from the
majority. "We all know instinctively," Plenge asserted, "that race is
a reality, and no sophistic arguments by blinkered biologists can
erase that problem."

Plenge considered the typical life of members of this race as guided
by animalistic "greed and dissipation." Although he conceded that
Jews had sharper minds, better ability to think abstractly, and admirable energy, those positive qualities were paired with a craven need
for social recognition, a lack of human warmth, an "intense will to
power," and an inability to "create things in positive, organic fashion."
To top off his summary of racial psychology, the Social Democratic
professor invoked the two-headed threat posed by Jewry, economic
and Bolshevik: "the fantastic triumph of Jews at the pinnacle of

capitalism" as well as the "ghetto resentment of capitalists" that had caused the revolution of 1917.

Despite his negative analysis, Plenge did not think that Jewish procapitalist and anticapitalist extremism was the end of the world. While he did think that the "shifting of political interests" to the benefit of Jews was inevitable, he advised his students in 1919 to pursue a third path between the "Jewish extremes" of unfettered capitalism and class hatred. Gentiles, Plenge proposed, could rally non-Jewish forces to "an alliance of unexpected strength" and create a "consciousness of unity among its thus enlightened members."

Though his rhetoric sounded objective, Plenge was defining Jews as fundamentally different from Christian Germans and declaring the differences to be irreconcilable. "We are not admitted inside, into the internal nature of Jews," Plenge complained. Here the Social Democratic professor effectively took up the "scientific" anti-Semitism preached by the right-wing intellectuals of his day. Right-wing anti-Semites, after all, usually also claimed to have nothing against individual Jews per se but only to be resisting the general encroachment of a group "intrinsically alien to us."[61]

The Hamburg philosopher and women's rights activist Margarete Adam, who wrote her dissertation with Ernst Cassirer, displayed a similar level of resentment, although its rough edges were smoothed over for bourgeois sensibilities. In 1929, in a "discussion of the Jewish question" that she conducted with the Jewish historian and sociologist Eva Reichmann-Jungmann, she was at pains to stress: "The Jew in his very nature is perceived by the Aryan as a different type of human being." Gentile antipathy toward Jews, Adam argued, was based on reciprocal feelings of foreignness, stemming historically from the terrible acts of persecution that Christians had visited on the minority with its old-fashioned faith and based more recently on the "teeth-gnashing disdain" that Jews felt for Christians. As evidence for her claims, Adam cited the mighty Jewish press, which was "rife with insults and scorn hurled at the great personages of the German past." Adam explained: "This press is what causes people to speak repeatedly of 'Jewish solidarity' in the worst sense." She dismissed the Weimar Republic's lifting of restrictions on Jews' occupying high civil service positions, calling it "an experiment contrary to history and nature."

In parliamentary elections on September 14, 1930, Adam voted for the Nazi Party, explaining her decision in a public statement. Her ballot had been cast not for the Nazis' harsh anti-Semitism, she said, but in support of their uncompromising demands for the revision of "the insane peace treaties" and the subsequent agreements that had extended Germany's reparations payments. She also felt that the democratic parties were incapable of recognizing the danger of communism and that a sudden, violent end to the Weimar Republic was preferable to a slow demise accompanied by endless parliamentary speeches. She told herself and her readers: "We know that for our children—and they are the ones at stake—a new and better future will arise from such a violent end." Toward that aim, she argued, it was worth tolerating crude Nazi anti-Semitism. Her tolerance was hardly surprising, since she herself advanced ideas quite close to Nazi anti-Semitism, merely in more polite language.

Comfortable bourgeois Germans often had mixed motivations for voting for Hitler. In the years after 1933, Adam joined the Catholic anti-Nazi resistance and was persecuted for it. In 1937, she was sentenced to eight years in prison for treason, and she died in January 1946 from the consequences of her imprisonment. Her debate partner, Eva Reichmann-Jungmann, survived the Holocaust in British exile. She did not respond in detail to Adam's justification of her vote for the Nazis, remarking only that she hoped that Nazi Jew hatred would be temporary and that "German history would wipe the slate clean of it in the next ten years."[62]

SOCIAL CLIMBERS: MY GRANDFATHER AND THE GAULEITERS

Industrial productivity rose spectacularly in Germany between 1925 and 1929 by rates of 25 to 40 percent—levels equaled only in the

United States.[63] As was typical for Germany, growth vacillated between periods of tremendous expansion and crisis-inducing stagnation. In the final third of the nineteenth century, a period of conspicuous reticence toward progress had been followed by extremely rapid economic modernization unaccompanied by adequate political reform. After a brief stretch of internal calm, the Germans stumbled into the difficult and self-destructive task of waging war and maintaining a wartime economy. Following the defeat, they sank into six years of torpor, only to hurtle again into a short-lived and similarly self-destructive prosperity.

What most upset the economic equilibrium between 1925 and 1929 was the rapid pace of modernization. It made human labor redundant, increasing unemployment and putting pressure on people who were looking for calm and security after the suffering of the war. Such people had few ways of compensating for the stress. Moreover, the national recovery that Germany painstakingly achieved during the middle years of the Weimar Republic went up in smoke with the Great Depression. "After a brief and frightening period of flourishing, everything is breaking down," local Berlin historian Hans Grantzow wrote. "Every seventh Berliner is without a job (655,000 in all) in January 1933. Our demise seems inevitable since all the measures available to the parliamentary state have failed."[64]

Beginning in 1929, the NSDAP profited from the global economic crisis, the quarreling among Germany's governing political parties, and the massive social changes in the Weimar period. Statistics suggest how much the traditional social order was shaken. In 1925, there were 32 million people in the German empire with a job, and two-thirds of them—whether laborers, white-collar workers, or civil servants— were dependent on a single employer. The number of white-collar employees working on permanent contracts had increased from 1.5 to 3.5 million between 1907 and 1925, so that they represented some 11 percent of the total workforce. A third of all employed people now were women, many of whom had risen from the lower classes to take up newly created office jobs. There were also around a million new civil servants, working for the post office, the rail system, various government administrations, and the power and water utilities. Laborers, on the other hand, now made up only 45 percent of the workforce.

As these statistics show, social mobility was becoming the rule in Germany. But climbing up the social ladder not only offered the promise of a better life but also entailed risk and stress. The parvenus had nothing inherited, in either the material or the intellectual sense, to fall back on. They lacked family support, role models, confidence in their new status, and full acceptance by society. Social climbers gave up old habits and subjected themselves to the alien demands of office culture, while losing what had been sources of security. Those who had risen were scared of slipping back down; the pioneers of families whose fortunes had improved were insecure and agitated. They felt themselves at the mercy of invisible forces that could either promote them further or set them back.

Moreover, the new middle classes—uncertain as they were in terms of their social behavior and their faith in the future—had a destabilizing effect on the entire structure of society. They constantly pressured the established bourgeoisie from below, blurring social boundaries and creating a kind of updraft in which ever more members of the lower classes tried to rise: the arrivistes usually had siblings, in-laws, or even spouses who were members of the proletariat. Changing social conditions, too, played a role. World War I and the end of the Hohenzollern monarchy, together with the Weimar Republic's improvements in public education and the rapid modernization of German industry, had increased social flux and weakened class restrictions. The hyperinflation of 1923 also reshuffled the social deck by obliterating fortunes that had been made. The path had been cleared for the industrious and ambitious. Nonetheless, the Treaty of Versailles did not just drastically restrict the German state's options. In the minds of the populace, it also put severe limits on the social ambitions and efforts that had finally been awakened in ordinary Germans. And such feelings were greatly intensified by the Depression, which many Germans saw as a plot hatched by foreign powers. The economic crisis blocked their sudden—if belated—social ambitions, driving young people, industrious social climbers, and everyone who wanted a better life for their children into the arms of National Socialism.

On the eve of the Great Depression, economist and sociologist Emil Lederer feared that fundamental tensions might tear society apart and lead to civil war. The crisis took its fateful course, and in early 1930 sociologist and cultural critic Siegfried Kracauer published a well-known study on white-collar workers. In it, he wrote: "The masses of white-collar employees can be distinguished from the laboring proletariat insofar as the former are spiritually homeless. For the time being there is no bridge between them and the SPD, and the house of bourgeois concepts and emotions in which they dwelt has collapsed, its foundation removed by economic developments."[65]

The various statistics and theories become more concrete if we look at individual biographies. Since the early eighteenth and nineteenth centuries, my paternal ancestors were solidly bourgeois Prussian merchants, clergymen, officers, forest superintendents, high school principals, and civil servants, and there was little change in the social status of this side of my family in the twentieth century. But my maternal grandparents, Friedrich (1888–1963) and Ottilie (1892–1968) Schneider, illustrate the tensions created by people's social rise in the early twentieth century, tensions that made many Germans into followers of the Nazi Party.

My grandfather Friedrich was baptized as a Catholic and spent his early childhood in a tiny village with a one-room schoolhouse. At the age of ten he had to move in with complete strangers to continue his education, which would allow him to learn a trade. His marks were poor. After four years, Friedrich quit school and became a salesman, moving first to Frankfurt and then to Munich. He was excused from military service because of a bad leg. My grandmother Ottilie grew up in the village of Mörfelden in central Germany, the youngest of five children. Her mother died young, and her father worked his way up to apothecary's assistant. (He continued to work during World War II even as a ninety-year-old.) The family was Protestant. Ottilie dreamed of becoming a schoolteacher but was sent instead at the age of fourteen to do an apprenticeship in a Frankfurt grocery store. There she took night courses to learn stenography, which at the time was a new profession. A curious young woman, she eventually found a job in Munich, where she met and married Friedrich. In 1921, to celebrate the birth of the couple's second daughter, Friedrich bought a piano. Two years later a third daughter was born. The Schneiders lived in a respectable part of Munich, and their daughters were given the posh-sounding names Dorothea, Auguste Viktoria, and Cecilie. They were raised as Protestants and took music lessons; all of them completed their *Abitur*, the high school qualification necessary to study at university. "Study so that you can become something," I can still hear my grandmother Ottilie say.

Friedrich worked in an office of the Rathgeber company, which produced train cars. There was no shortage of work immediately after World War I, since the Versailles treaty compelled Germany to deliver trainload after trainload of goods to France and Belgium. But by 1925 the contracts had dried up. The German national rail company didn't have any money to invest, and Rathgeber was forced to let most of its employees go. Friedrich Schneider lost his job, and Ottilie opened a small store to keep the family's heads above water. She also had an abortion. Friedrich joined the NSDAP. He never held an official position within the party, and during his de-Nazification proceeding in 1948, he told Allied authorities: "I became unemployed on April 1, 1926. As the provider for a family with children ages six, four, and two, I faced a dire situation. I went to a meeting of the NSDAP at which the Munich city counselor, Dr. Buckeley, spoke about how to alleviate unemployment, and because I believed what he said I joined the party." The Allies' file on Friedrich Schneider depicts him as a harmless, industrious, and honest person. The de-Nazification committee also regarded him as such.[66]

In the fall of 1926, Friedrich found a new job working as a sales-man on commission for the coffee-substitute company Imperial Fei-genkaffee. Later he was given a permanent contract as a traveling representative, making the rounds of retailers in northern Bavaria. Every Saturday afternoon he would come home laden down with cheap groceries, and every Monday morning he would set off again. In 1931, his salary was 3,960 marks a year. In 1939, he started work-ing from the company's headquarters, and by that time he was earn-ing 4,560 marks a year, with around 800 marks extra annually during the war for overtime and working nights and Sundays. At Ottilie's insistence, he bought a small row house on the outskirts of Munich that had been newly built by the German Workers' Front. The pur-chase price was 16,475.20 marks, of which 13,000 was financed on credit. The family scrimped and saved, going without butter and eating meat only on Sundays. But the children's school fees, music lessons, and university studies were paid for on time.

In 1919, the Schneiders had been a lower-middle-class family striv-ing to move up a rung on the social ladder. Their aspirations were repeatedly undermined by shortages of material goods, by war, revo-lutionary unrest, inflation, and then the Great Depression. That's one reason Friedrich Schneider found Nazi calls for the "social elevation" of the lower classes appealing. For him the NSDAP was a party of national self-respect that offered him the prospect of social better-ment and the promise of lowering class barriers.

In 1931, my then eight-year-old mother used to enjoy disappear-ing for a few hours in the nearby Jewish department store Uhlfelder's. The store contained a huge public attraction: Munich's first escalator, which half the city wanted to see. My mother was very impressed. But one day Friedrich told her: "We don't go to that store." In April 1945, a long line of concentration-camp inmates marched by the front door of his house. "That was the worst thing I've ever seen in my life," Friedrich told his daughter. Later, he added: "What was done to the Jews definitely went too far."

Friedrich Schneider's behavior was one of the little things that, taken together, led Germany down the path of historically unprecedented violence and annihilation. I myself remember my grandfather Friedrich as a man who was thoroughly good at heart.

The life of Friedrich Schneider is astonishingly similar to the lives of many NSDAP local leaders, the gauleiters. If we take as a sample the thirty leaders who served longest in the individual *Gaue*, as those areas were defined in 1937, we see that the vast majority came from villages and small towns.[67] Seventeen of them had fathers who were members of the working class, compared with ten from the lower middle class and only three from the bourgeoisie. In terms of religion, these gauleiters reflected Germany as a whole, with roughly three-fifths being Protestant and the rest Catholic.

If we examine indications of desire to improve social standing, we see that six of the gauleiters did their *Abitur* and studied at university. Twelve completed non-university-track diplomas, while twelve settled for halfway degrees or failed to complete high school. Only two were laborers, while six went into schoolteaching, a career that didn't require higher qualifications and was seen as an easy way of getting ahead. The others were merchants, civil servants, and white-collar workers. Thus, most of these gauleiters were people who were trying to rise above the traditional status of their families. This becomes particularly evident if we look at their individual biographical sketches. Here are the first ten, alphabetically, with the remaining twenty in the endnotes:[68]

Josef Bürckel (1895–1944): Catholic, son of an artisan, attended teacher training college and became a schoolteacher. 1926–44: gauleiter of Rhineland Palatinate.

Friedrich Karl Florian (1894–1975): Protestant, son of a senior railway worker. Trade school. Mining Department, Prussian Office for Mine Inspection. 1930–45: gauleiter of Düsseldorf.

Albert Foster (1902–1947): Catholic, son of a senior prison guard. Certificate from university-track academy, apprenticeship as a merchant and bank employee. 1930–45: gauleiter of Danzig.

Joseph Goebbels (1897–1945): Catholic, son of a manager. University-track academy, PhD in German literature. 1926–45: gauleiter of Berlin.

Josef Grohé (1902–1988): Catholic, ninth of twelve children of a part-time farmer and seller of groceries. Trade school. Worked in the family business, commercial school, company representative. 1931–45: gauleiter of Cologne-Aachen.

Otto Hellmuth (1895–1967): Catholic, son of a senior railway worker. Trade school, military service, PhD in dentistry. 1928–45: gauleiter of Lower Franconia.

Friedrich Hildebrandt (1898–1948): Protestant, son of an agricultural worker. Trade school, agricultural worker, railway worker, soldier, policeman, chairman of employees' association. 1925–45: gauleiter of Mecklenburg.

Rudolf Jordan (1902–1988): Catholic, son of a salesman and small-time farmer. Trade school, teacher training school, occasional factory work. 1924: schoolteacher; 1929: fired for right-wing extremism. 1931–45: gauleiter of Halle-Merseburg.

Karl Kaufmann (1900–1966): Catholic, son of a laundry owner. University-track high school until grade 7. Laborer, soldier, laborer. 1929–45: gauleiter of Hamburg.

Erich Koch (1896–1986): Protestant, son of a foreman. Middle school, trade school, salesman training, German national rail company, fired in 1926 for political reasons. 1928–45: gauleiter of Eastern Prussia.

The biographies of these gauleiters are representative rather than extreme. These men were not the embittered, antisocial failures that historians today often characterize them as. On the contrary, their backgrounds were typical of those of millions of Germans who had made their way up from various origins. In terms of their education, most of these future leaders displayed the ambition and ability, probably encouraged by their parents, to study their way up the social ladder. At the same time, the lack of intellectual and material support from their families meant that most of them suffered initial failures, like Friedrich and Ottilie Schneider did, and had to seek an alternate path toward social advancement. Almost all of their biographies led from the village or small town to the big city. As young men, most of the gauleiters took part in some capacity in World War I and were influenced by that conflict in ways typical of their generation. Their average age when they reached the position of local party leader was thirty-five.

As was the case with Hitler himself, these men did not possess an education adequate to the demands of leadership. The gauleiters had to develop leadership qualities on their own. Since the NSDAP was a young party, its full-time leaders were only recently assembled and were nowhere near as polished as the veteran functionaries of the bourgeois and social-democratic parties. On the other hand, the gauleiters displayed the enthusiasm of newcomers who, as oft-scorned outsiders without any external protection, had succeeded in creating a powerful organization. Because almost all of them came from the lower classes, they knew from their own experience and that of their families what it meant to lose one's job, to not be able to pay the rent, to see a brother die of tuberculosis, to hear the marshal ring the doorbell because of unpaid debts, or to be bullied as a foot soldier by some self-important officer. Unlike the members of the old elite, the gauleiters spoke the language of ordinary people and understood their concerns.

Hitler himself personally appointed the gauleiters, exclusively selecting men with backgrounds similar to his own who shared his own social ambitions. In the first pages of *Mein Kampf*, he pays tribute to his father, who was the son of an unmarried peasant in rural Austria. At the age of thirteen, Alois Hitler—then Alois Schicklgruber—left the narrow confines of his home village for Vienna, where he became a cobbler and then, despite lacking a formal education, a junior customs official. Adolf Hitler would later credit "an iron sense of industry" for his father's rise to full customs official, adding that "the pride of a self-made man" led Alois Hitler to insist that "his son have at least the same, if not a higher, position in life."[69] Alois wanted his son to attend university. Adolf didn't get the necessary grades and also failed to be admitted to art school. Nonetheless, the son did indeed climb the social ladder—at breakneck speed. In World War I, the twenty-five-year-old Hitler earned an Iron Cross, Second Class, for injuries suffered as a message runner, a post that required bravery, circumspection, and cleverness. (After he was discharged, Hitler's Iron Cross was upgraded to First Class on the recommendation of his Jewish regimental adjutant, Hugo Gutmann.) At the age of thirty-two, Hitler was the chairman of a political party. At forty-three, he became chancellor.

As the biographical data of the gauleiters show, the Nazi leadership did not come from those segments of the middle classes often described as petite bourgeoisie, who had been radicalized by their fear of losing social status. That may have been the case with some German anti-Semites and ordinary Nazi Party members. Nazi *leaders*, however, were typically men from the lower classes bidding to move up the social ladder. Far from representing those who had fallen down a notch, they spoke for social climbers whose ambitions were threatened by economic and political confusion. It mattered little which particular social class or trade individuals came from; their common denominator was the ambition to rise up from whatever specific social starting point. The Nazi Party represented the farmhand's son who wanted to become a skilled laborer, the worker's son who wanted to become a technician, the train conductor's daughter who wanted to become a photographer, the artisan's son who wanted to study law, the farmer's daughter whom fate had taken to the big city. The Nazi movement absorbed the ambitions and fears of those whose social status was in flux. By 1930, the mass group had millions of members, and they had only one thing in common: the desire to get ahead and earn social recognition.[70]

The functionaries of the Social Democratic Party, on the other hand, came from a middle-class caste of white-collar workers and state officials who had earlier risen up from the proletariat. Because their thinking was determined by Marxist paradigms, they were singularly unable to understand the precarious mentality of social climbers. SPD leaders talked about the noble proletariat, the contemptible petty bourgeoisie, and the malicious bourgeoisie proper. They weren't even capable of accurately describing their own social status. They lacked a realistic picture of the dramatic social changes that were continually easing class restrictions and making the borders between classes increasingly permeable. As political scientist Sigmund Neumann described it in 1932, SPD leaders could not comprehend "the peculiar intellectual and sociological structure of white-collar workers who had been energized by economic developments and now represented an active political force."[71]

YOUNG PEOPLE: FROM I TO WE

The upward social mobility of ordinary Germans during the Weimar Republic highlights an unsettling fact about Weimar education policy. As paradoxical as it may sound, better educational opportunities for the masses helped Hitler attract followers, provided the Nazi Party with functionaries, and enabled a wholesale change in the state elite in 1933. Between 1919 and 1931, democratically minded politicians created the conditions for a rapid increase in the number of people getting higher educational qualifications; the trend was especially pronounced between 1928 and 1931. The Weimar leadership opened up the German educational system to the lower classes as well as to women. They created new sorts of jobs, teacher training facilities, trade schools, polytechnic universities, and professional academies of all stripes. Yet from 1930 onward, well-educated young people had few or no opportunities to find work. Masses flooded the job market without any hope of success. The NSDAP benefited from their resultant frustration.

The Weimar Republic also revolutionized the idea of what constituted a course of study. At the beginning of the twentieth century, 80 percent of all students who earned the university-qualifying degree of *Abitur* did so at a classic liberal arts academy, or *Gymnasium*. Over the course of the Weimar Republic, that number fell to only 32 percent. Greater and greater resources were devoted to new, less elitist educational institutions, such as the more practically oriented *Realgymnasien* and *Realoberschulen*. This changed the social makeup of that group of Germans who could claim to be well educated. By 1929, children of low-level civil servants, white-collar workers, artisans, and small farmers accounted for roughly two-thirds of all students at higher secondary school institutions in Germany.

These young people, who thanks to democratic progress were the first in their families to get within sniffing distance of university, felt insecure in their new social roles.[72] Many doubted whether they were up to the task of facing unaccustomed challenges, which the Depression had made so severe as to be unbearable. The general opinion in the late 1920s was that institutions of higher education in Germany were overcrowded, and there was a lot of truth to this. The job prospects of university and polytechnic graduates were miserable. In 1931, some 325,000 college graduates were working in their chosen fields, while around 150,000 were waiting for positions commensurate with their qualifications. Of them, 40,000 to 45,000, according to official calculations, were considered "superfluous." In 1933, an educational superintendent in Breslau (today's Wrocław) estimated that to accommodate all the people who would soon have university degrees, Germany would need one million suitable jobs instead of the 330,000 that actually existed.[73] It matters little whether such gloomy prognoses were completely accurate. The important thing is that people believed them.

On graduating from trade schools, polytechnic academies, and universities, students were left empty handed. They couldn't even register as unemployed. Journalist Konrad Heiden, a critic of the Nazis who wrote in exile, summed up the logic of how this situation benefited Hitler. "If you see your professional path blocked and have to live the life of a proletarian even though you went to university, don't hang your head," Heiden wrote in his 1936 biography of Hitler. "Fight for the National Socialist state, in which everything will be better. The National Socialist state won't make high-level positions available on the basis of birth, wealth, and social status but according to the worth of the individual."[74]

Given this logic, it isn't surprising that the Nazis commanded majority support at universities, trade academies, and polytechnic colleges long before they were able to win over other segments of the populace. In the parliamentary elections of 1930, the Nazi Party got 18.3 percent of the vote. That same year the National Socialist German Students' Association polled 34.4 percent in student representative elections. The party was particularly popular at polytechnic colleges, which had a disproportionate number of would-be social climbers among their students.[75] From its very inception, the NSDAP developed special strategies for appealing to young people concerned with scaling the social ladder. Those who were still in high school were encouraged to rebel openly against democratically inclined teachers and figures of authority. "The best weapon in their fight against the state," advised Gotthart Ammerlahm, the leader of the Hitler Youth in Berlin in 1930, "is for students to laugh at the knee-jerk democratic teachers." Even the awarding of diplomas, those "scraps of paper," was to be greeted with a "contemptuous smirk."

Around the same time, at a meeting of the National Socialist German Students' Association, Joseph Goebbels described the academic work of most professors as "sophistry." The German professorship consisted of old elites who had been educated under the Wilhelmine system, and Goebbels encouraged class resentment of them among younger generations of students from humbler backgrounds. He accused professors of "sitting on their high thrones" and "haughtily judging their students." Germany's future propaganda minister raged that the country was being sunk by "science, statistics, careerism, cal-

culation, hair-splitting, and . . . the churlish arrogance of 'the educated' toward the people."

As an alternative ideal, Goebbels encouraged Nazi students to
topple class barriers. Only a student who was willing to go down in
the mines and dig for coal alongside regular miners to increase Germany's supply of natural resources, Goebbels said, would blaze new
paths connecting the lecture halls with real life. To achieve this sort of
progress, Goebbels predicted, "things untold will have to be shattered
and destroyed," but he promised that once the dirty work had been
done, life would be a joy. "Someone has to make a start," Goebbels
cried. "Overturn the altars! Extirpate the old man from your head
and your heart! Take an ax in your hands and smash the lie of an old,
false world! Start a revolution inside yourself! The end result will be
a new sort of man!"[76]

People who want to create a new sort of man inevitably come into
conflict with the authorities. Nazi students would fondly remember
their street-fighting days of 1930 as a time when they faced down
"cops with their rubber batons drawn" and been driven from campus
for anti-Semitic agitation on the orders of the head of Berlin's police
force. "He was worse than Ivan the Terrible sending in his brutes
among the students," wrote one self-proclaimed Nazi warrior. In the
end, the dean of the University of Berlin had to intervene as a media-
tor. The police troops were ordered to retreat, and in an act of local
appeasement, three Nazi agitators who had been detained were
released. But no sooner had a compromise been reached than the Nazi
student newspaper *Die Bewegung* ("The Movement") once again
began beating the war drum: "After incidents like these, the men who
call the shots can be absolutely certain that their ears will be boxed
much harder in the near future."[77]

Jewish professors such as Theodor Lessing at the University of
Hannover experienced firsthand—as early as 1925—what Nazi students meant when they promised to box people's ears. In a Prague
newspaper, Lessing had criticized the leading conservative candidate

in the upcoming presidential election, Paul von Hindenburg, as an instrument of highly dangerous antidemocratic forces. Hindenburg, Lessing argued, was not the sort of independent guardian of the state that the presidency required but rather "a representative symbol, a question mark, a zero." He underscored his point with a pun: "Better a zero than a Nero, some might say. Unfortunately history shows that there's always a Nero lurking behind every zero."

In response to the article, which turned out to be prescient, radical right-wing students founded a "battle committee against Lessing." They encouraged their peers to boycott his lectures, disrupted the classes that did take place, and ultimately, with the help of some like-minded professors, forced Lessing to give up his chair in the summer of 1926. Lessing could do nothing to counter being "shouted down, threatened, insulted, and denigrated" by student protests. Later he would write that he had no weapon "against the murderous bellowing of youngsters who accept no individual responsibilities but pose as spokesmen for a group or an impersonal ideal, always talking in the royal 'we,' for example, while hurling personal insults . . . and claiming that everything is happening in the name of what's true, good, and beautiful."[78]

Young people reaching adulthood around 1930 had been conditioned by the war and were used to thinking in black-and-white, friend-or-enemy categories. In an age when the vast majority of people were unable to afford the fees charged by secondary schools, to say nothing of the costs of a university education, point 20 of the Nazi Party platform explicitly addressed the interests of young adults as well as the parents who wanted better lives for their children. It read: "In order to ensure that every capable and industrious German has access to higher education and the possibility of attaining top positions, the state is responsible for fundamentally expanding our entire public education system. We demand that particularly gifted children from poor families be educated at state cost, without consideration of class or profession."

Around 1930, almost all young Germans felt themselves drawn to romantic movements that rebelled against the smug, overfed bourgeoisie. In youth organizations all along the political spectrum, from extreme left to extreme right, young people were attracted by slogans like "From I to We," "Subjugating I to You," and "Putting Communal Use before Selfishness." The members of these movements mocked the private pursuit of happiness as hopelessly retrograde. They heaped contempt on the "profitariat," rejected materialism in favor of ideals, and wanted to eradicate social differences and redistribute income to laborers, farmers, and ordinary citizens. During the campaign for the 1930 parliamentary elections, Hitler promised such idealistic young revolutionaries: "Bourgeois weakness will be replaced by German strength of will. Youthful heroism will overcome the geriatric sterility of our current bourgeois national life."[79] On the left and on the right, the battle cries of the postwar generation were the same. Down with bourgeois liberalism! Down with individualism! Up with the collective!

The 2.5 million first-time voters in 1930 were all born in the final years before the war. They had spent their early childhoods living in difficult circumstances, mostly with their fathers away at the war. Now most of them wanted to join the newly expanded middle classes. Many had enjoyed a better education than their parents had, and many felt drawn to the NSDAP. Most of the Nazi Party's functionaries were under forty, and they promoted themselves as fighters who had stayed young. The average age of the 114 NSDAP parliamentary deputies elected in 1930 was just under thirty-eight, compared with forty-six for the Reichstag as a whole.[80] From the perspective of young voters, Nazi candidates belonged to the previous half generation—people ten to fifteen years older, who always serve as guides for those younger. The National Socialists were men of action, determined to enact radical change. To put it in the youthful slang of the 1930s, the Nazis showed that they didn't have "chalk coming out their pant legs"—that is, that they weren't ossified old farts.

The greatest contrast was between the NSDAP and the democratic parties of the political center. In 1930, only 8 percent of card-carrying SPD members were under the age of twenty-five. By contrast, the Nazi Party consisted almost exclusively of young people. In 1927, the average age of new Nazi Party members was twenty-five. Between 1928 and 1930, it was twenty-nine.[81] The NSDAP seemed like a fresh, flexible, youthful force, while the SPD and the other centrist parties were reminiscent of an old folks' club. Moreover, SPD representatives emphasized policies over personalities. They did not go in for emotional appeals but rather, in the words of Sigmund Neumann, stressed "rationalism, pragmatism instead of fantasy, and level-headed and often middle-of-the-road calculations." The Social Democrats were, in the best sense, a pillar of the state, a reliable and responsible political institution. But these were times in which rationalism was increasingly rejected, in which most young Germans demanded acts of passion, not pragmatism. The new generation wanted to see ruthless activism, not compromise; utopia, not political realism, accompanied as the latter always was by complications and setbacks.

The result was a political climate in which fewer and fewer people were able to appreciate the major achievements, reached under extremely difficult circumstances, of mainstream politicians like Friedrich Ebert, Walther Rathenau, or Gustav Stresemann. Their names were dragged through the mud by high school and college students who, in the words of journalist Friedrich Franz von Unruh, "were learning their ABCs during the war and now, in their boundless ignorance, mock the men who laid the foundation from which they today launch their gripes." This young generation, Unruh pointed out, owed a lot to the Weimar Republic. Nonetheless, for them, concepts like peace and freedom of speech were just "refuse to be tossed on the dung heap by Hitler's hordes."[82]

By the 1920s, the down-to-earth petty bourgeoisie that had

existed in the nineteenth century had almost totally fragmented. For that reason alone, there is no credence to the idea that the NSDAP drew most of its support from "petty bourgeois circles." Statistics showing how many NSDAP voters or members belonged to this or that profession or class are misleading. As the example of my maternal grandparents attests, traditional German class structures were shaken to their foundations during the Weimar Republic. The NSDAP recruited members and voters from the broad class of would-be social climbers. This highly fluid category, which included millions of people pressing for social change, was extremely susceptible to the pressures and tensions that war, the economy, and technological change exerted on individuals, families, professions, and entire regions.

The political behavior of those who were caught up in the competition for upward social mobility depended directly on their expectations for the future. Social climbers wanted an activist political leadership that would create opportunities for them. That was the backdrop behind popular demands for colonies and "living space" (*Lebensraum*), for a halt to immigration, and for the removal of so-called alien peoples from German society—especially when the aliens in question were perceived as competition. National Socialism channeled the aggression and desperation of those who feared what was coming, projecting it onto Jews, and that provided a welcome sensation of relief.

From its very first day in power in 1933, the Hitler government tried to create social space for younger generations of Aryans. By 1938, it had succeeded in banning Jews from any and all professions. The Nazi policy of self-sufficiency took the pressures of the global market off the shoulders of farmers. The state bureaucracy, the economy, and the military all expanded. And Germany's imperialistic adventures in trying to grab "living space" in Eastern Europe held out the promise of a better future for millions of people. All of this was in keeping with the primary goal of a National Socialist state as formulated by Hitler in *Mein Kampf*: "Its end is the preservation and the promotion of a community of physically and psychically equal living beings." For that reason, it was the responsibility of the German state of the future to rally "Germanic ur-elements" and "raise them to a dominant position."[83]

7

THE NATIONAL SOCIALIST
PEOPLE'S PARTY

CONTAGIOUS FANATICISM

In the final chapter of the first part of *Mein Kampf*, Hitler spelled out
the recipe for his party's success: the nationalization of the masses.
Soberly, the Führer analyzed class structures in Germany and concluded that the German people were divided into two groups. The
smaller of the two was the bourgeoisie, which was superficially nationalistic but essentially undecided, even cowardly. The far larger group
was made up of agricultural and above all proletarian laborers. The
latter were close to moderate and radical Marxist movements: the
SPD, the trade unions, and the German Communist Party, the KPD.
Yet for that very reason, Hitler commanded his followers not to reject
"those who are tortured by suffering, those who are without peace
and unhappy and discontented," but rather to compete for their
hearts and minds. The people who "worked with their fists," as Hitler
somewhat oddly put it in 1925, may have been on the wrong side,
but without them "a national resurrection would be unthinkable and
impossible."

Hitler demanded that his followers take an interest in the welfare and concerns of every "ethnic comrade." The enemies of the German people, in the mind of the then thirty-six-year-old Hitler, included Jews, democrats, Moscow's agents, German and French politicians who supported the Treaty of Versailles, fat cats who lacked a social conscience, wartime profiteers, and pacifists. From the very beginning, he demanded that businessmen make sacrifices for "our workers," explaining that "the national education of the great masses can take place only by elevating their social status." That required a "contagious fanaticism": the masses respected strong statements that set out a clear direction and despised weak, halfhearted proposals. Having proposed a redistribution of wealth from entrepreneurs to workers, Hitler quickly moved on to excoriate the "international poisoners" of the people: "Without the clearest recognition of the race problem and, with it, the Jewish question, there will be no rise of the German nation."

Throughout *Mein Kampf*, Hitler sought to couple race and class, as shown by his assertions that Jews were to blame for class divisions within Germany. These divisions, in Hitler's view, "could not be resolved by lowering the station of the upper classes, but only by elevating the lower ones." He added: "Moreover, the focus of this process can never be the upper classes. On the contrary, it has to be the lower classes, which are fighting for equality." This meant that the party would have to recruit its followers and voters from the proletariat above all and would have to try to win over every individual worker "by deliberately elevating his social and cultural position." The social betterment of Aryan Germans was a constant element of Hitler's speeches and propaganda. He did not demand a dictatorship of the proletariat. Instead, he envisioned an ethnically defined population that had been "de-proletarianized" and that trusted completely in its leader. What Hitler promised was a state devoted entirely to the welfare of its (racially select) people, a state that would keep all enemies at bay and offer equal respect to physical and mental labor.

In Hitler's view, the national and social questions in Germany could be traced to the historical German problem of internal division. According to his logic, the two questions could only be answered together, through the rise of a national socialism. For the project to become a reality, all those who ostensibly obstructed German unity— first and foremost, the Jews, and less tangibly the international socialists—would have to make way. Both groups threatened the community of national destiny and solidarity that Hitler envisioned, although the strategies to be used against them differed. As far as the Jews were concerned, the idea was to expel them completely from the German *Volk*. Workers who had been led down the false paths of socialism and communism, on the other hand, were to be disabused of their "internationalist delusion" and initiated into the ideology of national solidarity. Internationalist thinking, in any case, had already been shaken by the war and the Treaty of Versailles.

In December 1926, some two thousand men and women made their way to an auditorium in Stuttgart to hear what the leader of the NSDAP had to say on "The Social Mission of National Socialism." Addressing his audience as "ethnic German comrades," Hitler launched into an attack on the way that Germany had been enslaved by the Treaty of Versailles and suggested that Germany could end its sub-jugation "if its sixteen million fanatical left-wing nationalists and its fourteen million passionate right-wing adherents of social justice joined together." Anyone who opposed this unity was a member of "the political bourgeois guild," which deserved to be eradicated "by the proletarian masses, who have been whipped into a complete frenzy and are willing to do anything." When it came to Communists and radical socialists, by contrast, Hitler had to grant that they at least were "fighting . . . for a larger idea, if a crazy and deadly one."

In 1929 Joseph Goebbels, then the gauleiter of Berlin, pursued much the same rhetorical strategy, proclaiming that young workers would become the new elites of the Third Reich. "The battle will sig-nal a choice for a new aristocracy!" Goebbels prophesied. "Smash the equality of democracy that blocks the path of fulfillment for the young working classes. Defend yourself against being put on the same level as every fool!"[1] Goebbels devoted much of his novel *Michael* to visions of the German proletariat's being united with pro-Hitler students. Modeled on Goethe's *Sorrows of Young Werther*, Goebbels's novel was a nature-fetishizing, slightly erotic, and above all political work.

The novel's protagonist is a university student from Heidelberg searching for greater meaning in life. One day in Munich he encounters an orator—the Prophet—who gives the people, from whom God has withdrawn his blessing, a much-needed sense of direction. "That man up there," Michael thinks. "Piling block upon block into a cathedral of the future. . . . Revelation! Revelation!" Michael's face turns red with excitement, and he feels like standing up and shouting "We are all comrades. We have to stick together." He renounces the affection of his politically unscrupulous, stereotypically bourgeois girlfriend and leaves the university. "I hate this genteel Heidelberg," he proclaims, trading in the lecture halls and dusty tomes of academia for physical labor. "I want to go down into the mines and become a miner," Goebbels has him say. "Sacrifice will lead to salvation!" After some initial setbacks and a period of feeling like an intruder, Michael wins over the miners' trust. In the end, he dies tragically underground.

The political target of Goebbels's novel is neither the Communists nor the socialists but rather the bourgeois, who belong to an already anachronistic class that is gradually breaking down under attacks from the proletariat. "We are all soldiers of the revolution of labor," Goebbels writes. "What we want is the victory of the laboring class over money. That is true socialism. It is still headed in differing directions, but the will is the same everywhere."[2]

Not all of those who turned to National Socialism did so with equal eagerness, and not all Germans heeded the call in the first place. There were a number of associations with utopian worldviews vying for the attention of the masses between 1920 and 1932. Yet despite their differences, all such groups constructed their faith from four common elements. All had a single, simplistic explanation for the state of the world. All advocated the exclusion of a hostile foreign element. All elevated their poorer adherents or those threatened with poverty into a chosen, morally superior group to whom the future would belong. And all of them promised that a rosy future would arrive after considerable sacrifices were made in one final battle. Such strong similarities, by no means superficial, meant that the content of the new political salvation ideologies was largely interchangeable. A given message could easily be framed in a new way or even discarded at a moment's notice. The appeal of utopian thinking lay not in this or that concrete goal but rather in the powerful organizations and their charismatic leaders, which provided a liberating sense of faith to the many insecure and disoriented people at the time. "I'm standing on a fixed point," Goebbels's Michael tells his youthful love Hertha, "and if the point is right, and the perspective straight, one's view of the world is clear and good. If they aren't, it's blurred and bad."[3]

Moral compasses that had been set in this fashion seemed to show many a befuddled German the best way to get through the jungle of everyday life, the darkness and emergencies of a difficult epoch. Those who had been uprooted looked for new ground in which to plant themselves and found it in the fiction of race. Those who had been driven apart sought unity, and found it in the fiction of the *Volk*. The path may have looked dangerous, but they told themselves and others that it would lead to the paradise of social harmony and freedom from care. The masses who had suffered and shed their blood for nothing in World War I now saw a worthwhile goal within reach, one that would bolster their interests. They could win this battle and erase past defeat and humiliation. What was needed was a guiding individual will, someone to determine the direction that society would take: Il Duce, the Führer, the Romanian Conducător, the Hungarian Regent of Empire, the anti-Bolshevik General Pilsudski, or the Communist patriarchs Lenin and Stalin. All of these dictators, at least in the early years of their rule, could draw on majority support within their respective societies. And all of them promised essentially the same things: social betterment, justice, and a battle for the general welfare against the enemies of the people.

The great role models for Hitler and his movement were the Italian Fascists, with their Partito Nazionale Fascista. Mussolini's PNF arose in the wake of World War I, under circumstances similar to the ones that saw the rise of the NSDAP in Germany. In 1917, shortly before the end of the war, the Italians had suffered a major defeat by Austro-Hungarian forces on the Isonzo front and required assistance from British and French divisions to avert complete collapse. Italy may have nominally been one of the winners in 1918, but the country had not earned victory. And then, already mentally and materially exhausted, staggered by the loss of 700,000 Italians who fell in the war, the country was shaken by economic crises and social unrest.

In March 1919, groups of unemployed ex-soldiers joined together in the Fascio dei Combattenti, or "association of veterans," the origin of the Mussolini-led Italian Fascist Party. Faced with a country deeply split into north and south, town and country, the Fascists made the overcoming of divisions—through the vague but nonetheless extremely effective idea of *Italianità*, a unique essence of Italianness—into the centerpiece of their political agenda. They turned against those who considered class antagonisms an integral part of socialism and against the parts of the bourgeoisie deemed to be parasitic or usurious, promoting the idea of a great communal productive push that would get the country back on track.

One of the main aims of Italian Fascism was to destroy Italy's liberal constitution and depict liberal thinking as hopelessly outmoded. In the Fascist mind, parliamentarianism was a synonym for internal division, disorientation, corruption, decay, indecisiveness, and lack of political energy. To achieve its goals, the Fascists had to use violence. As in all other totalitarian utopias, the end justified the means, and the means in this case included a brutal party militia. In 1940, German historian Theodor Schieder celebrated the militia's many misdeeds, including murders and "punitive expeditions." "With these actions, which continued uninterrupted until August 1921, Italian Fascism and its leader, Mussolini, not only refined the art of harnessing elementary forms of violence from civil wars or street battles to the great, overarching revolutionary plan," Schieder wrote. "Fascism also emerged, in place of the failed government, as the restorer of productivity and the avenger of socialist attacks."[4] This was a long-winded way of saying that Mussolini used organized armed gangs to usurp the state's monopoly on the legitimate use of force.

In 1922, thanks to compromises and concessions, the Fascist Party became part of Italian government. Mussolini was made prime minister and was able to consolidate his power, becoming Italy's lone ruler within a few years. Most of the Fascist Party elite were veterans of pre-1914 socialism; Mussolini himself had been the editor of the socialist newspaper *Avanti*. Mussolini came from a humble rural family in the north of the country. His father was a blacksmith who was imprisoned multiple times for alleged involvement in socialist unrest. His mother was a local schoolteacher. Mussolini himself qualified as a teacher but emigrated to Switzerland, where he lived as a transient laborer. The simple man of the people became first a socialist, then a fascist politician.

The first members of his party were agricultural laborers, small-time farmers, and intellectuals who had been radicalized by the war. Union-organized industrial workers were reluctant to join before 1923. At that point, though, they made their peace with the Mussolini-led government. In late 1923, German journalist Fritz Schotthöfer concluded: "Fascism has caused considerable turmoil among workers. It has found a lot of supporters." It wasn't long before the fascist organization of unions in Italy represented some 2,000,000 members, compared with only 170,000 members for the social-democratic unions. Revived national prestige, the state's job creation and investment programs, and the fascists' energy, decisiveness, and youth all appealed to Italian workers. For them, the nationalist-fascist alternative seemed "the easier and quicker way to raise their collective sense of self-worth." In any case, it was definitely preferable to interminable syndicalist infighting—that was how Hendrik de Man, one of Europe's leading socialist intellectuals, saw the situation in 1931. De Man concluded that Mussolini's *democrazia totalitaria* had "organized an unbelievable transformation of energy that has converted class consciousness into national pride."

The result was a classless unity party whose only platform was the revival of Italy. The means toward that end included national pride, economic protectionism, social reconciliation, massive state investment programs, and funds that came from German reparations payments. Marxist organizations were banned, parliamentary debates gradually ended, and elites were replaced one by one. In 1932, Mussolini himself described the transition from socialist to fascist collectivism as a simple progression from false to true consciousness: "He who marches is multiplied by all those who march with him. As in Russia, we are for the collective sense of life, and we will strengthen it at the cost of individual life." The ultimate goal was "the autonomous creation" of a new "we." "Seen psychologically," wrote de Man, "class consciousness is nothing other than an imaginatively augmented sense of self-worth to compensate for social humiliation."[5]

According to Fascist Party doctrine, an effective government required the support (though not the participation) of the masses. Under Mussolini's leadership, Italy was restyled as a beautiful and youthful nation, sprinting toward the future with a racing pulse and the party anthem on its lips: "Youth, youth, / Springtime of beauty, / Fascism is the savior, / The savior of freedom." Compared with the "Horst Wessel Lied," the Nazi anthem that was named after one of the party's early martyrs, the Italian anthem was almost breezy and certainly less threatening and much more self-confident.

Leaving aside the uniforms, the party slogans, and the paramilitary trappings, Italian Fascism and German National Socialism resembled each other in two main respects. To cite a phrase coined by Emil Lederer, both strove to replace a class-based state with a mass-based one, and the membership structure of both the PNF and the NSDAP showed how successful they were. Moreover, both Mussolini and Hitler quickened the pace of political and military activity to unprecedented speed. Il Duce and the Führer won over the masses not just as charismatic leaders but as the directors of a furious process of social and bureaucratic transformation. They ruled as manic men of political action, manipulating the masses through "enthusiasm and fascination," as Mussolini put it. No day should be without a new entry in the history of the nation—that was fascist-style politics. "His nature is one of constant energetic internal activity," a German observer wrote after seeing Mussolini at work in 1924. "He keeps the machinery of state running at full steam."[6]

Germans likewise experienced the years of National Socialist rule as a period of perpetual activity. "To me it always seems like a movie," the diarist Victor Klemperer quotes a merchant as saying when Germany annexed the Sudetenland in 1938. A year later, nine days before Germany invaded Poland, Hermann Göring would assure metalworkers in Berlin that they could rely on a leadership that was "racing" with energy. In a diary entry from spring 1941, Goebbels used much the same language in referring to Germany's planned attack on Russia: "Full speed the entire day; the furious offensive is starting again. . . . I spent the whole day in a feverish state of happiness."[7]

Hitler, too, was a proponent of the principle of perpetual action. In 1938, Emil Lederer noted from American exile: "The masses have to be kept in a state of excitement and activity. One can't allow them to become apathetic, disinterested, or bored." That would be "nearly as dangerous as opposition" for the sort of dictatorships that could maintain their equilibrium only while in constant motion.[8] Constantly increasing the political and military velocity allowed the leaders of the National Socialist revolution to maintain power. Mass mobilization, threats, artificial crises, propaganda campaigns, wars, and territorial expansion left people simultaneously dizzy, afraid, joyous, and numbed. The Nazi leadership promised a people at the end of their rope—a people who had lost all confidence and felt that they had

been unfairly treated—that together they could teach their internal
and external enemies a thing or two.

1930: PROFITING FROM CRISIS

The start of the Great Depression marked the NSDAP's arrival on the
national stage. In the parliamentary elections of September 14, 1930,
what had been a party of the lunatic fringe succeeded in mobilizing
millions of people, including many first-time voters and those who
were unsure of whether to cast their ballots at all. The NSDAP owed
its sudden popularity to its image as a party of national unity against
the backdrop of general economic decline. "Protest against the November Revolution of 1918 and parliamentarianism, protest against military defeat and Versailles, protest against the economic system, and
protest against the dominance of rationalism and materialism"—that
was how Sigmund Neumann summed up Hitler's party. In particular,
Neumann stressed the party's broad social foundations. To isolated
individuals who perceived the world as empty and cold, the NSDAP's
multifaceted mass organization offered a sense of belonging. This
could take the form of women's and youth associations; student and
trade organizations; music, automobile, glider, and social clubs; or
the pseudomilitary marching and street-fighting brigades known as
storm divisions. No one was left standing on the sidelines. Everyone
could feel included.

The appeal of the National Socialist movement was based on a
vague but socially holistic program, the promise of radical action,
discipline, party work, and the authority of the Führer. Neumann
spoke of an "entirely new type of modern party" that brought together
"the most heterogeneous elements" in the name of "a total *Volk* community."[9] That was one side of the coin. At the same time, the NSDAP
owed its breakthrough in large part to the exhaustion of the Weimar
Republic's established governing coalition. Democratic politicians
had expended their energy for ten years battling problems that were
almost impossible to solve: the legacy of war and the unreasonable

demands of the victors, a populace that was unaccustomed to the rational procedures and rule of law in a republic, and finally the Great Depression. As had happened before the war, the economic crisis seemed to refute the idea that an individual by his own actions could keep from sinking into the morass. Nothing helped—neither individual industriousness nor a good education, neither years of company loyalty nor voluntary wage reductions. Fully a quarter of non-self-employed German workers lost their jobs. Those who kept their positions worked fewer hours and had to accept drastic pay cuts. German industrial production sank by 40 percent. Real income declined by a third.

To understand the economic and political context of the Depression, it helps to review the effects of German hyperinflation in the early 1920s. The hyperinflation reached a peak in 1923 and was ended only by a radical revaluation of the German currency. The German state had financed 83 percent of its war costs on credit, specifically with war bonds purchased by patriotic citizens. The inflation that devalued the German mark also destroyed the value of these bonds, de facto releasing the state from its debts. But in essence this meant that wartime debts had been transferred from the public to the private sector. At the same time, inflation destroyed confidence in the new state and undermined the political foundations of the Weimar Republic, precisely as Keynes had predicted in his 1919 critique of the Treaty of Versailles.

In practical terms, German industry and agriculture's capital resources and capacity for investment sank in direct proportion to the rate at which the state defaulted on its debts in 1923. To avoid chaos, provide people with jobs, and make reparations payments, the economy had to be reinvigorated. This was a challenge. With capital in short supply, the average interest rate in Germany in 1924, immediately after inflation, was a staggering 25 percent. Even in the boom years of 1927 and 1928, the rate for normal loans to industry was 9 to 10 percent, with the rate somewhat higher for real estate financing. Yet thanks to the high interest rates, relative political stability, innovation, and the industriousness of German workers, the undercapitalized economy attracted massive amounts of foreign investment. The influx of capital, achieved at the cost of overly high interest rates and delayed repayments on the reparations, drove the small-scale German "economic miracle" of 1925 to 1928. The accompanying speculation by those hoping for windfall profits helped precipitate the worst economic crisis in history.

This was the situation in which Hitler's propaganda was effective, directed as it was against foreign influences that allegedly wanted to enslave Germany, as well as against "greedy Jewish capital" with its exorbitant interest rates. The Nazis were careful to distinguish that from "productive," largely Aryan capital, which was supposedly based on industry. In Germany, many people came out on the losing end of the economic rationalization that took place from 1924 to 1928. Above all, high interest rates punished farmers, since they had to finance their seeds, fertilizer, machinery, and labor in advance and then hope that they could sell their weather-dependent harvest in a favorable market. The combination of high interest rates and falling prices on the international grain markets drowned many farmers in debt. Indeed, almost all German farmers were sucked into "an increasingly hopeless struggle for survival," as economist Wilhelm Röpke put it in a 1931 book entitled *The Path to Calamity*.

Röpke compared the situation of the German economy—burdened by reparations, inflation, a lack of capital, and dependence on foreign investment—to an overloaded, barely seaworthy ship. Röpke wrote: "Laden with this heavy freight, the ship was able to set sail, slowly and unsteadily, but the voyage could not continue for long. As early as 1928, the first minor emergencies occurred. In 1929, the storm of the Depression blew up, and in 1930 and the first half of 1931, the overloaded and leaking ship was fighting desperately to stay afloat, battered by the giant waves of global crisis. By summer 1931, the ship had run aground, and could only wait and see whether it would be saved or left to sink."

Starting in 1930, foreign investment in Germany dried up dramatically, despite the extremely high interest rates on offer. Lines of credit, which were mostly short-term, were called in, and domestic liquid capital was withdrawn as well. In New York, German bonds fell from 90 to 30 percent of their initial value. International faith in the economic and political future of the first-ever German republic collapsed. The outward flow of capital reached its height directly after the election of September 14. Almost 50 percent of voters that day had cast their ballots for either the NSDAP, the KPD, or the radical right-wing German National People's Party—those political forces whose express goal was to dismantle the Weimar Republic. The subsequent withdrawal of capital only deepened the crisis. Tax revenues declined sharply, while the state was forced to provide for some six million unemployed people. Germany was on the verge of bankruptcy. City treasurers and state finance ministers were forced to take out hugely expensive lines of credit. At the same time, Röpke recounted, "expenditures were ruthlessly curtailed and taxes raised equally ruthlessly."

Against this backdrop of economic crisis, all Germans felt that the burdens of the Treaty of Versailles were a massive injustice. "It is impossible," Röpke wrote, "to pay a sum, year after year, generation after generation, that amounts to many times the capital stock of all the larger German banks. It is impossible to pay an annual sum that would be sufficient to solve the problem of providing adequate housing for poor people in big cities. And to pay that sum by way of confirming, year after year, that one behaved like a scoundrel . . . that is truly impossible." The sense of being treated unfairly led Germans to become increasingly bitter and made the country ungovernable. The emergency ordinances with which the final governments of the Weimar Republic tried to keep Germany above water smacked of a dictatorship "whose entire raison d'être was to subjugate the country to foreign influences."

Röpke acknowledged that the burden of reparations payments had not unleashed the worldwide depression. But he did blame them for pushing Germans to their psychological limits and preventing the possibility of global economic recovery. "They have put Central Europe in the eye of the storm," the economist wrote of the reparations requirements. "They are what has increased people's uncertainty day after day, destroyed economic and political peace in the world, and left our current economy less and less able to function, as a crisis of faith spreads from country to country. They are what has at last triggered the avalanche of Germany's foreign debts that has swept England as well and shaken the entire world. Reparations have proven to be a sand bar. At high tide, they are far enough below the surface that, although they may slow shipping, they don't prevent it entirely. At low tide, they're a source of disaster."

When we consider the connections between the particularly harsh effects of the Depression on Germany, the NSDAP's surprising electoral triumph in September 1930, and the continuing withdrawal of foreign capital because of Germany's political instability, it's clear that Hitler's breakthrough heralded a phase in which the Depression and political disintegration spurred each other in a vicious cycle. The economic crisis made Hitler's program of national self-sufficiency and retreat from global markets seem plausible. The farmers' desperate situation demanded a radical solution to the problem of debt, and it needed to come at the expense of creditors. If the creditors were foreign or Jewish, so much the better. By 1931, even the war's victorious powers were talking about the necessity of canceling reparations payments. Many Germans, though, thought that the discussions were just talk. Indeed, the Allies ultimately couldn't bring themselves to take this step, even though, as Röpke argued, forgoing reparations was the only practical way out of a potentially calamitous situation.

Instead, every debt moratorium only worsened the crisis, destroying what faith remained, since the unmanageable reparations repayments were merely deferred with more interest added. Why shouldn't Germans take matters into their own hands, as the Nazis demanded, and simply refuse to pay? Why shouldn't they export a bare minimum of goods, since all the money earned went straight back into reparations payments anyway and the producers, apart from having work, realized no profit? Why shouldn't young people in this situation be attracted to slogans like "Better Dead Than Enslaved"? And why shouldn't national self-interest triumph over the foreign elements within the country?

Given the dangers at hand, Röpke urged the world to regain a sense of common interests and solidarity. The crisis, Röpke argued, was no longer about individual countries, or debts, or the past. It was about the future. And the necessary condition for a better future was responsible, far-seeing statesmanship that would "finally give Europe economic and political peace." Twenty-six months before Hitler took power, Röpke concluded his plea with the words: "Let us not deceive ourselves. Our economic system, and with it the whole of Western civilization, is on its last legs. Before the gates there are barbarians who would love to inherit our legacy if we choose the wrong path at this crossroad."[10]

It was in this climate that Hitler had launched his campaign. The results of the balloting on September 14, 1930, demonstrated for the first time his ability to sway masses of people with his depiction of Jewish high finance, international free-market capitalism, and the Treaty of Versailles as a nightmarish three-headed monster that was devouring Germany. "Farming and industry may be destroyed, our artisans may go to the devil, and our small businesses may disappear, but big-time capital and the Jew who is behind it must remain untouched," Hitler snorted sarcastically. He accused the governing parties of playing various groups against one another "with true Jewish skill" in order to expose the German population, weakened as it was, "to the manifold influences of various international poisons and plagues."

The antidote to those poisons, Hitler proclaimed, lay in returning to Germany's traditional strengths, discovering new ones, and ending all halfhearted compromises. In the months leading up to the election, he confidently predicted that future generations would look back on it as a "turning point" in German history: "On this day, the young movement that would later liberate Germany pounded for the first time on the door of the German Reichstag and called out: 'Open up. It's time for the special interests to make way. The German people are moving in.'" Hitler also announced that the time was coming when people would no longer believe "the Jew." He thundered: "Then he'll be at his wit's end. The time is already at hand when he'll be treated as he was treated hundreds of years ago." Hitler whipped up his followers' passions for "a ruthless offensive against the entire front of 'young parties.'" He meant the democratic parties of the political middle who favored domestic and international compromise. He blamed them for Germany's misery: "The nation is slowly bleeding to death. Workers can't afford bread, and the government is stuffing the bellies of supranational financial spiders."[11]

Reading Hitler's articles and speeches from this period, one is struck by the way that certain themes recur over and over again: "the humiliation of 1918," "dictated terms of peace," "reparations," "two thousand years of German history," and "the suffering of the people." On the other hand, it was relatively rare for Hitler to talk about the Jews, and when he did do so, it was often in asides and seldom at length. In Hitler's speeches from 1930 to 1933 and in the official plat-form of the NSDAP, anti-Semitism provided "the emotional founda-tion," a sort of basso continuo. An occasional mention was sufficient. My uncle August R., who was studying in Munich at the time, described an appearance by Hitler on June 12, 1931: "Hitler's speech was so entirely free of hateful statements and so cautious that the audience had to add the usual Nazi interjections—'Jews,' 'traitors,' 'scoundrels,' etc."[12] Anti-Semitism was an interactive spectacle played out between speaker and listeners.

Hitler demanded that all members of the NSDAP be actively involved and make material sacrifices for the cause. That distin-guished the NSDAP from other parties and local political associa-tions, which had much more relaxed concepts of membership. It cost two marks to join the Nazi Party, and monthly membership fees were one mark, with an additional thirty pfennigs going into the insurance fund of the storm divisions, known as the SA (*Sturmabteilung*). The minimum fees for joining the SPD, by comparison, were only half as much.[13] And the NSDAP members who could afford it were often called on to make other financial contributions. In 1929, looking ahead to the coming election year, Hitler required all members to loan the party at least ten marks for a period of twelve months, at an interest rate that was half a percent below the going minimum rate. Audience members also usually had to pay entrance fees to political events. Depending on the quality of the seats, as in a theater, these fees ranged between fifty pfennigs and two marks. (A ticket to the movies cost thirty pfennigs.) These were no small sums, considering that the average monthly wage for a worker at the time was around 180 marks, while a student or an unemployed family man usually had around eighty marks a month at his disposal.

For the 1930 election, Goebbels organized three events in a row at Berlin's spacious Sportpalast arena. They were staged as political sparring matches and spectacles. Admission was one mark. With the arena's twelve thousand seats immediately selling out, the organizers added a supplementary charge of a mark for the third evening, with the extra proceeds going to the SA. The NSDAP's political events filled the party's coffers and allowed it to expand its organization and finance future gatherings.

It is true that Hitler, like the leaders of other parties, received contributions from industrialists. But the financial foundation of the party depended much more on membership and admission fees, as well as the sale of newspapers, books, uniforms, and badges to members and sympathizers. By exploiting these sources of income, the NSDAP became an unusually well-funded political organization. At the same time, treating individual material sacrifice as a party imperative encouraged solidarity, loyalty, willingness to do battle, and a passion for the cause.

Significant sums always went to the storm divisions. As of 1930, the SA had around seventy thousand members. They organized election events and showed up to wildly applaud speakers; they distributed leaflets, put up posters, and started fights at rival political meetings.

For those "services," every SA man was paid one to two marks a day plus expenses. This was a considerable amount of money when one considers that weekly unemployment benefits amounted to only around twenty marks, and young people who had failed to find a first job got nothing at all.[14] Writing about one of Hitler's events in the immediate aftermath of the 1930 election, journalist Friedrich Franz von Unruh described the diverse makeup of the SA, several hundred of whose members had been placed on stage behind their Führer: "A lot of weak-looking people, puny wartime youths, and guys who didn't get outside enough; next to them some students, taut and athletic; a handful of veterans; a lot of unemployed people, fanatics, and sturdy-looking fellows." In the audience, the reporter observed "men who had risked everything on the front lines, . . . youths, . . . and old people whose hearts were with the young."[15]

At the start of 1930, the Nazi Party had 200,000 members. By the end of the year, that number was 350,000, even as the party leadership purged the membership rolls of dissenters and people who had failed to pay their dues. In the election of May 20, 1928, the National Socialists had won only 800,000 votes and 12 seats in parliament. Just over two years later, the NSDAP got 6.5 million votes and 107 seats—an increase of more than 800 percent. The Nazis were now the second-largest faction in the Reichstag. It was an unexpected, overwhelming triumph. In comparison, the KPD increased its share of the vote by 40 percent and now had 77 seats. The SPD lost 20 percent of its vote, although it remained the largest parliamentary faction with 143 seats. The Catholic Center Party held steady with 68 parliamentary seats, while the liberal parties were all but dead. Two years later, in the national elections of 1932, Germans made the NSDAP the most powerful party by far. Even at the height of the Depression, Hitler never succeeded in attracting all of the thirty million working-class voters whom he had spoken of in Stuttgart in 1926 and whom he'd pledged to forge into "fanatic nationalists and fervent supporters of social justice." But those he did succeed in reaching were enough.

Electoral results tell only half the story. Feeling the pressure of the

National Socialists, the Communists had added some "folkish" and nationalistic elements to their own platform. By getting workers to think of themselves in nationalist terms, the KPD thus began readying them mentally for the Third Reich. Three weeks before the 1930 vote, the KPD issued a "Proclamation about the National and Social Liberation of the German People"—the German people, it should be noted, not German workers. That statement also accused the SPD, in Nazi-like tones, of pandering to French demands and committing "high treason against the interests of Germany's working masses." Using rhetoric similar to that of the NSDAP, the KPD declared: "We Communists are fighting against . . . the larcenous Treaty of Versailles, the beginning of the enslavement of all working people in Germany." The KPD promised that "in the event we achieve power, we will declare all Germany's pledges in the Treaty of Versailles to be null and void." Hearing such promises parroted, many working-class people probably asked themselves whether they wouldn't be better off simply voting for the original.

The KPD's proclamation also contained passages capable of appealing to anti-Semites: "The big merchants, the magnates of commercial capitalism, are driving small merchants to ruin, throwing thousands of employees out onto the street, destroying hundreds of thousands of middle-class existences, exploiting farmers, and driving up the prices of articles of mass consumption." The Communists promised that they would immediately nationalize the banks and the German wholesale trade, free working people "from criminal profiteers," and "smash all speculative investment with an iron fist." Phrases like these sounded a lot like Adolf Hitler. In the spring of 1932, the KPD went on to echo his demands that Germany leave the League of Nations and lead the fight against the "plundering invasion of international finance capital and its German money collectors." The Communists also insisted on the return of all the lands Germany had lost after the war, when it had been "territorially mutilated."[16]

Having adapted some of the ideology of the NSDAP, the Communists decided to cooperate with the Nazis on certain other issues as well. For instance, in the summer of 1931, the KPD supported a referendum demanding the dissolution of the regional Prussian parliament (*Landtag*), which had been one of the most stable bastions of the Weimar Republic. The referendum was a radical right-wing initiative aimed at forcing new elections that would strip the SPD and the centrist parties of their parliamentary mandate. Of twenty-six million Prussians eligible to vote, almost ten million cast their ballots for this measure supported by both Communists and Nazis.[17]

Significantly, the KPD's efforts to court the right wing came after Hitler's party had begun attracting increasing numbers of votes in working-class districts. In June 1932, around 24 percent of workers (defined as those who paid into the state pension fund set up for the working classes) voted for the NSDAP. By the March 1933 elections, that number had gone up to 33 percent. Depending on exactly how one defines *working class*, support for the Nazis in that demographic may have run as high as 44 percent. That was roughly the same level of support that the Nazis enjoyed among white-collar employees in the dying days of the Weimar Republic.[18]

In spite of being called the National Socialist German Workers' Party, the NSDAP conceived of itself not as a party for workers but rather as a party for the entire German people. It triumphed in elections not as the caste-based mouthpiece for any particular class but as a political movement that attracted increasing support from all segments of society. That was the difference between the NSDAP and its competition. The KPD and SPD drew their support mainly from the working class (which made up about 28 percent of the German electorate) and to a lesser extent from low-level white-collar employees. The Center Party was a party for Catholics, the Liberals were the party of the bourgeoisie, and there was no shortage of fringe parties representing various specific regional and professional interests. In stark contrast, the NSDAP emphasized the common element binding all "blood Germans" together. Its party platform allowed the Nazis to stand above domestic conflicts of interest, to transcend traditional rivalries between regions, classes, and religions. That was what made the NSDAP attractive. In two elections with unusually high turnout, 37.5 percent of voters cast their ballots for the NSDAP in July 1932, and 44 percent in March 1933. The corresponding numbers for the KPD were 14.5 and 12.3 percent, the far-right German National People's Party attracted 6.3 and 8 percent support, and the SPD polled 21.6 and 18.3 percent. The Nazis became by far the largest party in Germany, and by 1933 two-thirds of all Germans were voting against the republican form of state.

Hitler promised a lot of things before becoming German chancellor. He was going to do away with the Weimar Republic, annul the Treaty of Versailles, help those hardest hit by the Depression to feed themselves and find work, and apply the power of the state to putting the theories of racial and genetic hygiene into practice. Some small demographic differences notwithstanding, impressive numbers of Germans—northerners and southerners, farmers and bourgeois, laborers and office workers, Protestants and Catholics, men and women—put their faith in the NSDAP. By 1933, it was this party, and this party alone, that could claim to represent a cross section of Germany as a whole.

DULL, ALMOST INARTICULATE POPULAR HATRED

Not all of those who voted for the NSDAP shared the party's aggressive anti-Semitism, but they all tolerated it. Indeed, most Germans, including many who did not vote for Hitler, maintained a genteel, embarrassed aversion to the Jewish minority. It was not uncommon to hear otherwise well-mannered people opine that pushy Jews deserved to get the odd knock on their heads or that Jews, being such know-it-alls, would surely know how to help themselves out of their situation. Many people viewed the Jewish plight with no small amount of schadenfreude. Such people considered Jewish Germans as aliens within Germany and welcomed the chance to strip them of their rights and drive them out of society.

Because Jews tended to have better jobs, those who were initially most likely to exploit anti-Semitism to their advantage were the aspiring classes. In 1933, mass firings of Jewish teachers meant that 60 percent of the 1,320 non-Jewish applicants for teaching jobs were hired, despite cuts in public budgets. At Germany's universities, more than 5,000 regular positions likewise suddenly became available for the politically receptive graduate students, adjunct lecturers, and research assistants who had long been looking for their first permanent posts in academia. Jobs and apartments were everywhere: Jews forced to emigrate had no choice but to sell off their households and the rest of their possessions cheap.

Merchants and entrepreneurs, promoting their companies as "pure German," profited from the demise of their Jewish competitors. Gentiles took over the Jews' public contracts and their customers and could expand by purchasing the warehouse stores that Jewish businesses, driven into bankruptcy, had to auction off at rock-bottom prices. The pressure put on Jewish businesses relieved the economic pressure on the Gentile middle classes, transferring their burden to a disadvantaged minority. Manufacturers, bank managers, and insurance company heads all benefited in their own ways from the racial discrimination. In 1932, there had been 1,350 private banks in Germany. By the end of 1935, there were just 915 banks, of which 345 were considered non-Aryan. By 1939, all of those 345 had been absorbed, without exception, by Aryan financial companies, and the total number of private banks declined to just 520.[19]

In the spring of 1933, Jews found themselves tacitly marginalized and then removed from thousands of German associations and hundreds of newspaper editorial boards, bureaucracies, and cultural institutions, in precisely the fashion that Siegfried Lichtenstaedter had envisioned in his parable of the Anthropopolitan marshal. In April, a doctor and psychotherapist, Hertha Nathorff, wrote a diary entry about her final visit to the conference of the Association of German Women Doctors in Berlin: "There was a colleague I knew well as my predecessor at the Red Cross, someone very left-wing for the time.

She had been fired for incompetence and other not very attractive qualities. She stood up and said: 'I would ask my German colleagues to join me next door for a discussion.' Colleague S., a good Catholic, stood up and asked: 'What's that supposed to mean, German colleagues?' 'Everyone who's not a Jew, of course,' came the answer. That was the wording. Silently we Jewish and half-Jewish doctors stood up, together with some of the 'German' doctors. Silently we left the room, pale and outraged to our very cores."[20]

That same month, Cardinal Michael Faulhaber of the archbishopric of Munich and Freising answered a letter from a Catholic who had written to express his deep concern about the spread of Jew baiting. Faulhaber argued that it was a Catholic's duty to look the other way: "This course of action against the Jews is so un-Christian that every Christian and not just every priest would have to oppose it. But the higher Church authorities have far more urgent questions to address at the moment. The issues of schools, of the continued existence of Catholic associations, and of sterilization are more important to Christianity in our homeland, especially since we can assume the Jews will be able to help themselves and thus that we have no call to give the government a reason to turn their persecution of Jews into a persecution of Jesuits."[21] Statements like this illustrated the truth of an observation made in 1932 by a Protestant clergyman, Otto von Harling, who ran a mission aimed at converting Jews to Christianity. Harling pointed out that the increasingly crass anti-Semitism of the Nazis was "hardly viewed anymore as a scandal and an injustice by broad segments of the population." The constitutional lawyer Franz Böhm, who would become a conservative member of parliament in postwar West Germany and a leader of reparation talks with Israel, later remarked about the final years of the Weimar Republic: "Anti-Hitler slogans in those days, insofar as they existed, never expressed contempt for anti-Semitism."[22] The overwhelming majority of Germans remained silent about the state's persecution of Jews. Despite intensive research, historians have not been able to find many private letters or diaries in which Aryan Germans comment or reflect on—to say nothing of condemn—the anti-Semitic campaigns of the first years of the Nazi regime.

Even active Nazis didn't waste very many words on what they were doing. I have in my possession around a hundred letters by my uncle August R., who was born in 1910 and fell in World War II in 1944. In 1931, during his third semester at university, he joined the Nazi Party, and he would remain an enthusiastic member of it until the day he died. In his mind, he was defending Germany—first as a small-time functionary, then as an officer in the news corps. His correspondence runs some five hundred pages and covers the period between September 1930 and December 1944, yet it contains a grand total of only two anti-Semitic remarks. In November 1930, his mother, in desperate need of money, asked him if it was all right for her to let his room to a Jewish woman who was studying at university. August, whose tone was often brusque, answered: "As long as I'm not home I don't care whether there are bedbugs or Jewesses in my bed. The main thing is that she pays." The only other anti-Semitic remark occurred eight years later. In October 1938, after Germany's annexation of Sudetenland, August noted, among his impressions of the "beautiful city" of Karlsbad, that "Jews have dominated everything there without exception (160 doctors, 120 Jewish)."[23]

Aside from those two comments, there is not one further sentence about Jews in the entire fourteen-year correspondence of a passionate and without doubt actively anti-Semitic Nazi. This silence is of a piece with the behavior of the "German" doctors described by Hertha Nathorff and the answer that Cardinal Faulhaber provided to the worried Catholic's letter. As Jakob Wasserman put it, the "popular hatred of Jews" was "dull, rigid, almost inarticulate." As of 1933, this silent majority provided the social basis for state policies toward Jews. Deep-seated, often off-hand aggression made people look the other way and shrug their shoulders at the growing injustice. In 1933 a strange moral insensibility gained ascendancy, expanding the horizons within which state anti-Semitism could operate. Conversely, every ratcheting up of the state's anti-Jewish measures only increased the moral torpor of the populace.

A NEW MORALITY OF LARCENY AND MURDER

The preceding pages have detailed the social preconditions by which anti-Semitism could become an official goal pursued by the German state. It took eight years, however, from the time Hitler assumed power until the Nazi government started to pursue the "final solution to the Jewish question." The Holocaust was by no means a given, nor was it based on a plan that was hatched long in advance. There is no doubt about that. The new anti-Semitic policies in Germany in 1933 may already have gone far beyond the usual forms of discrimination against minorities in many countries. But as Holocaust historian Raul Hilberg has written, "no bureaucrat in 1933 could have predicted what kind of measures would be taken in 1938, nor was it possible in 1938 to foretell the configuration of the undertaking in 1942."[24]

The decisions between 1933 and 1941 that progressively stripped Jews—initially in Germany and later in occupied countries—of their rights and property were made by various institutions and individuals, first and foremost, of course, by Hitler. Both the individuals and the institutions were guided by ideological group hatred, material interest, and political calculations. Nonetheless, to turn those plans into reality, the decision makers needed both the approval of the minority of Germans who were politically active and the silent tolerance of the vast majority. Focusing as I do on the period from 1800 to 1933, I won't go into the details of this process. But I would like to sketch out some of the major factors that encouraged such a criminal collaboration between the people and their political leadership.

The majority of Germans profited materially in either direct or indirect fashion from the expropriation of Jews. Allowing ordinary people to benefit from discrimination made it easier for them to accept their role as tacit accomplices. I have already discussed this phenomenon at length in my book *Hitler's Beneficiaries* and won't repeat

myself here. What is important for this investigation is how the peculiar German theory of genetic and racial hygiene, based on massive
feelings of inferiority and envy, created a new morality that justified
wholesale discrimination, larceny, and murder.

The concept of race not only reduced groups of human beings to
the level of animals. The academic and political proponents of racial
theory also declared that there were good and bad races, and that the
good races needed to be protected—if necessary, with violence.
According to this logic, a good race had a right to self-defense against
the constant threat posed by bad races. This outlook also encouraged
a hard-line approach toward people deemed to be congenitally ill
within the ranks of the good race itself, and such aggression against
the weaker members of the good race further legitimized and bolstered aggression against those perceived as outsiders. In both cases,
the protection of one's own race served the higher purpose of ensuring the permanent genetic health and thus the happiness of future
generations. Finally, racial theory held out the promise of social harmony, since a nation composed of ethnically identical individuals was
presumed to function more smoothly than a diverse one. These were
the arguments with which adherents defined genetic and racial hygiene
as self-defense and self-purification. "We will recover full health," Hitler proclaimed succinctly in 1942, "when we eliminate the Jews."[25]

From a social-psychological perspective, the most important tenet
of racial theory was that individual attributes were determined by
race and thus exempt from subjective experience or evaluation. The
specific characteristics of an individual Jew no longer had to be
explained in the context of religion, political outlook, personal success,
or behavior. The category of race allowed Germans to ignore or negate
all the good things that Jews might have done as well-educated citizens, clever entrepreneurs, artists, scientists, work colleagues, or owners of the shop on the corner. Goebbels, for instance, has his hero,
Michael, proclaim: "The Jew is in his very being the opposite of us. I
cannot hate him. I can only despise him." A bit later Michael gives
the following answer to the rhetorical question of whether peaceful

coexistence is possible: "Peace? Can the lung make peace with the tubercule bacillus?"[26]

In 1930, one NSDAP gauleiter responded to recurring objections that not all Jews were the same with a brutal analogy: "That may be. But if someone is lying on a hotel mattress infested with bedbugs, he doesn't ask: 'Are you a good or bad bedbug?' He simply crushes them all." Clearly pleased with his colorful example, the gauleiter offered a second, no less graphic one. It might be the case that Jewish babies were as adorable as Aryan ones, he said; still, "a little piglet may be cute, but it grows up to be an old sow." This gauleiter's words were preserved in a pamphlet written by a high-ranking civil servant who supported the Nazis; it was meant to win over a bourgeois readership for Hitler's cause. Admittedly, the civil servant wrote, comparisons of human beings with bedbugs and swine might cause "embarrassment" among educated readers, and he himself, the author, had encountered honest Jews who had heroically sacrificed themselves for the fatherland in the war. But that, the author declared, represented only a minor tragedy, one that had to be ignored in order to deal with the "greater tragedy" threatening the German people.[27]

"Death to the Jews" and similar slurs may have been unacceptable in polite academic society. But people like Eugen Fischer, the director of the Kaiser Wilhelm Institute for Anthropology, Human Heredity, and Eugenics, translated them into language that was professorial and yet still murderous. "The world thinks that we are fighting the Jews only to rid ourselves of financial and intellectual competition," Fischer wrote in 1934 in the magazine *Mein Heimatland* ("My Homeland"). "On the contrary, our struggle is to save the race that created Germanness and to cleanse it from foreign, racially alien elements, which threaten to divert, and in part already have diverted, its spiritual development in other directions. The consequences will be hard, indeed terrible for many quite honorable individuals. But is that too great a sacrifice to save an entire people?"[28] This was the same line of argument that had been employed by the fictional Dr. Schwertfeger in Bettauer's 1922 satire *City without Jews*. Schwertfeger, too, professed admiration for the special talents of the minority. But he also posed a rhetorical question: "The fiddler beetle with its glimmering wings may be, in and of itself, a lovely and worthy creature, but does not the gardener, who cares more for roses than bugs, still eradicate it?"[29]

Anti-Semites had traditionally justified violence, even murder, in terms of self-defense. All the way back in 1841, the poet Franz Dingelstedt wrote: "Wherever you go, grab a Jew, / God's supposèd chosen few! / Christians, stick him in his ghetto / Before he does the same to you!"[30] Berlin's court preacher Adolf Stoecker entitled an anti-Semitic sermon of 1879 "Emergency Defense against Modern Jewry." That same year, Wilhelm Marr's newly founded League of Anti-Semites began publishing a magazine whose title, German Watch (as in keeping watch in the military), implicitly called on readers to defend themselves. In his most widely read pamphlet, Marr depicted a nightmare scenario in which Jewishness triumphed over Germanness. In response, outraged Catholics began to demand that the rights of Christians, and not of Jews, should be explicitly guaranteed.[31]

Hitler entitled the last chapter of Mein Kampf "The Right of Emergency Defense." The law that justified the removal of thousands of German Jews from public jobs in 1933 was called the Law for the Restoration of the Professional Civil Service, as though those persecuted by the law had tried to destroy something that was now being saved at the last second. The draft law drawn up by the Finance Ministry in summer 1937 that aimed at partially expropriating Jews was entitled the Law on the Compensation for Damage Done to the German Empire by Jews. The decree of November 12, 1938, that sentenced Jews to a collective punishment of one billion reichsmarks after Kristallnacht was known as the Decree concerning the Compensatory Payment by the Jews of German Nationality.[32]

Hitler also used the emergency self-defense argument in his speech on January 30, 1939: "Should international finance Jewry inside and outside of Europe succeed in plunging the world's peoples into another global war . . . it will lead to the destruction of the Jewish race in Europe."[33] He would repeat this threat with stupendous regularity.

Party propaganda chief Hermann Esser used similar arguments. "Anti-Semitism is nothing else but justifiable self-defense," he said, and Germany was compelled to avert "an impending danger" in the interest of the survival of the nation, or Germans' "right to life."[34] On May 9, 1943, Goebbels told the public at large: "The day the Jews drew up their plan for the total destruction of the German people, they signed their own death sentences. History will be the judge here."[35] Ten years into the Third Reich, the German public was not at all taken aback by such statements.

In a private speech Heinrich Himmler delivered to upper-level SS leaders on October 4, 1943, he offered the following justification for the "extermination of the Jewish people": "We have the moral right and the duty to our own people to kill this people who wanted to kill us." Two days later, at a speech to gauleiters and other high-ranking Nazi officials, he explained the murder of millions of Jewish women and children: "I did not consider myself justified in getting rid of the men—that is, killing them or having them killed—only to have their children grow up and avenge themselves on our sons and grandsons."[36]

In his 1926 book *Antisemitica*, Siegfried Lichtenstaedter quoted an article that had appeared in the magazine *Heimatland* ("Homeland") on October 15, 1923. The magazine's subtitle read "Patriotic Weekly— Organ of the German Battle Association (Federal Director: Adolf Hitler)." At the beginning of that month, police authorities had banned the magazine's distribution, having deemed it to be a stand-in for the already prohibited *Völkischer Beobachter*.[37] In any case, one of the longer articles in that issue, "Mustapha Kemal Pascha and His Work," attracted Lichtenstaedter's attention. The author was Sergeant Hans Tröbst, a German mercenary who in 1920 to 1922 had fought alongside Turkish troops in the Greco-Turkish War. Tröbst described how Turkish soldiers had brutalized "foreign populaces," especially Greeks, and imagined what the Osman massacres of Armenians from 1915 to 1917 must have been like. "In the field of battle," Tröbst wrote, "foreigners had to meet their maker, almost without exception, and it would be no exaggeration to put their number at 500,000." They were done away with without regard for age or sex." Civilians who did not reside in or near battle areas were driven from their homes.

The article appeared three weeks before Hitler's unsuccessful Beer Hall Putsch of November 9, 1923. Lichtenstaedter was drawn to the article as a contemporary, but several passages from it are particularly striking for readers today, with the benefit of hindsight. Tröbst's experiences in Turkey led him to conclude that political leaders who wanted to emulate young Turkish national revolutionaries' "unified internal front" and "ethnic purity" would have to burn their bridges behind them. "They have to be aware that they're risking their necks," Tröbst wrote. "This awareness will give them the ability to eliminate, ruthlessly and permanently, anything and anyone working against them, no matter how much more sensitive minds may lament about cruelty, barbarism, or worse. The act of rendering enemies harmless has to take a form that is final and obvious to everyone. That's the way to give the movement a terrifying advance reputation. Only the starkest form of fear can make an impression on the frayed nerves of jaded humanity."

What had the Armenian and Greek minorities in Turkey done to merit such terrible punishment? "The Armenian and the Greek reproduced very quickly in comparison with the Turk," wrote Tröbst. "Commerce and reform were exclusively in their hands, and they understood how to sap, in the most perfidious manner imaginable, the strength of the population, which had been helplessly delivered up to them." For Tröbst, mass murder was a justifiable response to the "constant exploitation of the working people." Indeed, it was more than justifiable: "Common sense alone forced the Turk to do a thorough job of it while he was cleaning house, so that he would not have to fear once again facing the same necessity a generation down the road."

Those with foreign backgrounds who were not slaughtered by Turkish soldiers were forced to "emigrate," leaving behind the property that "they had swindled their way into owning over the years." They were allowed to take along only what they could physically carry, and in the end Turks and Kurds relieved the refugees of "all the stuff they had lugged away." Districts and whole towns were left empty. Often, Tröbst reported, "you couldn't find a single soul" apart from the Turkish police. The abandoned properties, the sergeant noted with approval, were quickly put to good use: "All the towns and empty houses have been set aside for fellow Turks who live in Bulgaria, Macedonia, and Greece. Their return will provide a welcome boost to the strength of the Turkish people."

Tröbst cautioned readers against sentimentality and summed up the moral of his story for Germany: "Turkey has shown that it is possible to cleanse a people, in large-scale fashion, from alien elements of every sort." A policy of what we would now call ethnic cleansing, carried out by troops of "fresh and courageous" volunteers, had created the "foundation for the national rebirth of a people." And that, for Tröbst, raised the question of how things stood in Germany. "When will our country see the savior who can translate the needs of the hour into action?" he asked. "Comrades! We must close ranks! Our time will come!"

Reading Tröbst's essay in 1926, Lichtenstaedter interpreted his words as a call to murder the 600,000 Jews in Germany and the 200,000 in Austria and to redistribute their possessions to "Aryans." To justify that, Lichtenstaedter noted drily, a new morality was needed, one that permitted the murder and expropriation of people of "alien origin (i.e., alien religion)."[38]

Hans Tröbst put forward Turkey as an example of how *racial* hygiene could be maintained by mass murder. But Germany was to witness a different radical innovation in inhumanity in 1933, as violence was carried out against German citizens in the name of *genetic* hygiene. In order to maintain the health of the race, Hitler had stated unequivocally in *Mein Kampf*, Germans who were "genetically ill or handicapped in any way" had to be prevented from reproducing, and the "social preconditions" had to be created for healthy people to have lots of children. These aims, according to Hitler, required "the harshest and most invasive decisions," but the Führer had no time for moral scruples: "The demand that it should be impossible for defective people to produce equally defective offspring is one of purest rationality. It will spare millions of creatures undeserved suffering and lead to increased health in general." Hitler admitted that for those "unfortunate enough to be affected," the means by which he planned to raise the general quality of life would seem "barbaric." Nonetheless, he argued, the "temporary pain of a century" would liberate subsequent generations from "millennia of suffering."

What Hitler demanded was a "pitiless" act of cleansing carried out on the corpus of the German people itself. Only by going to such an extreme, he said, could Germans move beyond all hesitation and scale new heights. "If the strength to fight for one's health is no longer present," Hitler proclaimed, "one has no right to exist in this world of struggle." In another passage, he demanded that ill, physically weak, and malformed children be "exterminated" in the name of "controlled racial hygiene." Such drastic measures, Hitler promised, would liberate the German people from "degenerates," and they were "a thousand times more humane" than the "pathetic insanity of our times that wants to save the lives of even the sickest of human subjects."[39]

In polished academic language, Nazi medicine was confronted with a duty to "negatively conserve the race"—that is, to sterilize the mentally, psychologically, and physically disabled. Nazi logic held that such measures would serve the long-term cause of a happy future for the majority of Germans by permanently increasing the German people's ability to fight for survival. In late 1932, Erwin Baur, a geneticist and botanist, drew an analogy with an originally heterogeneous breed of rabbits released on a fictional island. According to Baur, birds of prey would begin culling the weaker members of the group, whereupon the rabbits, threatened with extinction, would respond through natural selection. "Nature" would lead all the rabbits in the colony to develop the same camouflaging fur color and the same short ears, harder for the birds to spot. A "race" of rabbits, thus formed, would be optimally adapted to its environment and would be able to defend its existence and habitat. Human beings, Baur contended, differed from rabbits because civilization allowed them to disrupt the process of natural selection in the name of humanity. For that reason, he asserted, the state had to take over the racially purifying function of the predator.[40]

According to this line of thought, the various human races evolved along Darwinian lines, aiming solely to preserve themselves. In his 1917 essay "Race as a Value," Fischer and Baur's colleague Fritz Lenz argued that such a recognition had to lead to a new set of ethics: "In the long run, the only forms of life that can survive are those whose race can also be preserved." The ethical imperative was therefore to ask of every action or nonaction: "'Is it good for our race?'" Fischer reaffirmed those ideas in 1934 and even formulated a new legal and ethical principle: "The destiny of a people must take precedence over the right of individuals." From that, Fischer concluded: "Just as we seek to remove alien genetic strains, we reject the genetically ill. Here too a sacrifice is required, unconditionally required."[41]

Before the majority of Germans committed or at least permitted the murder of six million Jews, they cleansed their own ranks. "Pitilessly" and "unconditionally," they invaded the lives of hundreds of thousands of members of their own native group. Beginning in 1934, German doctors sterilized more than 350,000 German men and women—an act of unprecedented radicalism. In the women's case, the operation required cutting open their abdomens, and some 6,000 of them died of infections in the immediate aftermath.

In 1941, Siegfried Koller and Heinrich Wilhelm Kranz, medical statisticians, calculated that approximately 1.6 million Germans deemed to be "unfit for community life" would have to be subjected to "special treatment" in order to keep the corpus of the German people free from impurity. This group, which the two statisticians described on occasion as "biological Bolshevists," included those unwilling to work and those happy to live off handouts, as well as state traitors, those who had sex with people of other races, women who had opted for abortions, nymphomaniacs, drug addicts, alcoholics, and prostitutes.[42]

Germans who wanted to get married were now required to apply for permission and supply increasing numbers of documents attesting to their family lineage and biological health. Candidates for the SS also had to meet strict genetic and biological criteria, and would-be-upper-level civil servants had to document their family trees. An alcoholic uncle, an epileptic grandfather, a brother who was clinically depressed, or a handicapped child could be enough to destroy a career and render a life's ambition inconsequential. Given the pressures Germans were subjected to, problematic relatives—and who didn't have one in their extended family?—led many people to worry that perhaps not all was right in their own genealogies and that they themselves might be made to suffer negative consequences. Such concerns were one reason for Germans' very tentative resistance to Nazi euthanasia policies.

Forced sterilizations were not the only result of the Nazi obsession with genetic hygiene. By September 1939, a secret decision had been taken to mass murder mentally ill and disabled Germans. From January 1940 to summer 1941, the Reich regime (*Reichsregierung*) sent more than seventy thousand mentally and physically disabled Aryan Germans to the gas chambers. A special organization had been set up in 1939 to exterminate handicapped children. These two groups, whose true functions were partially concealed from the public at large, carried out their murderous work in close conjunction with national, state, and local health authorities. Mayors, councilors, and registry offices were informed about what was happening, as were courts and doctors' organizations. Euthanasia procedures resembled the later extermination of European Jews in some respects—for instance, in the use of poisonous gas and the sale of gold from fillings removed from the teeth of the victims.

By the summer of 1941, opposition to the murder of patients in hospitals and mental institutions began to coalesce among the general public, particularly in Catholic circles. Euthanasia procedures were not abandoned, but from that point on they were better disguised and decentralized. During the second half of World War II, doctors and nurses would murder an additional hundred thousand German patients in psychiatric institutions, mostly by administering lethal doses of sedatives.

The doctrine of genetic hygiene that led to such ruthless and often lethal encroachments on the corpus of the German people can only be understood as a massive instance of collective aggression. Autoaggressive behavior often takes place in conjunction with aggression against others. From this perspective, it seems as though the culling of its weaker members was a trial to which Nazi Germany submitted in order to toughen itself up sufficiently to exterminate other races. Historians have thus far underestimated the extent to which forced sterilization and euthanasia functioned as an act of self-conditioning crucial for the wholesale murder of Jews. Someone who allows his own relatives to be sterilized, labeled as dead weight, and deported to locations unknown because they have the wrong genetic makeup is also going to accept his government's making members of a supposedly foreign race disappear.

One of the few sources of opposition to racist and geneticist justifications for murder was the traditional Christian morality of many Germans. For Nazis, that was a hurdle that needed overcoming, and the government and its bureaucracy honed its techniques for doing so in the violence it exercised against Germans. For instance, sterilizations were ordered in closed hearings of special genetic health courts made up of one lawyer and two doctors, who rendered their judgments in the name of science. Leading psychiatrists often served as judges, and the procedure was generally known and considered scientifically objective. By contrast, the murders of sick and permanently disabled people on the recommendations of doctors took place in a gray area between public knowledge and willful ignorance. Notifications containing the transparently euphemistic phrase *patient transfer* sufficed to reassure family members and help them accept the news, delivered a short time later, that their loved one had died of natural causes. The pragmatic justification for withholding more precise information was to "prevent ethnic comrades from being morally over-taxed." That, predicted one official document from the time, would have been the effect on the vast majority of "our ethnic comrades, if their conventional and probably Christian morality were to be confronted with the facts."[43]

The man who recommended this way of proceeding was Hitler's personal physician, Theo Morell. With war fast approaching in summer 1939 and with the government drawing up plans to murder handicapped Germans as "useless mouths to feed," Morell stumbled across a survey from the 1920s that had been carried out among parents of seriously handicapped children in a Protestant home. The parents had been asked whether, in specific circumstances, they would be willing "to agree to a painless shortening of their child's life." Morell was struck by one pattern that emerged from their answers. "In principle, they agree," Morell noted. "But parents must not be asked. It's difficult for them to condone a death sentence for their own flesh and blood. If the news is that the child died of some illness, however, everyone is relieved." Nothing remained completely secret, of course, but Hitler's ethnic comrades assuaged their scruples about mass murder of the disabled by relegating what was going on to the realm of suspicions, tempered by a vague belief in higher racial-political necessity. Because family members, caregivers, and nurses weren't *supposed* to know how "transferred patients" died, they didn't *need* to know it. The procedure spared them pangs of conscience.

The later "evacuation" and "resettlement" of Jews used the same techniques that had been tested on the Aryans with genetic defects. That was the reason, to cite but a single example, 2,171 Jews could be rounded up in a school in downtown Darmstadt in September 1942 and deported to Eastern Europe. The deportation was carried out in broad daylight, and it became a topic of discussion among both adults and children, who had been given two weeks off from school. When the children asked what was going to happen to the people who had been held in their school building, the answer was: "Those people are being taken away for work duty." Their parents avoided the word *Jews*. In any case, there was no protest. The good people of Darmstadt didn't want to know what was happening, although it was plain for them to see.[44]

Hitler and Goebbels took care, at regular intervals, to intimate that something terrible was being done to the deportees. In their speeches, they repeatedly mentioned the "destruction of the Jewish race." This created a growing, semiconscious sense among Germans that they were collectively culpable and involved in a terrible crime. This sort of half knowledge and willful ignorance quashed any moral qualms that Hitler's ethnic comrades might still have felt. In a November 1941 speech broadcast by the BBC to German listeners, Thomas Mann analyzed the criminal symbiosis between the German people and their leadership: "You know of the unspeakable things happening in Russia and being done to Poles and Jews. But you would prefer not to know, and for good reason, namely your justified horror at the equally unspeakable hatred that will come raining down on your heads when the power of Germany's people and machinery is exhausted. That hatred will have swelled to gigantic proportions, and you have every reason to be horrified by it. Your leaders exploit this fact. They who have led you to commit all these shameful deeds constantly tell you: 'Now that you have committed them, you are inseparably chained to us, and you'll have to persevere to the very end. Otherwise, hell will break over you.' "[45]

The vast majority of Germans did not raise their voices in protest, and did fight to the bitter end—all the way until May 8, 1945, when massive military force liberated them from themselves. They had accepted the morally outrageous offer of their leaders. For years they had benefited from the expropriation of Jewish citizens, tolerated the forced sterilization and murder of the weaker, defenseless members of their own families, and witnessed the deportation of Jews. They had heard a lot, only to flee down the escape route offered them: You're not allowed to know everything, so learn to forget! As a result, when the Third Reich fell, Germans could not explain either to others or to themselves how things had really been. Instead, they claimed with the deepest conviction that they hadn't known very much at all.

A STORY WITH NO END

THE WEAK AND THE DANGEROUS

Crisis does not explain crisis, nor does war account for war. The same is true of the Holocaust. Anyone who proposes that the German anti-Semitism that resulted in the mass murder of six million people was the result of anti-Semitism in general is merely painting a picture of the devil without accounting for the forces that conjured him and gave him such massive power. In this book, I have tried to recount when and in what circumstances Germans developed their particular brand of anti-Semitism, with its particular results. My guiding questions were the following: How did German anti-Semites justify their resentment, envy, and hatred? What did contemporaries, both Jewish and Gentile, think about the motivation and burgeoning popularity of the anti-Semitic movement? In which social, political, economic, and war-related situations did animosity toward Jews especially increase, and why?

Up until 1933, asking empirical questions of this sort about history was standard. After 1945, however, those who survived and those who were born into a different epoch were confronted by the unspeakable. Most people initially kept silent. And even after two, three, or four decades had passed, the almost indescribable, unimaginable murderous actions of the Germans mostly provoked tautological explanations along the lines of "evil begets evil." Where people had once stayed silent, they now glibly explained things away. Yet as inhuman as those German crimes were, their preconditions were nothing if not human.

For historical reasons, Germans had a difficult time coalescing into a nation. As late as the early nineteenth century, it was still unclear whether the Upper Saxon dialect of today's eastern Germany or the Lower Saxon one of the central regions would serve as the basis for High German. It was only thanks to the intensive efforts of linguists and historians that a unified language was codified, that sagas and fairy tales were collected, that Lutheran Protestantism was reinterpreted as a religious expression of German identity, and that medieval records were strung together into popular German ancient history.

How different that story was from the story of the Jews, broadly scattered in exile. They possessed what Germans so sorely lacked. Their myths were the most significant stories of all, even for Christianity. Those stories stretched back to Eden and told of ancient laws, wise men, wars, and determined efforts to establish a state able to defend itself. Jews had a language, an alphabet, a tradition, and a religion that were thousands of years old and belonged to them and them alone. Decried as vagabonds, Jews in fact possessed the sort of deep, meaningful roots that patriotic Germans were forever frantically digging for. Often enough, Jews had been forced to adapt and change, but they always preserved what was their own. By contrast, Germans, who always claimed to be bound to their own kind, quickly forgot their language and culture when they emigrated.

The Nazis' conviction that the German people had a historically permanent racial core addressed Germans' historical lack of a nation-state. During the Great Depression, two Nazi slogans proved particularly resonant: "Don't forget you're German" and "Germany, awaken!" Slogans like these seem more appropriate to a people who are disoriented and lethargic than to muscle-flexing hypernational-ists. "What is German does not exist, it first has to become," observed author Arnold Zweig, writing about Nazified youth in 1927. In 1933, when Friedrich Sieburg, the cultural correspondent of the *Frankfurter Zeitung*, published an article kowtowing to his new Nazi masters, he similarly entitled it "Germany Will Become." In 1932, the Zionist Hein-rich York-Steiner explained the Nazis' growing popularity and increas-ing animosity toward Jews since the 1930 elections as the continuation of an older story: "From the era of the Hohenstaufens on down to today, Germany's political and cultural position has been uncertain, unstable, and erratic. . . . This position in world history accounts for Germans' ambivalence toward foreigners. What they lack is the strength that comes from constant development, from a naturally evolving self-confidence. The German today is a helot, tomorrow a conqueror, and he acts out his feelings in displays of ethnic hyperbole."[1]

For a short time at the beginning of the nineteenth century, German demands for national unity and popular democratic emancipation went hand in hand. Unlike England or France, the part of Europe inhabited by German speakers—which was split into tiny feudal states and whose margins were culturally open—had no corresponding governmental form. Political unity remained a pipe dream, so the van-guard fighters for personal liberty were forced to take up the national cause as well. They were defeated by the old aristocratic powers in 1814, 1830, and 1848. In 1870, most democrats made their peace with the Prussian-dominated, antirepublican Wilhelmine Empire. Germans achieved remarkable intellectual and (somewhat later) economic and technological breakthroughs in the nineteenth century. But as a nation they remained immature, formless, and unsure of themselves.

Jews in Germany had to overcome five separate obstacles that stood in the way of their emancipation: traditional religious prejudice, the established social castes' fear of progress, a bourgeoisie interested more in state protectionism than in personal liberty, xenophobia among German national revolutionaries, who defined the German people as an exclusive religious, historical, and linguistic community, and reform-minded German Christian romantics. The common elements in all these anti-Jewish perspectives were fear of change, lack of self-confidence, and panic in the face of competition. Particularly in intellectual circles, as York-Steiner wrote, "the fight for survival created resentment."[2] Meanwhile, automatic rejection of everything foreign was considered a sign of faithfulness to one's convictions.

Educational reforms of the Enlightenment had improved German universities and academies by the early nineteenth century, but this sort of progress did not reach ordinary German schools until 1875. Thanks to their better preparation and mental agility, Jewish children were able to profit from the improved institutions of higher learning, while poor elementary education and a lack of parental role models meant that Gentile children fell further and further behind. These trends continued until the beginning of the twentieth century. On the whole, Jews were well acquainted with the risks and opportunities of the new economy and the conditions of life in rapidly expanding cities, whereas most Christians who moved to those cities were barely literate unemployed agrarian laborers, impoverished farmers, or struggling artisans, fit only for menial industrial work.

Despite the many roadblocks that Jews encountered on the path to legal equality, Germany offered them excellent opportunities to throw off historical restrictions.[3] Relative to their Christian peers, they overcame the initial obstacles to social betterment with ease, even though legally they became fully equal everywhere in Germany only in 1918. Conversely, Christian social climbers were in an inferior position vis-à-vis Jews, who were objectively disadvantaged but subjectively better equipped to deal with new social demands. As Gentile Germans began to call for state protection from economically and intellectually superior Jews, laws were passed and administrative procedures were found to secure the privileges of the Christians. But such protectionism only highlighted how slow and incompetent many Gentiles were. Public failure was embarrassing, and people who were fearful, who had emerged as the losers of social change, and who were plagued by feelings of inferiority became modern anti-Semites. Sometimes it's the weak who are dangerous.

A handful of intellectual agitators like Constantin Frantz and Heinrich von Treitschke led the way in the fight against Jews. They appealed to the silent unskilled majority within society. This was fertile social ground for the growth of anti-Jewish resentment, and it exploded in intensity after Germany's defeat in World War I and the disastrous Treaty of Versailles. Anti-Semitism became a common, accepted part of German culture.

In September 1932, six months before he would leave Germany forever, Jewish activist Kurt Blumenfeld spoke to a group of German Zionists. He laid out the reasons the Nazis would come to rule the country, including "the world war, the swift increase in the European population, the decline of the former ruling and propertied classes of Europe, the miserable living conditions of the masses, the mechanization of life, and the suppression of intellectual and cultural interests." All these factors, as Blumenfeld saw things, would help the National Socialists seize the reins of government. Blumenfeld also analyzed why post-1875 German nationalists had opposed the idea of the liberal state and devalued individual liberty in favor of "equality of the historic group, the German people." "Paradoxically," Blumenfeld concluded, "a longing for dictatorship has arisen by democratic means among the majority of the people." This desire became all the more fervent "as the postwar generation proved increasingly unable to shape their lives and learn trades that would bring them security."

The liberal idea that individual citizens had to be responsible for their own welfare had been completely supplanted by faith in a state organized along collective ethnic lines. The pluralistic state theory of the Anglo-Saxon world, Blumenfeld emphasized, had been fundamentally and violently rejected in Germany. "Any assertion that individuals have a variety of social ties and responsibilities and that membership in a religion, a nation, a trade union, and a family can create ties of various sorts is seen as a negation of the necessary unity of the state," Blumenfeld said. "People demand the 'total' state in which there are no parts of life that are outside politics." With the imminent triumph of the National Socialist revolution, Blumenfeld added, the legal system would become a "purely technical expression of the greatest source of power of the total state, and the destruction of Jews will be one of the main goals."[4]

In parallel with its attacks on Jews, the Hitler government redefined its constituency as a racial unit of ethnic comrades. Because the Nazis promised "equality" to all members of this homogeneous group, Blumenfeld expected the NSDAP to attract considerable support. This was all the more likely since many Germans had jettisoned the values of modern liberal society long before the 1930s. In the 125 years prior to Hitler's assumption of power, the ideas of individual liberty and equality before the law had been drained of their content and converted, one by one, into collectivist slogans. In 1945, Thomas Mann put the problem this way: "The German concept of freedom was always directed externally. It means the right to be German, only German, and nothing but." The German concept of liberty meant liberty only for the German fatherland, not for the individual. It was, Mann said, the expression of "collective ethnic egotism and militant pride in servitude."[5]

As early as 1810, the nationalistic movement was already heading down an unhappy path. A bit later, economic reformers would encourage the German tendency toward protectionism. Between 1876 and 1879, Bismarck broke radically with the ideas of the liberal state and deliberately destroyed the theretofore relatively principled National Liberal Party. Afterward, the powerful, well-organized Social Democrats put the might of the masses above the cause of individual liberty, idealizing state socialism as a guarantee of a happy future. On the bourgeois front, too, the national-social component and imperial, bellicose aims only increased the lure of collectivist nationalism. The German aristocracy may have been at best halfhearted supporters of political and economic enlightenment, but it was the bourgeoisie, the working classes, and the new intermediate stratum of aspiring social climbers who ultimately destroyed the rule of law and reason. As sharply defined as the conflicts between those groups may have been, they were united in their hatred for British-style liberalism.

All of the anti-Semitic associations and parties that appeared in Germany between 1880 and 1933 favored economic and political protectionism. They all demanded "justice" for the Christian majority and insisted that those who had fallen behind be put on equal footing. They expected the state to shower the masses with material security. As they saw it, the state existed to guarantee people's welfare and protect the proverbial man in the street from economic crises, wage cuts, foreign competition, and Jews. Anti-Semitic propagandists promised that happiness would be attained via the collective, and they demonized individualism. They did not just stir up resentment against Jews—they encouraged ordinary Germans not to trust themselves to make their own way in the world.

The diametric opposite of the German man in the street was the Jewish pauper from Eastern Europe. He came from the eastern German province of Posen or the Russian part of Poland and settled in Berlin, where he lived with his extended family in one-room apartments for fifteen years or so while he worked himself up the social ladder. He then became a self-employed businessman and sent his children to university-track academies.[6] In the same span of time, a not-quite-so-poor but also disadvantaged Christian might make the leap from starving farmhand to an assistant in an apothecary. The outer limit of his ambitions was to secure his son a job as a postman so that he might qualify for a state pension.

World War I and German defeat massively increased the pace of this century-old process. The commanders of Kaiser Wilhelm's army exploited the social-democratic virtues of solidarity, discipline, collective fighting spirit, clear recognition of the enemy, and willingness to sacrifice everything for a good cause, transforming them into military virtues. The war dragged on and on, claiming increasing numbers of victims, as the million-strong popular armies sank their teeth into each other. The brutality of the fighting left soldiers intensely dependent on one another. As economist and sociologist Emil Lederer observed in 1915, "society reverted to community" and "all previously distinct, fundamental social groups disappeared into a limitless unity of the people" who were defending their native soil.[7]

Social amalgamation was a phenomenon affecting all the societies that took part in the war, but it soon dissipated in the victorious Western democracies. The situation was different in post-1918 Germany, which continued to feel and act like a besieged fortress. The result was a second amalgamation, encouraged by conditions that had been building for a hundred years but that would never have been unleashed without the corrosive force of war. Nationalist and socialist movements, which had begun to merge in the nineteenth century yet still remained distinct, now "mutually influenced one another and sought to become one." That was how historian Friedrich Meinecke described the situation. With reference to Hitler, Meinecke added: "In him, the fusion of nationalist and socialist movements found its most fervent herald and its most determined executor."[8]

A strong third political force committed to the idea of personal liberty might well have been able to halt this fateful process. But that force was lacking. The NSDAP became the party of the masses, its path to popularity cleared by the hated peace treaty, inflation, foreign military interventions, armed uprisings, and finally the Great Depression. Hitler promised his supporters uncompromising antiliberalism and muscular state capitalism. He pledged absolute national-socialist justice for the racially homogeneous and genetically healthy. He elevated the state above the individual. He transformed the existing social, religious, and regional contradictions in German society into national and racial conflicts.

In the spring of 1945, against the backdrop of the impending, long-desired defeat of his homeland, Wilhelm Röpke wrote a book entitled *The German Question*. The burning question of his title was straightforward: "How could the German people ever have come to this pass?"[9] By the time an expanded new edition was published in 1948, Röpke had already rejected the excuse, adopted by so many Germans at the time, that capitalism and the bourgeoisie had helped National Socialism to its triumph. Nevertheless, that excuse still remains somewhat popular today, even though it forestalls any serious investigations into the deeper causes of the Third Reich.

The "capitalism thesis" can be understood as an attempt to lay the blame for the crimes of Nazi Germany at the feet of as few people as possible, thereby relieving the historical burden on the majority. But we would be well served to remember the words of Röpke: "There are countless examples of how short the step was from Socialists to National Socialists. The legend of the evil capitalists who raped the masses with the help of National Socialism cannot be dispelled vigorously enough. Without broad support from the German masses, National Socialism would neither have come to power nor been able to retain power. The fact that these same masses previously voted for Socialists and Communists, and once more vote for them today, does not change the facts. One cannot make a graver mistake regarding National Socialism than to deny its mass character."[10]

THE POISON OF ENVY

Anti-Jewish resentment had begun bubbling up in the nineteenth century after trade restrictions on Jews were lifted and Jews began to have economic success. Gabriel Riesser observed in 1831: "The true Jew haters of today envy the rich man his wealth, the busy man his employment, and the beggar his rags. This is not a rhetorical exaggeration. There are Jew haters who are not embarrassed to complain that poor Jews are much better cared for [than Gentiles] thanks to their coreligionists' generosity."[11]

Although individuals could not admit it either to themselves or to others, gnawing envy, together with a collectivist longing for a life among equals, paved the way for racial theory. This ideology was just what Germans, so beaten down and unhappy with themselves, needed.

Untalented Christian students, noninnovative entrepreneurs, and businessmen who got their numbers mixed up couldn't keep on simply complaining about the better results achieved by their Jewish competitors. That undermined their own morale and worsened their fear of failure. It was only logical to transform anti-Semitism based on social envy into a theory that would impugn a purported race.

In his 1797 treatise *The Metaphysics of Morals*, Immanuel Kant discussed the sins associated with human hatred: "They comprise the contemptible family of envy, ingratitude, and schadenfreude. Hatred here is neither open nor violent. It is secret and concealed. It is cowardly, in addition to violating our duty to love our neighbors." Kant characterized the sour sensation of envy as the feeling "that our own welfare is being diminished by the welfare of others." When not constrained by a sense of ethical responsibility, envy develops into "the abominable vice of a grim and self-flagellating passion aimed, at least in the realm of wishes, at destroying others' happiness." Those who felt schadenfreude, Kant argued, coveted the sensation of contrast, the "feeling that one's own welfare and even rectitude were all the greater when others' misery or descent into scandal was laid under them as a reflective foil, bathing them in an even brighter light." For Kant, schadenfreude was a shabby compensatory mechanism for small-minded, eternally complaining people, a "horrific sign of one's secret hatred for one's fellow man and an indication of one's intellectual impoverishment."[12]

Envy thrives in concealment, since it throws a disadvantageous light on the enviers themselves. For that reason, the enviers prefer it when others can deliver arguments or act on their behalf. They like to hide their base instincts behind political programs, state laws, abstract concepts like justice, or purported objective truths, such as those of scientific racial theory. A subconscious, never fully acknowledged recognition of one's own failure, and the accompanying feeling of shame, is a crucial component of envy. The anti-Semitism that determined the aims of the German state beginning in 1933 relieved individual Germans of feeling shame and responsibility. To this end, dictatorship was a particularly good form of government. Actions that were bureaucratically organized and legally sanctioned allowed the average German citizen to watch events from behind the curtains, his arms folded, refusing to intervene. That explains how most Germans, who did not themselves directly exercise violence toward Jews, could think it legitimate for their government to do so. To paraphrase Kant slightly, most Germans nurtured their envy of Jews not in open and violent but in secret and concealed form. This passively expressed anti-Semitism gave the German government the latitude it needed to press forward with its murderous campaigns.

The phenomenon is the topic of American sociologist Everett C. Hughes's essay "Good People and Dirty Work." In 1948, Hughes toured postwar Germany and recorded his conversations with Germans, most of whom were still extremely distraught. In his essay, he writes of an encounter with an architect from Frankfurt am Main who told him: "I am ashamed. But you see, we had lost our colonies, and our national honor was hurt. And these Nazis exploited that feeling. And the Jews, they *were* a problem. They came from the east. You should see them in Poland; the lowest class of people, full of lice, dirty and poor, running about in their Ghettos in filthy caftans. They came here and got rich by unbelievable methods after the first war. They occupied all the good places. Why, they were in the proportion of ten to one in medicine and law and government posts." At this point, the architect lost his train of thought. Hughes jogged his memory, and he continued, though only with the most indirect reference to the Holocaust: "Well, of course that was no way to settle the Jewish problem. But there *was* a problem, and it had to be settled some way." In Hughes's analysis, by accepting that Jews were a problem, the architect and many like him were accepting the fact that others should do the dirty work of solving that problem, work about which he would later refuse to speak. The architect himself had not committed any Nazi crimes. But at the time when they were being committed, he was indifferent toward them.[13]

In 1946, Friedrich Meinecke, then eighty-three years old, advanced similar arguments. In his book *The German Catastrophe*, he even blamed to some extent the very people who had been driven into exile and murdered. In the nineteenth century, Meinecke wrote, "Jews who had tended to freely enjoy the favorable winds of fortune had caused considerable offense when fully emancipated." Meinecke also saw Jews as partially responsible for anti-Jewish agitation during the Weimar Republic: "There were many Jews among the people who were too quick and greedy to drink from the cup of power that had been given them. In the minds of all anti-Semites, they looked like the beneficiaries of German defeat and revolution."[14]

Although there were setbacks in times of crisis, general German prosperity had steadily increased since 1870, and many millions of Germans were developing a determination to work their way up in life and give their children a better education—a will to do what Jews had historically done. The material gap between German Jews and Gentiles had begun to close as of 1910. The period of hyperinflation saw the impoverishment of large parts of the German bourgeoisie, and since Jews were disproportionately represented in this class, as a group they lost a commensurately larger amount of wealth. War, crisis, and republican policies leveled social differences. A decline in Jewish birth rates preceded that in Christian ones.

Slowly at first, but with ever-increasing tempo, Gentiles narrowed the education gap, got a better handle on life in big cities, and became more vertically mobile. Conversely, as Arthur Ruppin determined, Jews faced "ever-increasing Christian competition." In 1886–87, 10 percent of all university students in Prussia were members of the Jewish faith. By 1930, despite the mistaken impressions of the Frankfurt architect, that figure was only 4 percent. In 1914, Jews earned five times as much on average as Gentiles. In 1928, Jews earned only three times as much—a significant step toward parity. Social scientists at the time observed "that the age of the Jew's leading role in German economy is over."[15] Yet ironically, the shrinking gap between Jewish and Gentile prosperity did not alleviate Jew hatred. On the contrary, Jewish social stagnation and advances made by Gentiles only increased the tension that was already present. That may seem paradoxical, but the explanation is really quite simple. Envy is usually much stronger between neighboring groups that differ only moderately in material welfare and success than between groups that are more socially differentiated and spatially separated. Proximity is what enables constant comparisons, be it within families, among work colleagues, or in larger social groups. Popular envy-based anti-Semitism was directed primarily not against Jewish bankers, revolutionaries, department store owners, or racial and religious enemies but rather against neighbors, classmates, colleagues, and fellow club members who were somewhat better off. As philosopher Max Scheler observed early in the twentieth century, "it is only the new feeling of equality of the climber that gives social resentment its edge."

In 1927, Arnold Zweig went searching for reasons behind the growing popularity of anti-Semitism. He hit upon increasing social proximity as an explanation. "Emotion was sparked by intense contact between Jews and non-Jews along an obviously long line of friction," Zweig wrote. "It has combusted, permanently raising temperatures to abnormal levels."[16] If we were to formulate this as a general rule for ethnic conflicts motivated at least in part by social competition, it would be: As soon as an economically and socially backward majority catches up somewhat and narrows the gap with a more quickly advanced minority, the danger of hate and violence increases instead of disappearing.

The anti-Semitism that began to reach a boil in Germany in the 1920s was energized by the dynamic of upward social mobility among the Christian majority. Popularized racial science also added fuel to the fire, providing arguments and instruments to highlight differences between Jews and Gentiles. The doctrine of the German people as a biologically superior collective, which became popular around 1900 and which began to be taught in 1922 at German universities and schools, gave individuals who felt humiliated and threatened a sense of safety and allowed them to release their repressed aggression. In 1933, political philosopher Erich Voegelin wrote that this doctrine used the concept of race as a "tool for interpreting one's own life and the larger life of the community."[17] The theory of a racially pure people, or *Volk,* became part of everyday praxis and anchored a utopian vision of a better life to come.

Today's generations of Germans owe a lot to their ancestors' desires to get ahead in the world. Precisely for that reason, there is no way for them to divorce anti-Semitism from their family histories. On account of their own continuing social rise, the murderous anti-Semitism of their forefathers now appears incomprehensible and alien. But in one major regard, the answer to the riddle posed by German anti-Semitism is terribly easy. Arthur Ruppin formulated it in a single, pointed sentence in 1930: "The mentality displayed by the Jews of today is the mentality of the Gentiles of tomorrow."[18]

Envy, fear of failure, resentment, and greed fueled German anti-Semitism. These were forces of evil that mankind has feared and has tried to rein in with civilization since the dawn of time. Germans, connected as they were to the traditions of Christianity and Roman law, were aware of the base motivations behind their Jew hatred and were rightly ashamed of it. That, however, made them all the more receptive to racial theory. Biopolitical pseudoscience disguised hatred as insight and made one's own shortcomings seem like virtues. It also provided justification for acts of legal discrimination against others, allowing millions of Germans to delegate their own aggression, born of feelings of inferiority and shame, to their state. Representatives of that state relieved people of their responsibilities as individuals and transformed individual malice into a collective need to find a "final solution to the Jewish question."

Cain killed his brother, Abel, because he felt disadvantaged and unjustly treated by God. The first murder in the history of humanity was born of envy and the need to feel equal. The mortal sin of envy—together with a belief in collective happiness, modern science, and specific techniques of political rule—is what made the systematic mass murder of European Jews possible. There is no way around the pessimistic conclusion that evil can never be quarantined once and for all in a way that would rule out such horrors. Another event structurally similar to the Holocaust could still occur. Those who want to reduce the danger of its happening should work to understand the complex human preconditions of the Holocaust. And they should not kid themselves into thinking that the anti-Semites of the past were completely different from who we are today.

NOTES

INTRODUCTION: THE QUESTION OF QUESTIONS

1. Marcus, pp. 20–21.
2. Lichtenstaedter, *Zionismus*, p. 37.
3. Lichtenstaedter, *Täuschung*, p. 61.
4. Lichtenstaedter, *Jüdische Politik*, pp. 21, 56.
5. Ibid., pp. 21–27, 56.
6. Hitler, *Zweites Buch*, p. 220.
7. Fröbel, p. 170.
8. Treitschke quoted in Fröbel, p. 30; Sforza, p. 18.
9. Quoted in Görtemaker, p. 357.
10. Quoted in Kraus, *Walpurgisnacht*, p. 12.
11. Zweig, p. 13.
12. Oehme and Caro, pp. 107–8.
13. Lestschinsky, *Bilan de l'extermination*; World Jewish Congress, *Memorandum to the United Nations Special Committee on Palestine*; Lestschinsky, "Migrations," pp. 1565–66.
14. Heuss, "Mut zur Liebe," p. 123.

1: JEWISH EMANCIPATION

1. Meinecke, *Zeitalter*, p. 95.
2. Riesser, "Über die Stellung," p. 9; *Die gegenwärtig beabsichtigte Umgestaltung der bürgerlichen Verhältnisse der Juden in Preußen*, p. 14.

3. Treitschke, *Deutsche Geschichte im Neunzehnten Jahrhundert*, vol. 1, p. 377.

4. Cabinet order of Dec. 14, 1822, quoted in Jost, pp. 56–57; Riesser, "Über die Stellung," p. 9.

5. *Bundesgesetzblatt des Norddeutschen Bundes* (1869), no. 319, p. 451.

6. *Die Preußische Staatsverwaltung und die Juden*, pp. 10, 22, 28. See Loewenthal; Sombart, *Zukunft*, pp. 77–78.

7. Quoted in Aly, *Im Tunnel*, p. 47.

8. Ruppin, *Juden der Gegenwart*, p. 114.

9. Lackmann, p. 17.

10. Those were the words used at the founding of a Jewish school in Frankfurt am Main in 1794. Quoted in Scholtzhauer, pp. 8–9.

11. Schnabel, vol. 1, p. 422.

12. Sack, "Gegen die Prügelpädagogen," pp. 73–92.

13. Dittes, pp. 203–10, 258–59; Dittes, 1890 ed., pp. 259–67.

14. Sack, "Schlaglichter," pp. 174–75, pp. 196–97, 209n.

15. Dittes, p. 47.

16. Schottlaender, p. 8.

17. *Preußische Statistik*, vol. 102, pp. 66ff.; Thon and Ruppin, pp. 21–47; "Unterrichtswesen in Preußen," *Zeitschrift für Demographie und Statistik der Juden* 1 (1905): 11; Ruppin, "Begabungsunterschiede christlicher und jüdischer Kinder," *Zeitschriff für Demographic and Statistik der Juden* 8–9 (1906): 129–35; Ruppin, *Gegenwart*, pp. 119–32; Jarausch, "Universität und Hochschule," p. 325; D. Müller, table 12.3, p. 218; Herrmann, table 3.5.3, pp. 242–43, table 3.5.8, pp. 252–53. On the numbers of Jewish academy and university students, see Kampe, pp. 77–81. The relative numbers of advanced Jewish and Christian pupils remained basically unchanged in 1911; see May, pp. 6–9.

18. Paulsen, pp. 195–200; Hammerstein, p. 12.

19. Kohn, *Bürger vieler Welten*, p. 63.

20. Quoted in Slezkine, p. 137.

21. Ruppin, *Juden der Gegenwart*, p. 114; Weizmann, *Trial and Error*, pp. 19–45.

22. Scholem Alejchem, p. 70.

23. Němeček, pp. 7–8, 12–16, 26, 29–34.

24. Bamberger, "Deutschtum und Judentum," p. 25.

25. Open letter by Suttner, Jan. 25, 1893, quoted in Simon, pp. vi–vii.

26. Oettinger, p. 5.

27. Jost, p. 7.

28. Börne, *Briefe*, p. 512; Jost, p. 56; Silbergleit, pp. 74–77; Toury, pp. 119–20.

29. Silbergleit, pp. 74–77, 11–12.

30. Ruppin, *Juden der Gegenwart*, p. 129 and n. 9.

31. Segall, p. 70; May, pp. 33, 36.

32. Pohlmann, pp. 21–22.

33. Volkov, pp. 53–54; Sombart, *Die Juden und das Wirtschaftsleben*, pp. 217–21; Sombart, *Die Zukunft der Juden*, pp. 33–36; Marcus, pp. 11–15; Lestschinsky, *Das jüdische Volk im neuen Europa*, pp. 43–44; Weinryb, pp. 54–55; Ruppin, *Die Juden der Gegenwart*, pp. 51ff.; Segall, pp. 72–75.

34. Bahr, pp. 28–29; Rieger, p. 7.

35. Friedrich and Schmieder-Friedrich, pp. 23, 48; Toury, p. 119.

36. Quoted in Schnabel, vol. 1, p. 471.

37. Von der Marwitz quoted in Erb and Bergmann, p. 19; letter from Wilhelm to Caroline von Humboldt, June 4, 1815, in Humboldt, vol. 5, pp. 565–66. There is no reason to suspect Wilhelm von Humboldt of being a covert anti-Semite. See Rosenstrauch, pp. 225–44.

38. Schnabel, vol. 2, p. 225; Graetz, vol. 6, pp. 245–52; on Frankfurt, see Börne, "Für die Juden," p. 280.

39. Börne, *Über den Antisemitismus*, pp. 55–56.

40. Quoted in Erb and Bergmann, p. 109.

41. Hundt-Radowsky, "Judenspiegel," quoted in Fasel, pp. 165, 275–77; Hundt-Radowsky, "Juden und ihr Schachergeist," quoted in Fasel, pp. 270–71. See also Fasel for biographical details about Hartwig von Hundt-Radowsky (1780–1835).

42. Dann, pp. 14, 100.

43. Quoted in Riesser, "Rede gegen Moritz Mohls Antrag," p. 103.

44. Edler, pp. 1–56.

45. Schwarz, p. 14; Philippson, p. 73.

46. Eckstein, p. 13.

47. Landau, *Die Petition des Vorstandes der israelitischen Gemeinde zu Dresden*.

48. Auerbach, pp. 24, 26, 28–29, 54; Bamberger, *Erinnerungen*, p. 27.

49. Wagner, pp. 9–32.

50. "Die bürgerlichen Verhältnisse der Juden in Deutschland," pp. 353–55. The German writer and rabbi Ludwig Philippson described this document as "apparently from the pen of a Prussian Christian who approached the affair neutrally."

51. Riesser, "Über die Stellung der Bekenner," pp. 22–23; Riesser, "Vertheidigung der bürgerlichen Gleichstellung der Juden," pp. 6–7, 30.
52. Goldstein, *Deutsche Volks-Idee*, p. 94.

2: THE ANXIETY OF GERMAN NATIONALISM

1. Friedrich Oertel to Thomas Mann, Feb. 16, 1947, in Hübinger, pp. 598–99.
2. Virchow, p. 17.
3. Villers, pp. 5–71.
4. Bisky, pp. 356–62. For the translation of Kleist, see Dennis F. Mahoney, *The Literature of German Romanticism*, Rochester, 2003.
5. Bamberger, "Deutschtum und Judentum," pp. 25–26.
6. Arnim, *Texte der Deutschen Tischgesellschaft*, pp. 114–20, 153–54, 159, 179–84. See also Grab, *Der deutsche Weg*, pp. 16–17; Brumlik, pp. 125–31.
7. Arnim, *Texte der Deutschen Tischgesellschaft*, pp. 114–20, 151–59, 179–84.
8. See especially the conclusion of Arnim's *Majoratsherren*.
9. Aretin, p. 50.
10. Arndt, "Noch etwas über die Juden," *Ein Blick*, p. 192.
11. Arndt, *Noch ein Wort über die Franzosen*, pp. 4, 13.
12. Arndt, *Deutsche Volkwerdung*, pp. 115–16; Arndt, *Reden und Glossen*, pp. 37–38; 70–71; Arndt, *Versuch*, pp. 427–28.
13. Arndt, "Noch etwas über die Juden," *Blick*, pp. 180–204.
14. Arndt, *Reden*, pp. 36ff.; Arndt, *Versuch*, pp. 427–28; Arndt to Heinrich Eugen Marcard, quoted in Herzig, "Brandstifter und Biedermeier."
15. Arndt, *Entwurf einer teutschen Gesellschaft*, pp. 25–26.
16. Arndt, "Auch ein Wort über die auf dem preußischen Reichstage," p. 1853.
17. Arndt, "Phantasien zur Berichtigung der Urteile über die künftige deutsche Verfassung," quoted in Puschner, p. 191.
18. T. Mann, *Deutschland und die Deutschen*, pp. 24–25; "Polen, Franzosen, Pfaffen," quoted in Sterling, p. 164.
19. Ascher, *Die Germanomanie*, pp. 13–14.
20. Fries, *Von Deutschem Bund*, pp. 41–43, 61–63, 71–72.
21. Fries, "Über die Gefährdung," pp. 3, 18–21; on Fries's biography, see Brumlik, pp. 227–31.
22. For a brief overview, see Sterling, pp. 190–92.

23. Richarz, pp. 471–72 (testimony of Isaak Bernstein, born in 1824 in Schildberg, died in 1893 in Berlin); "Bericht des Landrats und Parlamentärs Edmund von Bärensprung über das Gefecht bei Sokolowo vom 3.5.1848 und Schreiben des Generalleutnants Friedrich Wilhelm von Brünneck vom 18.7.1848," *Deutsche und Polen in der Revolution von 1848–1849*, pp. 317–20, 410–11.

24. Quoted in Kohn, *Das zwanzigste Jahrhundert*, pp. 25–26.

25. Dann, p. 205; Bamberger, *Erinnerungen*, pp. 528–29.

26. Hoffmann von Fallersleben, vol. 4, pp. 207–8.

27. Wilhelm to Caroline von Humboldt, June 4, 1815, in Humboldt, vol. 4, p. 566.

28. See Metternich, *Die deutsche Frage*, and Metternich's letter to the Prussian minister of police, Prince zu Sayn-Wittgenstein, May 25, 1832, quoted in Glossy, pp. viii–viv.

29. Heine, *Ludwig Marcuse*, p. 276; Heine, *Ludwig Börne*, pp. 84–85.

30. Heine, *Zur Geschichte der Religion und Philosophie in Deutschland*, p. 119.

31. Heine to Moritz Embden, Feb. 2, 1823, in Heine, *Briefe*, vol. 1, p. 42.

32. Heine, preface, *Französische Zustände*, p. 67.

33. Bamberger, *Erinnerungen*, pp. 416–17, 524, 534–35.

34. Börne, "Eine Kleinigkeit"; Scheuer, pp. 43–44.

35. Hamann, pp. 160–68; "Sturm des Jubels und der Freude. Die alte Kaiserstadt huldigt dem Gründer des neuen Reiches," *Völkischer Beobachter*, April 2, 1938.

36. Cited in Botz, pp. 184–85.

3: ANTI-SEMITISM AS A POLITICAL FORCE

1. The proportion of Jews within the Prussian population remained nearly constant between 1811 and 1933. In 1816 it was 1.2 percent. It rose to 1.4 percent in 1861 and by 1925 fell back to 1.1 percent. See Silbergleit, p. 25.

2. Quoted in *Die Judenfrage im Preußischen Abgeordnetenhause*, p. 100.

3. Weinryb, p. 48; Kautsky, *Rasse und Judentum*, p. 62.

4. Frantz, p. 27.

5. Max Bewer, quoted in *Abwehr-ABC*, p. 90.

6. Stoecker, Feb. 11, 1880, in *Preußischen Abgeordnetenhaus*, quoted in *Die Judenfrage im Preußischen Abgeordnetenhause*, p. 158.

7. Frantz, pp. 20, 37–44, 64.

8. Marr, *Der Judenkrieg*, pp. 29–31; Marr, *Der Sieg des Judenthums*, pp. 3, 33, 45–46. See also *Die Verjudung der höheren Schulen*; Boeckel, *Nochmals: "Die Juden,"* pp. 6–9.

9. Frantz, p. 20.

10. Pohlmann, p. 26; Dann, p. 199.

11. Wirth, p. 454; 1890 ed., pp. 450–614.

12. Lestschinsky, *Das jüdische Volk im neuen Europa*, pp. 81–83.

13. Ludwig Bamberger on Bismarck's *Unwillen zur inneren Strukturierung des Kaiserreichs*, in Bamberger, "Die Sezession," p. 62.

14. Röpke, *Die deutsche Frage*, pp. 199–203; Hobrecht, quoted in W. J. Mommsen, pp. 376–84; Rürup, p. 106.

15. Treitschke, "Unsere Aussichten," pp. 570–76.

16. Bamberger, "Die Sezession," p. 132; Marcus, p. 147.

17. York-Steiner, *Kunst*, p. 559; Bamberger, "Deutschtum und Judentum," p. 16.

18. "The Jews in Germany," *Times* (London), Nov. 16, 1880. See also Bürger, pp. 110–13.

19. Quoted in Wassermann and Franz, pp. 127–28.

20. Quoted in Boehlich, pp. 202–4; for a list of signees, see Liebeschütz, pp. 341–42.

21. T. Mommsen, p. 218; T. Mann, pp. 242–46.

22. Treitschke, "Unsere Aussichten"; Treitschke, *Ein Wort über unser Judenthum*, pp. 2–3.

23. Treitschke, "Das constitutionelle Königthum," pp. 49–93.

24. *Die Judenfrage. Verhandlungen des Preußischen Abgeordnetenhauses*, pp. 50–52; Stoecker, *Das moderne Judenthum*, pp. 16 ff., 38.

25. *Die Judenfrage. Verhandlungen des Preußischen Abgeordnetenhauses*, p. 58 (Hobrecht), p. 149 (Kröcher), pp. 85–95 (Bachem).

26. Ibid., pp. 62–63.

27. Ibid., p. 68.

28. Ibid., p. 89.

29. Ibid., p. 83; "The Jews in Germany," *Times* (London), Nov. 16, 1880.

30. *Die Judenfrage*, pp. 137–38.

31. Ibid., p. 117.

32. Marr, *Der Sieg des Judenthums*, pp. 43–46.

33. E. Bernstein, pp. 59, 106.

34. "Programm der Christlich-Sozialen Arbeiterpartei (Januar 1878)," quoted in Wilhelm Mommsen, pp. 71–73.

35. Massing, p. 42.

36. "Grundsätze und Forderungen der Antisemitischen Deutsch-sozialen Partei," quoted in Wilhelm Mommsen, pp. 73–78.

37. Claß, "*Wenn ich der Kaiser wär*," pp. 30–38, 74–78.

38. "Ernst Moritz Arndt über die Juden, Judeneinwanderung und Judene-mancipation," *Germania*, Aug. 29, Aug. 30, and Sept. 1, 1879. These are essentially quotations of Ernst Moritz Arndt. I owe the reference to Rybak, p. 129.

39. Friedrich Kosnik, "Über meine Vorfahren," Aly Family Archive, I 5.

40. Fritsch, *Die Juden im Handel*, pp. 128, 196.

41. Fritsch, *Die Stadt der Zukunft*, p. 29.

42. Sombart, *Die Zukunft der Juden*, p. 47; Stoecker, pp. 3, 16–17, 36–37; *Die Judenfrage. Verhandlungen des Preußischen Abgeordnetenhauses*, p. 118.

4: THE MAINSTREAM'S DANGEROUS INDIFFERENCE

1. Quoted in Massing, pp. 218, 273; see also Osborn.

2. *Der Sozialdemokrat*, Jan. 9, 1881.

3. Mehring, *Herr Hofprediger Stöcker*, pp. 64–76.

4. See Mehring, "Kapitalistische Agonie," pp. 545–48; "Drillinge," p. 581; "Im Wechsel der Zeiten," p. 2; "Anti- und Philosemitisches," pp. 586–87. More generally, see Rürup, pp. 110–11, 118; Leuschen-Seppel, pp. 165–67. "Change is the true God of the Jews," Karl Marx wrote. "We have to emancipate ourselves before we can emancipate others." For more about Marx's brief text "On the Jewish Question," see Silberner, pp. 119–23.

5. Mehring, introduction to Marx and Engels ("Einleitung"), pp. 352–56.

6. This phrase was quite common among Social Democrats. See Kautsky, "Das Massaker," p. 304.

7. Silberner, pp. 203–7; *Der Sozialdemokrat*, May 22, 1881; Bebel, pp. 20–21; Liebknecht, p. 224; "Die Stichwahlen," *Vorwärts*, June 26, 1893; Mehring, "Sauve qui peut," p. 163; Mehring, "Zu den preußischen Land-tagswahlen," p. 803; Braun, pp. 513–14.

8. Naumann, *National-sozialer Katechismus*.

9. Naumann, *Mitteleuropa*, pp. 4, 112–13, 147, 174–78.

10. Hitler, *Zweites Buch*, esp. ch. 9, pp. 117–32; Hitler, *Mein Kampf*, esp. ch. 14.

11. Protocol of Reichstag session, March 23, 1933, *Verhandlungen des Reichstags*, vol. 457, pp. 23–45.

5: WAR, DEFEAT, AND JEW HATRED

1. Arendt, Philippson, and Holländer quoted in Blumenfeld, *Erlebte Judenfrage*, pp. 45, 51, 55.
2. Weltsch, p. 40.
3. See Hirschfeld; Goldmann; Nathan, p. 33; Lewin, p. 2.
4. May, p. 9.
5. Wassermann, *Mein Weg*, p. 8.
6. Wolfgang Aly, "Das Leben eines deutschen Professors 1881–(1962). Erinnerungen und Erfahrungen," privately published, pp. 145, 154–55.
7. Stenographic report of the annual meeting of the association in 1917, pp. 14–18, 30–32.
8. See Oppenheimer; York-Steiner, *Die Kunst*, pp. 520–26; Max Warburg to Hugo Stinnes Jr., Jan. 3, 1923, Stiftung Warburg Archive, Max Warburg/Carl Melchior Estate. I owe this last reference to Dorothea Hauser.
9. Naumann, *Mitteleuropa*, pp. 70–71.
10. Walther Rathenau to Wilhelm Schwaner, Aug. 4, 1916, quoted in Jochmann, p. 111.
11. Röpke, *Der Weg des Unheils*, p. 33.
12. Sieferle, pp. 106–31.
13. Lensch, *Drei Jahre Weltrevolution*, pp. 29–30, 87, 211–21. For a critical account of Lensch, see Hayek, *Der Weg zur Knechtschaft*, pp. 117–22.
14. Lensch, *Sozialdemokratie*, p. 177.
15. Meinecke, "Die deutsche November-Revolution," p. 213.
16. Sieburg, p. 18.
17. Goebbels, *Michael*, p. 62.
18. W. Aly, "Leben eines deutschen Professors," pp. 152, 156–57, 171–72.
19. Hindenburg, p. 89.
20. Plessner, *Die verspätete Nation*, pp. 322–33.
21. Jünger, preface, *Der Kampf als inneres Erlebnis*, p. xii.
22. Sforza, pp. 86–91.
23. Keynes, *A Revision of the Treaty*, pp. 3–4.
24. See NSDAP party program (1922).
25. Keynes, *Revision*, pp. 14–18.

26. Keynes, *The Economic Consequences of the Peace*, pp. 225, 235–36, 267–68; Heuss, *Hitlers Weg*, p. 152.

27. Lloyd, p. 105; Sforza, pp. 93–95.

28. Jünger, "Revolution und Idee," *Völkischer Beobachter*, Sept. 23–24, 1923, quoted in Jünger, *Politische Publizistik 1919–1933*, p. 36.

29. Keynes, *Economic Consequences*, pp. 249, 268, 216–17. It is likely that the negotiator Keynes cites was the German Jewish delegate Carl Melchior.

30. Keynes, *Revision*, pp. 179–202.

31. Sforza, pp. 103–16.

32. Geyer, p. 71.

33. Kautsky, *Die Welt am Montag*, Spring 1920, quoted in Fendrich, p. 6; Kautsky, *Rasse und Judentum*, pp. 5–10.

34. Geyer, pp. 78, 88–89.

35. Wassermann, *Mein Weg*, pp. 38–39, 118; on Löwenthal, see Hammerstein, 291n.

36. Hitler, "Warum sind wir Antisemiten," p. 201.

37. See Bloch, "Hitlers Gewalt."

38. Michel, pp. 29–30, 34.

39. Ibid., 3–4, 29–30, 34.

40. Goebbels, introduction, "Der Nazi-Sozi."

41. Quoted in Heiden, *Geschichte des Nationalsozialismus*, p. 243.

42. Stapel, *Antisemitismus*, p. 5; Hildebrandt, p. 51.

43. See Feder.

44. Quoted in Jäckel and Kuhn, pp. 906–9.

45. Max Warburg to Hugo Stinnes Jr., Jan. 3, 1923.

6: WEAK MASSES, STRONG RACE

1. Riemer, p. 208.

2. Riesser, "Über die Stellung," p. 24.

3. Bamberger, *Deutschtum und Judentum*, p. 18; York-Steiner, *Die Kunst*, p. 412; York-Steiner, "Wie entsteht," p. 395; Adam and Reichmann-Jungmann, p. 35.

4. H. Mann, pp. 83–84.

5. Rosenberg, p. 82; Jarausch, "Universität und Hochschule," pp. 313–45. The 1881 Kyffhäuser speech is quoted in Jarausch, *Deutsche Studenten*, p. 82.

6. Kautsky also located pronounced anti-Semitism among those "who do

intellectual work rather than pursuing the trades of their fathers." See Kautsky, "Das Massaker," p. 304.

7. Bebel, pp. 18–20.

8. Sombart, *Die Zukunft der Juden*, pp. 82–83.

9. Ibid., p. 83; Sombart, *Die Juden und das Wirtschaftsleben*, pp. 284–87, 299; Sombart, *Deutscher Sozialismus*, pp. 144, 192–95.

10. Paulsen, p. 200; Hammerstein, p. 13.

11. Schmoller, pp. 423–34.

12. Quoted in Landmann, pp. 26–27.

13. M. Lenz, pp. 216–24.

14. Max Lenz volunteered for the military in the Franco-Prussian War of 1870–71. His mother, Johanna, torn between maternal concern and the desire for her son to become a hero, hoped that he would get "a nice flesh wound" and return home safely. Her wish was granted. See Frieda Erdmannsdörffer, "Ein Lebensbild von Grössing, Johanna Lenz, geb. Adlich (1827–1908)," Aly Family Archive. (Frieda was Johanna's granddaughter and Max Lenz's niece.)

15. See G. Lenz; Demelius.

16. Anna Erdmannsdörffer to Johanna Lenz, July 12, 1879, and March 16, 1881; Bernhard Erdmannsdörffer to Gustav Lenz, ca. 1886, quoted in F. Erdmannsdörffer. Frieda, Bernhard and Anna Erdmannsdörffer's daughter, was my great-aunt, and I got to know her well. Like her mother, she loved Mendelssohn, Heine, and the songs of Fanny Hensel-Mendelssohn. In 1947 she highlighted the passages in the letters of her parents that were about Jews and wrote a biography of her grandmother in which she clearly described her grandfather's anti-Semitism.

17. Sombart, *Die Zukunft der Juden*, p. 83; Sombart, *Die Juden und das Wirtschaftsleben*, pp. 284–87, 299; York-Steiner, *Die Kunst*, p. 412.

18. Kautsky, *Rasse und Judentum*, p. 60; Fraser, *The Conquering Jew*, p. 35, quoted in Slezkine, p. 76.

19. The person who may be meant is lawyer Jakob Friedrich Behrend, who was the dean of Greifswald University in 1882 and 1883.

20. See C. Müller, *Das Judentum in der deutschen Studentenschaft*.

21. Stapel, *Antisemitismus*, p. 47; Goldstein, *Deutsche Volks-Idee*, pp. 50, 110–11; Stapel, "Aphoristisches zur Judenfrage," pp. 172–73.

22. Quoted in Lichtenstaedter, *Antisemitica*, p. 115; *Verhandlungen des Bayerischen Landtags, Sitzungsperiode 1924–1928*, vol. 1: *Stenographische Berichte zu den öffentlichen Sitzungen 1–34*, 18th sess., Aug. 1, 1924, Rutz speech, pp. 205–14, esp. p. 212.

23. *Weltbühne*, March 3, 1925, p. 333.

24. Schottlaender, p. 39.

25. F. Bernstein, pp. 114, 144; T. Mann, *Der Zauberberg*, pp. 961–62.

26. Voegelin, *Rasse und Staat*, pp. 186–87. See also Faas and Mund; this essay quotes reactions to Max Liebermann's painting *The Twelve-Year-Old Jesus in the Temple* during the Second International Art Exhibit at Munich's Glaspalast Museum in 1879. Liebermann caused a furor by depicting Jesus, and not just the Pharisees, as Jews.

27. *Abwehr-ABC*, pp. 88–89.

28. Heuss, *Hitlers Weg*, pp. 42–43; de Man, pp. 15–17, 22; Voegelin, *Staat und Rasse*, p. 182.

29. T. Mann, "Zum Problem des Antisemitismus," p. 28; T. Mann, *Deutschland und die Deutschen*, pp. 9, 11.

30. Heuss, *Hitlers Weg*, pp. 42–43; de Man, pp. 15–17, 22; Hitler, *Mein Kampf*, pp. 329–32, 338.

31. Hitler, *Zweites Buch*, pp. 64, 129, 221.

32. Orders (Secret Commando) to 22nd Infantry Division on June 20, 1941, Bundesarchiv, RH 26-22/67 (the document is reproduced in *VEJ*, vol. 7); Hitler, *Monologe*, p. 293, entry for Feb. 22, 1942, evening. Heinrich Himmler was also present.

33. Compared with others deemed to have betrayed Stalin's Great Cause, Zamyatin got off lightly. He died in Parisian exile in 1937.

34. Bettauer, pp. 3–50.

35. Lichtenstaedter, preface, *Jüdische Fragen*, p. 7.

36. Lichtenstaedter, *Zionismus und andere Zukunftsmöglichkeiten*, p. 59.

37. Lichtenstaedter, *Das neue Weltreich*, vol. 1, pp. 22–23.

38. Lichtenstaedter, *Das neue Weltreich*, vol. 2, pp. 37–41, 59–60, 65–69, 105–10.

39. Lichtenstaedter, *Antisemitica*, p. 12.

40. See Conze.

41. Lichtenstaedter, *Antisemitica*, pp. 14–85.

42. See Erben.

43. Friedenthal, p. 125.

44. "Beischreibung zum Geburtsvermerk Lichtenstaedters im Geburtsregister der Israelitischen Kultusgemeinde Baiersdorf," p. 65, Staatsarchiv Nürnberg, Fremde Archivalien, no. 80 (Baiersdorf). Thanks to Horst Gemeinhardt for this reference.

45. In 1910 Eugen Fischer would bemoan how belatedly Germany had gotten involved in racial research. Fischer, *Sozialanthropologie*, p. 3.

46. Günther, p. 14.

47. Goldstein, *Rasse und Politik*, p. 63.

48. Giesen, p. 209; Kiefer, pp. 26–28.

49. Quoted in Sombart, *Die Juden und das Wirtschaftsleben*, p. 386.

50. Wilhelm II, p. 154; Kaltenbrunner, pp. 120–21.

51. Fischer, *Die Rehobother Bastards*, pp. 164–67, 296–99, 302; Fischer, *Rasse und Rassenentstehung*, p. 121.

52. Fischer, *Sozialanthropologie*, p. 20.

53. Wassermann, open letter to Richard Drews, publisher of the monthly magazine *Kulturelle Erneuerung* ("Cultural Renewal"), quoted in Wassermann, *Lebensdienst*, pp. 155–59.

54. Baur, Fischer, and Lenz, vol. 1, pp. 138, 162–63, 215, 290, 537–39, 547, 556–59.

55. See Gilsenbach.

56. Fischer, *Der völkische Staat*, pp. 10, 19.

57. Pommerin, pp. 78–79.

58. Hitler, *Zweites Buch*, p. 62; see also pp. 125, 129; Hitler, *Mein Kampf*, pp. 441–51.

59. Fischer, "Erbe."

60. Zollschan, p. 15.

61. Quoted in Herbert, p. 49.

62. Adam and Reichmann-Jungmann, pp. 3–24, 41. The authors conducted their discussion in spring 1929. It was published by the Central Association of German Citizens of the Jewish Faith in late 1931, with Margarete Adam's afterword, "Why Did I Vote National Socialist?" and an extremely short concluding remark by Eva Reichmann-Jungmann.

63. Wehler, p. 256.

64. Grantzow, p. 29.

65. Lederer, "Die Umschichtung des Proletariats"; Kracauer, p. 85; Speier, pp. 44–51, 161n7.

66. Staatsarchiv München, Spruchkammern, Carton 1668, XII/22/48 (Schneider, Friedrich).

67. The biographical sketches are based on Hüttenberger, *Die Gauleiter*; Höffkes, *Hitlers politische Generale*; and Lilla, *Die Stellvertretenden Gauleiter der NSDAP*.

68. *Hinrich Lose* (1896–1964): Protestant, son of a small farmer. Trade school, salesman. 1925–45: gauleiter of Schleswig-Holstein.

Alfred Meyer (1891–1945): Protestant, son of a government counsel. University-track academy, officer, studied economics, PhD, mine administrator. 1930–45: gauleiter of North Westphalia.

Wilhelm Murr (1888–1945): Protestant, son of a master metalworker. Secondary school, sales training, full-time employee, staff sergeant. 1928–45: gauleiter of Württemberg-Hohenzollern.

Martin Mutschmann (1879–1947): Protestant, son of a metalworker. Trade school, sales training, self-employed businessman. 1925–45: gauleiter of Saxony.

Carl Röver (1889–1942): Protestant, son of a salesman. Middle school, sales training, self-employed manufacturer. 1928–42: gauleiter of Weser-Ems.

Bernhard Rust (1883–1945): Catholic, son of a carpenter. University-track academy, studied philology, academy teacher. 1925–40: gauleiter of North Hannover.

Fritz Sauckel (1894–1946): Protestant, son of a postal assistant. Left university-track academy in grade 4, naval training, sailor. 1922–23: engineering academy. 1927–45: gauleiter of Thuringia.

Franz Schwede (1888–1960): Protestant, son of a forester. Secondary school, metalworker, naval maintenance mechanic, first mate for machinery, naval service aboard the *Kaiser Wilhelm II*. 1918: machinist deck officer, chief technical operating officer. 1934–45: gauleiter of Pomerania.

Gustav Simon (1900–1945): Catholic, son of a railway manager. Secondary education, teacher training, studied economics, instructor of commerce, student teacher. 1931–45: gauleiter of Koblenz-Trier.

Jakob Sprenger (1884–1945): Protestant, son of a farmer. Secondary education, telegraph school, superior postal inspector. 1927–45: gauleiter of Hessen–South Nassau.

Julius Streicher (1885–1946): Catholic, son of a teacher. Secondary education, teacher training, substitute teacher, teacher. 1930–40: gauleiter of Main-Franconia.

Emil Stürtz (1887–1945): Protestant, son of a rural laborer. Secondary education, sailor, soldier, wartime invalid, truck driver. 1936–45: gauleiter of Brandenburg.

Otto Telschow (1876–1945): Protestant, son of a court servant. Military school, low-level officer (cavalry). 1902–24: police official. 1925–45: gauleiter of Lüneburg-Stade.

Josef Terboven (1882–1945): Catholic, son of a farmer. Secondary school, aborted university course, bank apprenticeship. 1928–45: gauleiter of Essen.

Fritz Wächtler (1891–1945): Protestant, son of a watchmaker. Secondary education, teacher training, teacher. 1935–45: gauleiter of Bavarian Ostmark.

Adolf Wagner (1890–1944): Catholic, son of a miner. Secondary education, studied math and mining. 1919–20: administrative leader in Bavarian mining societies. 1930–42: gauleiter of Munich–Upper Bavaria.

Josef Wagner (1898–1945): Catholic, sixth child of a miner. Secondary education, teacher training, civil servant in finance. 1928–41: gauleiter of Westphalia; 1935–41 also gauleiter of Silesia.

Robert Wagner (1895–1946): Protestant, son of a farmer. Secondary education, teacher training, career military officer. 1925–45: gauleiter of Baden.

Karl Wahl (1892–1981): Protestant, the last of thirteen children of a train driver. Secondary education, metalworker, supplementary trade education, military nurse, noncommissioned officer, legal secretary. 1928–45: gauleiter of Swabia.

Karl Weinrich (1887–1973): Protestant, son of a shoe manufacturer. Secondary education, miner school, mining apprentice, military supply expert. 1928–44: gauleiter of Hessen–North Nassau.

69. Hitler, *Mein Kampf*, pp. 2–5.
70. See Merkl, pp. 62–76. A study by psychologist Bruno Bettelheim and sociologist Morris Janowitz demonstrated that anti-Semitism was particularly prevalent among people who either feared for their social status or hoped for upward social mobility. Bettelheim and Janowitz concluded that, in terms of how prejudiced individuals were, their social and economic status was less significant than the degree and extent of their social mobility. See Bettelheim and Janowitz, p. 165.
71. Neumann, pp. 34–35; Falter, "Die parteistatistische Erhebung der NSDAP 1939," p. 186.

72. On the rapid change in the social backgrounds of German university students between 1919 and 1932, see Jarausch, *Deutsche Studenten*, pp. 134–37.

73. Quotations and statistic taken from Langewiesche and Tenorth, pp. 155–257.

74. Heiden, *Adolf Hitler*, vol. 1, pp. 75–76.

75. Grüttner, pp. 54, 56.

76. Ammerlahn's speech to a student demonstration quoted in Oehme and Caro, pp. 29–30; Goebbels's speech at the leadership conference of National Socialist German Students' Association (ca. 1930), Bundesarchiv, NS 38/II/21, sheets 224–226; Goebbels, "Student und Arbeiter" (ca. 1930), ibid., sheets 18–24.

77. *Die Bewegung (Kampfblatt des Nationalsozialistischen Deutschen Studentenbundes)*, Jan. 27, Feb. 10, and Feb. 17, 1931.

78. See Lessing, "Hindenburg"; Lessing, "*Wir machen nicht mit*," pp. 67–68.

79. Hitler, *Reden, Schriften und Anordnungen*, vol. 3, part 3 (Aug. 3, 1930), p. 294.

80. Döring, pp. 407, 416. On the similar results achieved by the NSDAP in the Prussian election of 1932, see Möller, pp. 298–305.

81. Falter, *Hitlers Wähler*, p. 146.

82. Unruh, p. 43.

83. Hitler, *Mein Kampf*, pp. 433, 439, 447.

7: THE NATIONAL SOCIALIST PEOPLE'S PARTY

1. Quoted in Remmele, p. 19.

2. See Hitler's speech at the Nazi meeting of Dec. 16, 1925, in Stuttgart's Liederhalle, quoted in Hitler, *Reden, Schriften, Anordnungen*, vol. 1, pp. 239–62; see also Hitler, *Mein Kampf*, p. 451; Goebbels, *Michael*, pp. 64, 101–2, 122–23.

3. Goebbels, *Michael*, p. 42.

4. Schieder, p. 479.

5. Schotthöfer, p. 164; Mussolini, pp. 126–27; de Man, pp. 24–26; Michels, pp. 251–309.

6. Mussolini, p. 123.

7. Klemperer, p. 410 (May 25, 1938); *Völkischer Beobachter*, Sept. 11, 1939; Goebbels, *Tagebücher*, pp. 171, 229, 247 (March 5, April 6, April 14, 1941).

8. Lederer, *Der Massenstaat*, p. 143.

9. Neumann, pp. 73–86.

10. Röpke, *Der Weg des Unheils*, pp. 46–58, 71–75, 84–85, 112–15.

11. Hitler, *Reden, Schriften und Anordnungen*, vol. 3, part 3, doc. 76 (July 18, 1930), pp. 277–81; doc. 77 (July 24, 1930), p. 289; doc. 79 (July 27, 1930), p. 292; doc. 78 (Aug. 12, 1930), p. 332; doc. 89 (Aug. 16, 1930), p. 339n1; doc. 108 (Sept. 8, 1930), pp. 390–91.

12. August R. to his father, June 13, 1931, Aly Family Archive.

13. See the 1929 organizational statute of the SPD, in "Sozialdemokratischer Parteitag Magdeburg 1929. Protokoll," p. 297. Thanks to the Archive of Social Democracy at the Friedrich Ebert Foundation for alerting me to this source.

14. Oehme and Caro, pp. 90–93.

15. Unruh, pp. 6, 27.

16. Proclamation of the KPD Central Committee, Aug. 24, 1930; Declaration of the KPD Central Committee, Feb. 1932; both quoted in Berthold, pp. 229–38, 254–64.

17. Winkler, pp. 422–24; Möller, pp. 315–23.

18. Falter, *Hitlers Wähler*, pp. 224–26. On full employees, see pp. 232–42.

19. For more details, see the sources in *VEJ*, vol. 1, pp. 30–36 (introduction).

20. Hertha Nathorff, diary entry, April 16, 1933, quoted in *VEJ*, vol. 1, pp. 141–42.

21. Joseph Kardinal Faulhaber, April 8, 1933, quoted in *VEJ*, vol. 1, pp. 135–36.

22. *Kirchliches Jahrbuch*, 1932, p. 484, quoted in H. J. Kraus, *Die evangelische Kirche*, p. 259; Böhm quoted in Jochmann, p. 193.

23. August to the family, Nov. 27, 1930, to his father, Oct. 19, 1938, Aly Family Archive.

24. Hilberg, p. 50.

25. Hitler, *Monologe*, entry for Feb. 22, 1942, p. 293.

26. Goebbels, *Michael*, p. 57. Goebbels uses similar imagery in *Der Nazi-Sozi*, p. 8.

27. Cited in Eckehard, pp. 39, 44.

28. Fischer, "Erbe," pp. 149–51. See also Fischer "Die Fortschritte der menschlichen Erblehre," esp. p. 214.

29. Bettauer, p. 11.

30. This is the final strophe of the poem "Das Frankfurter Ghetto," quoted in Hoffmann and Passier, pp. 34–36.

31. Wawrzinek, pp. 28, 33.

32. *VEJ*, vol. 1, pp. 676–77; Ordinance of Dec. 12, 1938, quoted in *VEJ*, vol. 2, p. 403.

33. Hitler, Reichstag speech of Jan. 30, 1939, quoted in *VEJ*, vol. 2, pp. 678–80.

34. Esser, p. 78.

35. Goebbels, "Der Krieg und die Juden," *Der steile Aufstieg*, p. 270.

36. *Der Prozess gegen die Hauptkriegsverbrecher*, vol. 29, p. 146; Smith and Peterson, *Heinrich Himmler. Geheimreden*, pp. 169, 201–3.

37. *Heimatland: Vaterländisches Wochenblatt (für Bayern)*, Oct. 15, 1923, pp. 8–9.

38. Lichtenstaedter, *Antisemitica*, pp. 108–11 (Lichtenstaedter erroneously refers to 600,000 Austrian Jews. This is probably a printer's error); Tröbst, "Mustapha Kemal Pascha und sein Werk"; Tröbst, *Soldatenblut*.

39. Hitler, *Mein Kampf*, pp. 279–82, 433–48; Hitler, *Zweites Buch*, pp. 56–57.

40. Baur, *Die Bedeutung der natürlichen Zuchtwahl*, pp. 7–8, 10–11.

41. F. Lenz, *Die Rasse als Wertprinzip*, pp. 31, 39; Fischer, "Erbe," p. 150.

42. Aly and Roth, pp. 105–8.

43. Lübbe, p. 307.

44. Aly, "Medizin gegen Unbrauchbare," pp. 14–16.

45. T. Mann, *Deutsche Hörer!*, p. 44.

EPILOGUE: A STORY WITH NO END

1. Zweig, p. 353; York-Steiner, "Wie entsteht," p. 369.

2. York-Steiner, *Die Kunst*, p. 405.

3. Kohn, *Bürger vieler Welten*, p. 60; Ruppin, *Soziologie der Juden*, vol. 2, p. 53.

4. Blumenfeld, "Die zionistische Aufgabe," pp. 353–54; Röpke, *Die deutsche Frage*, p. 39.

5. T. Mann, *Deutschland und die Deutschen*, pp. 22–23.

6. For example, the condom manufacturer Julius Fromm. See Aly and Sontheimer.

7. Lederer, "Zur Soziologie des Weltkrieges," pp. 120–26.

8. Meinecke, *Die deutsche Katastrophe*, pp. 106–7.

9. Röpke, *Die deutsche Frage*, p. 12.

10. Ibid., p. 28.

11. Epstein, *Neid*, p. 76; Riesser, "Über die Stellung," pp. 22–23.

12. Kant, p. 596.

13. Hughes, pp. 4–7.

14. Meinecke, *Die Deutsche Katastrophe*, pp. 339, 356.

15. Ruppin, *Soziologie der Juden*, vol. 2, pp. 54–56; Marcus, p. 144.

16. Ruppin, *Soziologie der Juden*, vol. 2, pp. 53–54; Zweig, p. 221.

17. Voegelin, "Die Rassenidee in der Geistesgeschichte," p. 160.

18. Ruppin, *Soziologie der Juden*, vol. 1, p. 54.

BIBLIOGRAPHY

Abwehr-ABC. Published by the Verein zur Abwehr des Antisemitismus. Berlin, 1920.

Adam, Margarete, and Eva Reichmann-Jungmann. "Eine Aussprache über die Judenfrage" (1929). Afterword by M. Adam. *Warum habe ich (1930) nationalsozialistisch gewählt?* Berlin, 1931.

Aly, Götz. "Medizin gegen Unbrauchbare." *Aussonderung und Tod. Die klinische Hinrichtung der Unbrauchbaren. Beiträge zur nationalsozialistischen Gesundheits- und Sozialpolitik.* Vol. 1. Berlin, 1985. 9–74.

———. "Wohltaten der europäischen Gesittung. Ein rheinischer Fürst im albanesischen Dornengarten." *Rasse und Klasse. Nachforschungen zum deutschen Wesen.* Frankfurt am Main, 2003. 16–27.

———. *Im Tunnel. Das kurze Leben der Marion Samuel 1931–1943.* Frankfurt am Main, 2004.

———. *Hitlers Volksstaat. Raub, Rassenkrieg und nationaler Sozialismus.* Frankfurt am Main, 2005.

Aly, Götz, and Karl Heinz Roth. *Die restlose Erfassung. Volkszählen, Identifizieren, Aussondern im Nationalsozialismus.* Berlin, 1984.

Aly, Götz, and Michael Sontheimer. *Fromms. Wie der jüdische Kondom-fabrikant Julius F. unter die deutschen Räuber fiel.* Frankfurt am Main, 2007.

Arendt, Hannah. *Besuch in Deutschland.* Foreword by Henryk M. Broder. Portrait by Ingeborg Nordmann. Berlin, 1993.

Aretin, Johann Christoph Freiherr von. *Über die Gegner der großen Pläne Napoleon's besonders in Teutschland und Österreich.* 2nd exp. ed., Strasbourg, 1809.

Arndt, Ernst Moritz. *Ein Blick aus der Zeit auf die Zeit.* Frankfurt am Main, 1814.

———. *Entwurf einer teutschen Gesellschaft.* Frankfurt am Main, 1814.

———. *Noch ein Wort über die Franzosen und über uns.* Leipzig, 1814.

———. *Versuch in vergleichender Völkergeschichte.* Leipzig, 1843.

———. "Auch ein Wort über die auf dem preußischen Reichstage diesen Sommer besprochene und bestrittene Judenfrage." *Augsburger Allgemeine Zeitung,* Aug. 19–20, 1847, pp. 1844–46, 1852–53.

———. *Reden und Glossen.* Leipzig, 1848.

———. *Deutsche Volkwerdung. Sein politisches Vermächtnis an die deutsche Gegenwart. Kernstellen aus seinen Schriften und Briefen.* Ed. C. Petersen and P. H. Ruth. Breslau, 1934.

Arnim, Ludwig Achim von. *Werke und Briefwechsel. Historisch-kritische Ausgabe.* Vol. 11: *Texte der deutschen Tischgesellschaft.* Ed. Stefan Nienhaus. Tübingen, 2008.

———. *Die Majoratsherren.* 1820. Munich, 1920.

Ascher, Saul. *Die Germanomanie. Skizze zu einem Zeitgemälde.* Berlin, 1815.

Auerbach, Berthold. *Das Judenthum und die neueste Literatur, Kritischer Versuch.* Stuttgart, 1836.

Baas, Josef. "Die Juden bei Wilhelm Raabe," *Monatsschrift für Geschichte und Wissenschaft des Judentums* 54 (1910): 641–88.

Bahr, Hermann. *Der Antisemitismus. Ein internationales Interview.* Berlin, 1894.

Bakunin, Michael. *Gesammelte Werke.* 3 vols. Berlin, 1921–24; rpt. 1975.

Bamberger, Ludwig. "Deutschtum und Judentum." *Gesammelte Schriften.* Vol. 5: *Politische Schriften von 1879–1892.* Berlin, 1897. 3–37.

———. "Die Sezession." *Gesammelte Schriften.* Vol. 5: *Politische Schriften von 1879–1892.* Berlin, 1897. 38–134.

———. *Erinnerungen.* Ed. Paul Nathan. Berlin, 1899.

Barth, Hans Paul. "Gesellschaftliche Voraussetzungen des Antisemitismus." *Entscheidungsjahr 1932. Zur Judenfrage in der Endphase der Weimarer Republik.* Werner E. Mosse. Tübingen, 1966. 135–55.

Baur, Erwin. *Die Bedeutung der natürlichen Zuchtwahl bei Tieren und Pflanzen.* Berlin 1936.

Baur, Erwin, Eugen Fischer, and Fritz Lenz. *Menschliche Erblichkeitslehre und Rassenhygiene.* Vol. 1: *Menschliche Erblichkeitslehre,* Munich, 1927. Vol. 2: *Menschliche Auslese und Rassenhygiene (Eugenik),* Munich, 1923.

Bebel, August. *Sozialdemokratie und Antisemitismus. Rede des Reichstagsabgeordneten Bebel auf dem IV. Parteitag der Sozialdemokratischen Partei zu Köln a.Rh.* Berlin, 1894.

Benz, Wolfgang. *Was ist Antisemitismus?* Munich, 2004.

Bernstein, Eduard, ed. *Die Geschichte der Berliner Arbeiter-Bewegung. Ein Kapitel zur Geschichte der deutschen Sozialdemokratie.* Vol. 2: *Die Geschichte der Sozialistengesetze in Berlin.* Berlin, 1907.

Bernstein, Fritz. *Der Antisemitismus als Gruppenerscheinung. Versuch einer Soziologie des Judenhasses.* Berlin, 1926.

Berthold, Lothar. *Das Programm der KPD zur nationalen und sozialen Befreiung des deutschen Volkes vom August 1930. Die Grundlage der Politik der KPD zur Herstellung der Aktionseinheit und zur Gewinnung der Volksmassen für die Lösung der Lebensfragen der deutschen Nation.* Berlin, 1956.

Bettauer, Hugo. *Die Stadt ohne Juden. Ein Roman von übermorgen.* Vienna, 1922.

Bettelheim, Bruno, and Morris Janowitz. *Social Change and Prejudice: Including Dynamics of Prejudice.* 1950. London, 1964.

Bisky, Jens. *Kleist. Eine Biographie.* Berlin, 2007.

Bloch, Ernst. "Hitlers Gewalt." *Das Tage-Buch,* April 12, 1924, 474–77.

Blumenfeld, Kurt. *Der Zionismus. Eine Frage deutscher Orientpolitik (Sonderdruck aus den Preußischen Jahrbüchern).* Berlin, 1915.

———. "Die zionistische Aufgabe im heutigen Deutschland. Referat auf dem Delegiertentag der Zionistischen Vereinigung für Deutschland in Frankfurt a.M., gehalten am 1 September 1932." *Jüdische Rundschau,* Sept. 16, 1932, 353–54.

———. *Erlebte Judenfrage. Ein Vierteljahrhundert deutscher Zionismus.* Stuttgart, 1962.

Boeckel, Otto. *Die Verjudung der höheren Schulen in Oesterreich und Deutschland.* N.P., 1886.

———. *Nochmals: "Die Juden—Könige unserer Zeit." Eine neue Ansprache an das deutsche Volk.* Berlin, 1901.

Boehlich, Walter, ed. *Der Berliner Antisemitismusstreit.* Frankfurt am Main, 1965.

Börne, Ludwig. "Für die Juden." *Die Zeitschwingen,* Aug. 28, 1819, 280.

———. *Über den Antisemitismus. Ein Mahnruf aus vergangenen Tagen.* 1821. Vienna, 1885.

———. "Eine Kleinigkeit." *Börnes Werke.* 1821. Vol. 3. Berlin, 1911. 162–65.

———. *Briefe aus Paris. Sämtliche Schriften.* 1832. Rev. and ed. Inge and Peter Rippmann. Vol. 3. Düsseldorf, 1964.

Bornemann, Elke. *Der Frieden von Bukarest 1918.* Frankfurt am Main, 1978.

Botz, Gerhard. *Nationalsozialismus in Wien. Machtübernahme, Herrschaftssicherung, Radikalisierung 1938–39.* Rev. and exp. ed. Vienna, 2008.

Braun, Heinrich. "Zur Lage der deutschen Sozialdemokratie." *Archiv für soziale Gesetzgebung und Statistik* 6 (1893): 506–20.

Brumlik, Micha. *Deutscher Geist und Judenhass. Das Verhältnis des philosophischen Idealismus zum Judentum.* Munich, 2000.

Bürger, Curt, ed. *Antisemiten-Spiegel. Die Antisemiten im Lichte des Christenthums, des Rechtes und der Wissenschaft.* Vol. 3. Rev. and exp. ed. Berlin, 1911.

"Die bürgerlichen Verhältnisse der Juden in Deutschland." *Die Gegenwart. Eine encyklopädische Darstellung der neuesten Zeitgeschichte für alle Stände.* Vol. 1. Leipzig, 1848. 353–407.

Chasanowitsch, Leon, and Leo Motzkin, eds. *Die Judenfrage der Gegenwart. Dokumentensammlung.* Stockholm, 1919.

Christenschutz oder Judenschutz? Erwägungen über Ursprung, Umfang und Berechtigung der Judenfrage vom katholisch-conservativen Standpunkt. Linz, 1893.

Claß, Heinrich [Daniel Frymann]. *Wenn ich der Kaiser wär'. Politische Wahrheiten und Notwendigkeiten.* Leipzig, 1912.

———. *Wider den Strom. Vom Werden und Wachsen der nationalen Opposition im alten Reich.* Leipzig, 1932.

Conze, Werner. *Die weißrussische Frage in Polen. Schulungsbriefe des Bundes Deutscher Osten*, no. 6. Ed. Theodor Oberländer. Berlin, 1938.

Dann, Otto. *Nation und Nationalismus in Deutschland 1770–1990.* Munich, 1996.

de Man, Hendrik. *Sozialismus und National-Fascismus.* Potsdam, 1931.

Demelius, Gustav. "Rezension von Gustav Lenz' Über die geschichtliche Entstehung des Rechts." *Kritische Zeitschrift für die gesamte Rechtswissenschaft* 2 (1855): 164–84.

Denkler, Horst. "Das 'wirkliche' Juda und der Renegat. Moses Freudenstein als Kronzeuge für Wilhelm Raabes Verhältnis zu Juden und Judentum. Neues über Wilhelm Raabe." *Zehn Annäherungsversuche an einen verkannten Schriftsteller.* Tübingen, 1988. 66–80.

Deutsche und Polen in der Revolution von 1848–1849. Dokumente aus deutschen und polnischen Archiven. Ed. Hans Bohms and Marian Wojeciechowski. Boppard am Rhein, 1991.

Deutsche Schulerziehung. Jahrbuch des Deutschen Zentralinstituts für Erziehung und Unterricht. Berlin, 1940.

Dittes, Friedrich. *Geschichte der Erziehung und des Unterrichtes. Für deutsche Volksschullehrer.* 6th ed., Leipzig, 1878; 9th rev. ed., Leipzig, 1890.

Döring, Martin. *"Parlamentarischer Arm der Bewegung." Die Nationalsozialisten im Reichstag der Weimarer Republik.* Düsseldorf, 2001.

Eckehard, Kurt. *Fieberkurve oder Zeitenwende. Nachdenkliches über den Nationalsozialismus.* Munich, 1931.

Eckstein, Adolf. *Beiträge zur Geschichte der Juden in Bayern. Die bayerischen Parlamentarier jüdischen Glaubens.* Bamberg, 1902.

Edler, Carl F. *Stimmen der preußischen Provinzial-Stände des Jahres 1845 über die Emancipation der Juden.* Berlin, 1845.

Epstein, Josef. *Neid. Die böseste Todsünde.* Berlin, 2010.

Erb, Rainer, and Werner Bergmann. *Die Nachtseite der Judenemanzipation. Der Widerstand gegen die Integration der Juden in Deutschland 1780–1860.* Berlin, 1989.

Erben, Peter. *Auf eigenen Spuren. Aus Mährisch-Ostrau durch Theresienstadt, Auschwitz I, Mauthausen, Gusen III über Paris nach Israel. Jüdische Schicksale aus der Tschechoslowakei.* Konstanz, 2001.

Esser, Hermann. *Die jüdische Weltpest. Judendämmerung auf dem Erdball.* Munich, 1939.

Faas, Martin, and Henrike Mund. "Sturm der Entrüstung. Kunstkritik, Presse und öffentliche Diskussion." *Der Jesus-Skandal. Ein Liebermann-Bild im Kreuzfeuer der Kritik.* Ed. Martin Faas. Berlin, 2009.

Falter, Jürgen W. *Hitlers Wähler.* Munich, 1991.

———. "Die parteistatistische Erhebung der NSDAP 1939. Einige Ergebnisse aus dem Gau Groß-Berlin." *Weltbürgerkrieg der Ideologien. Antworten an Ernst Nolte. Festschrift zum 70. Geburtstag.* Ed. Thomas Nipperdey. Frankfurt am Main, 1993. 175–203.

Fasel, Peter. *Revolte und Judenmord. Hartwig von Hundt-Radowsky (1780–1835). Biografie eines Demagogen.* Berlin, 2010.

Feder, Gottfried. *Das Programm der NSDAP und seine weltanschaulichen Grundlagen.* Munich, 1925.

Fendrich, Anton. *Der Judenhaß und der Sozialismus.* Freiburg im Breisgau, 1920.

Fichte, Johann Gottlieb. "Beiträge zur Berichtigung der Urtheile des Publicums über die französische Revolution." *Fichtes Werke.* 1793. Ed. Immanuel Hermann Fichte. Vol. 6: *Zur Politik und Moral.* Berlin, 1971. 39–288.

Fischer, Eugen. *Sozialanthropologie und ihre Bedeutung für den Staat. Vortrag, gehalten in der Naturforschenden Gesellschaft zu Freiburg i.Br. am 8. Juni 1910.* Freiburg im Breisgau, 1910.

———. *Die Rehobother Bastards und das Bastardisierungsproblem beim Menschen.* Jena 1913. Abridged reprint, Graz, 1961.

———. *Rasse und Rassenentstehung beim Menschen.* Berlin, 1927.

———. *Der völkische Staat, biologisch gesehen.* Berlin, 1933.

———. "Die Fortschritte der menschlichen Erblehre als Grundlage eugenischer Bevölkerungspolitik." *Mein Heimatland* 20 (1933): 210–19.

———. "Erbe." *Mein Heimatland* 21 (1934): 149–51.

———. "Das Erbgut der Sippen." *Mein Heimatland* 22 (1935): 357–65.

Frantz, Constantin. *Der Nationalliberalismus und die Judenherrschaft.* Munich, 1874.

Freytag, Gustav. "Jacob Kaufmann." *Gesammelte Werke.* Vol. 16. 2nd ed. Leipzig, 1897. 9–20.

———. *Über den Antisemitismus. Eine Pfingstbetrachtung,* ed. vom Central-Verein deutscher Staatsbürger jüdischen Glaubens. Berlin, 1910. First printed in *Neue Freie Presse,* May 21, 1893.

Friedenthal, Herbert. *Die unsichtbare Kette. Roman eines Juden.* Berlin, 1936.

Friedrich, Eckhardt, and Dagmar Schmieder-Friedrich. *Die Gailinger Juden. Materialien zur Geschichte der jüdischen Gemeinde Gailingen aus ihrer Blütezeit und den Jahren der gewaltsamen Auflösung.* Konstanz, 1981.

Fries, Friedrich Jakob. *Über die Gefährdung des Wohlstandes und Charakters der Deutschen durch die Juden. Eine aus den Heidelberger Jahrbüchern der Litteratur besonders abgedruckte Recension der Schrift des Professors Rühs in Berlin, "Über die Ansprüche der Juden an das deutsche Bürgerrecht. 2., verb. Abdruck."* Heidelberg, 1816.

———. *Von Deutschem Bund und Deutscher Staatsverfassung.* Heidelberg, 1816.

Fritsch, Theodor [F. Roderich-Stoltheim]. *Die Stadt der Zukunft.* Leipzig, 1896.

———. *Die Juden im Handel und das Geheimnis ihres Erfolges.* Steglitz, 1913.

Fröbel, Julius. "Die deutsche Auswanderung und ihre nationale und culturhistorische Bedeutung." *Kleine politische Schriften.* Vol. 1. Stuttgart, 1866. 93–198.

Die gegenwärtig beabsichtigte Umgestaltung der bürgerlichen Verhältnisse der Juden in Preußen. Nach authentischen Quellen beleuchtet. Breslau, 1842.

Geiger, Theodor. *Die soziale Schichtung des deutschen Volkes. Soziographischer Versuch auf statistischer Grundlage.* Stuttgart, 1932.

Gelber, Nathan Michael. *Die Juden und der polnische Aufstand 1863.* Berlin, 1923.

Geyer, Curt. *Der Radikalismus in der deutschen Arbeiterbewegung. Ein soziologischer Versuch.* Jena, 1923.

Giesen, Bernhard. *Kollektive Identität. Die Intellektuellen und ihre Nation.* Frankfurt am Main, 1999.

Gilsenbach, Reimar. "Erwin Baur. Eine deutsche Chronik." *Arbeitsmarkt und Sondererlass. Beiträge zur nationalsozialistischen Gesundheits- und Sozialpolitik.* Vol. 8. Berlin, 1990. 184–97.

Glossy, Karl, ed. *Literarische Geheimberichte aus dem Vormärz.* Vienna, 1912.

Gobineau, Arthur de. *Versuch über die Ungleichheit der Menschenracen.* Stuttgart, 1897.

Goebbels, Joseph. *Wege ins dritte Reich. Briefe und Aufsätze für Zeitgenossen.* Munich, 1927.

———. *Michael. Ein deutsches Schicksal in Tagebuchblättern.* Munich, 1929.

———. *Der Nazi-Sozi. Fragen und Antworten für den Nationalsozialisten.* Munich, 1929.

———. *Der steile Aufstieg. Reden und Aufsätze aus den Jahren 1942–43.* Berlin, 1943.

———. *Die Tagebücher von Joseph Goebbels.* Ed. Elke Fröhlich. Part 1: *Aufzeichnungen 1923–1941.* Vol. 9: *Dezember 1940–Juli 1941.* Munich, 1998.

Goethe, Johann Wolfgang. *Maximen und Reflexionen.* 1832. *Goethes Werke.* Hamburger ed. Vol. 12. 6th ed. Hamburg, 1967. 365–547.

Goldhagen, Daniel Jonah. *Hitler's Willing Executioners: Ordinary Germans and the Holocaust.* New York, 1996.

Goldmann, Nahum. *Der Geist des Militarismus. Der Deutsche Krieg. Politische Flugschriften.* Ed. Ernst Jäckh. Vol. 52. Stuttgart, 1915.

Goldstein, Julius. *Rasse und Politik.* With an introduction by Heinrich Frick. 2nd exp. ed. Berlin, 1921.

———. *Deutsche Volks-Idee und deutsch-völkische Idee. Eine soziologische Erörterung der völkischen Denkart.* Berlin, 1927.

Görtemaker, Manfred. *Deutschland im 19. Jahrhundert. Entwicklungslinien.* Opladen, 1996.

Grab, Walter. *Der deutsche Weg der Judenemanzipation 1789–1938.* Munich, 1993.

———. *Zwei Seiten einer Medaille. Demokratische Revolution und Judenemanzipation.* Cologne, 2000.

Graetz, Heinrich. *Volkstümliche Geschichte der Juden.* 1888. Vol. 6: *Das europäische Judentum der Neuzeit bis zur Revolution von 1848.* Berlin, 1923.

Grantzow, Hans. *700 Jahre Berlin. Im Auftrage der Stadtverwaltung zur 700-Jahr-Feier der Reichshauptstadt.* Berlin, 1937.

Grüttner, Michael. *Studenten im Dritten Reich.* Paderborn, 1995.

Günther, Hans F. K. *Mein Eindruck von Adolf Hitler.* Pähl (Oberbayern), 1969.

Hahn, Hans Henning. "Polnische Freiheit oder deutsche Einheit? Vor hundertfünfzig Jahren führte das Paulskirchen-Parlament seine große Polen-Debatte." *Frankfurter Allgemeine Zeitung*, July 22, 1998.

Hamann, Brigitte. *Hitlers Wien. Lehrjahre eines Diktators*. Munich, 1996.

Hammerstein, Notker. *Antisemitismus und deutsche Universitäten*. Frankfurt am Main, 1995.

Hauptmann, Gerhart. *Der rote Hahn. Tragikomödie in vier Akten*. Berlin, 1901.

Haußherr, Hans. *Erfüllung und Befreiung. Der Kampf um die Durchführung des Tilsiter Friedens 1807–1808*. Hamburg, 1935.

Hayek, Friedrich A. *Der Weg zur Knechtschaft*. Erlenbach bei Zürich, 1945. Originally published as *The Road to Serfdom*. London, 1944.

Hegel, Georg Friedrich Wilhelm. *Grundlinien der Philosophie des Rechts*. Berlin, 1821.

Heiden, Konrad. *Geschichte des Nationalsozialismus. Die Karriere einer Idee*. Berlin, 1932.

———. *Adolf Hitler. Eine Biographie*. Vol. 1: *Das Zeitalter der Verantwortungslosigkeit*. Zürich, 1936. Vol. 2: *Ein Mann gegen Europa*. Zürich, 1937.

Heine, Heinrich. *Französische Zustände*. 1832. *Historisch-kritische Gesamtausgabe der Werke*. Vol. 12, part 1. Hamburg, 1980. 63–226.

———. *Zur Geschichte der Religion und Philosophie in Deutschland*. 1834. *Historisch-kritische Gesamtausgabe der Werke*. Vol. 8, part 1. Hamburg, 1979. 9–120.

———. *Ludwig Börne. Eine Denkschrift*. 1840. *Historisch-kritische Gesamtausgabe der Werke*. Vol. 11. Hamburg, 1978. 9–132.

———. *Ludwig Marcus. Denkworte*. 1844. *Historisch-kritische Gesamtausgabe der Werke*. Vol. 14, part 1. Hamburg, 1978. 265–75.

———. *Briefe. Erste Gesamtausgabe nach den Handschriften*. Vol. 1. Mainz, 1948.

Helfferich, Karl. *Deutschlands Volkswohlstand 1888–1913*. 6th ed. Berlin, 1915.

Herbert, Ulrich. "Generation der Sachlichkeit. Die völkische Studentenbewegung der frühen zwanziger Jahre." *Arbeit, Volkstum, Weltanschauung. Über Fremde und Deutsche im 20. Jahrhundert*. Frankfurt am Main, 1995. 31–58.

Herrmann, Ulrich G. *Datenhandbuch zur deutschen Bildungsgeschichte*. Vol. 2: *Höhere und mittlere Schulen*. Part 2: *Regionale Differenzierung und gesamtstaatliche Systembildung. Preußen und seine Provinzen, Deutsches Reich und seine Staaten 1800–1945*. Göttingen, 2003.

Hertz, Friedrich. *Rasse und Kultur. Eine kritische Untersuchung der Rassentheorien*. 3rd rev. and enl. ed. Leipzig, 1925. Originally published as *Moderne Rassentheorien. Kritische Essays*. Vienna, 1904.

Herzig, Arno. "Brandstifter und Biedermeier." *Die Zeit*, Jan. 20, 2010.

Heuss, Theodor. *Hitlers Weg. Eine historisch-politische Studie über den Nationalsozialismus*. Stuttgart, 1932.

———. "Mut zur Liebe. Rede, gehalten am 7. Dezember 1949 anlässlich einer Feierstunde der Gesellschaft für christlich-jüdische Zusammenarbeit in Wiesbaden." *An und über die Juden. Aus Schriften und Reden 1906–1963*. Ed. Hans Lamm. Düsseldorf, 1964. 121–27.

Hilberg, Raul. *The Destruction of the European Jews*. Chicago, 1961. 3rd ed. New Haven, 2003.

Hildebrandt, Kurt. *Staat und Rasse*. Breslau, 1928.

Hindenburg, Paul von. *Aus meinem Leben*. Leipzig, 1920.

Hirschfeld, Magnus. *Warum hassen uns die Völker? Eine kriegspsychologische Betrachtung*. Bonn, 1915.

Hitler, Adolf. "Warum sind wir Antisemiten? Rede in München am 11.8.1920." *Sämtliche Aufzeichnungen: 1905–1924*. Ed. Eberhard Jäckel and Axel Kuhn. Stuttgart, 1980. 184–204.

———. *Mein Kampf*. 31st ed. Munich, 1934.

———. *Zweites Buch. Ein Dokument aus dem Jahre 1928*. Stuttgart, 1961.

———. *Reden, Schriften und Anordnungen. Februar 1925 bis Januar 1933*. Vol. 1: *Die Wiederbegründung der NSDAP. Februar 1925–Juni 1926*. Ed. with commentary by Clemens Vollnhals. Munich, 1992. Vol. 3, part 1: *Juli 1928–Februar 1929*. Ed. with commentary by Bärbel Dusik. Munich, 1994. Vol. 3, part 3: *Januar 1930–September 1930*. Ed. with commentary by Christian Hartmann. Munich, 1995.

———. *Monologe im Führerhauptquartier 1941–1944. Die Aufzeichnungen Heinrich Heims*. Ed. Werner Jochmann. Hamburg, 1980.

Höffkes, Karl. *Hitlers politische Generale. Die Gauleiter des Dritten Reiches. Ein biographisches Nachschlagewerk.* Tübingen, 1986.

Hoffmann, Christhard, and Bernd Passier, eds. *Die Juden. Vorurteil und Verfolgung im Spiegel literarischer Texte.* Stuttgart, 1986.

Hoffmann von Fallersleben, August Heinrich. *Gesammelte Werke.* Vol. 4: *Zeit-Gedichte.* Berlin, 1891.

Hübinger, Paul Egon. *Thomas Mann, die Universität Bonn und die Zeitgeschichte. Drei Kapitel deutscher Vergangenheit aus de Leben des Dichters 1905–1955.* Munich, 1974.

Hughes, Everett C. "Good People and Dirty Work." *Social Problems* 10 (1962): 3–11.

Humboldt, Wilhelm von, and Caroline von Humboldt. *Briefen.* Vol. 4: *Federn und Schwerter in den Freiheitskriegen.* Berlin, 1910; Vol. 5: *Diplomatische Friedensarbeit 1815–1817.* Berlin, 1912.

Hüttenberger, Peter. *Die Gauleiter. Eine Studie zum Wandel des Machtgefüges in der NSDAP.* Stuttgart, 1969.

Jäckel, Eberhard, and Axel Kuhn, eds. *Hitler. Sämtliche Aufzeichnungen: 1905–1924.* Stuttgart, 1980.

Jarausch, Konrad H. *Deutsche Studenten 1800–1970.* Frankfurt am Main, 1984.

———. "Universität und Hochschule." *Handbuch der deutschen Bildungsgeschichte.* Vol. 4: *1870–1918. Von der Reichsgründung bis zum Ende des Ersten Weltkriegs.* Ed. Christa Berg. Munich, 1991.

Jochmann, Werner. *Gesellschaftskrise und Judenfeindschaft in Deutschland.* Hamburg, 1988.

Jost, Isaak Markus. *Legislative Fragen betreffend die Juden im Preußischen Staate.* Berlin, 1842.

Die Judenfrage. Verhandlungen des Preußischen Abgeordnetenhauses über die Interpellation des Abgeordneten Dr. Hänel am 20. und 22. November 1880. Separatdruck der Amtlichen Stenographischen Berichte des Hauses der Abgeordneten. Berlin, 1880.

Die Judenfrage im preußischen Abgeordnetenhause. Wörtlicher Abdruck der stenographischen Berichte vom 20. und 22. November 1880. Breslau, 1880.

Jünger, Ernst. *Der Kampf als inneres Erlebnis.* Berlin, 1926.

————. *Politische Publizistik 1919–1933*. Stuttgart, 2001.

Kaltenbrunner, Gerd-Klaus. "Wahnfried und die 'Grundlagen': Houston Stewart Chamberlain." *Propheten des Nationalsozialismus*. Ed. Karl Schwedhelm. Munich, 1969. 105–23.

Kampe, Norbert. *Studenten und "Judenfrage" im Deutschen Kaiserreich. Die Entstehung einer akademischen Trägerschicht des Antisemitismus*. Göttingen, 1988.

Kant, Immanuel. *Metaphysik der Sitten in zwey Theilen. Metaphysische Anfangsgründe der Tugendlehre*. 1797. *Werke in zwölf Bänden*. Vol. 8: *Schriften zur Ethik und Religionsphilosophie 2*. Wiesbaden, 1956. 501–634.

Kaplun-Kogan, Wladimir Wolf. *Die jüdischen Wanderbewegungen in der neuesten Zeit*. Bonn, 1919.

Kautsky, Karl. "Das Massaker von Kischeneff und die Judenfrage." *Die Neue Zeit* 21 (1902–3): 303–9.

————. *Rasse und Judentum*. 1914. 2nd rev. ed. Stuttgart, 1921.

Keynes, John Maynard. *The Economic Consequences of the Peace*. New York, 1920.

————. *A Revision of the Treaty: Being a Sequel to "The Economic Consequences of the Peace."* New York, 1922.

Kiefer, Annegret. *Das Problem einer "jüdischen Rasse." Eine Diskussion zwischen Wissenschaft und Ideologie (1870–1930)*. Frankfurt am Main, 1991.

Klemperer, Victor. *Ich will Zeugnis ablegen bis zum letzten. Tagebücher*. Vol. 1: *1933–1941*. Berlin, 1995.

Kohn, Hans. *Das zwanzigste Jahrhundert. Eine Zwischenbilanz des Westens*. Zürich, 1950.

————. *Bürger vieler Welten. Ein Leben im Zeitalter der Weltrevolution*. Frauenfeld, 1965.

"Kommunismus und Judenfrage." *Der Jud ist schuld . . . ? Diskussionsbuch über die Judenfrage*. Ed. Hermann Bahr et al. Basel, 1932. 272–86.

Kracauer, Siegfried. *Die Angestellten*. Allensbach, 1959. Originally published as *Die Angestellten. Aus dem neuesten Deutschland*. Frankfurt am Main, 1930.

Kraus, Hans-Joachim. "Die evangelische Kirche." *Entscheidungsjahr 1932. Zur Judenfrage in der Endphase der Weimarer Republik*. Ed. Werner E. Mosse. Tübingen, 1966. 249–70.

Kraus, Karl. "Warum vadient der Jude schneller und mehr Jeld als der Christ." *Die Fackel*, 668–75 (1924): 149–52.

———. *Die Dritte Walpurgisnacht*. 1933. Munich, 1967.

Lackmann, Thomas. *Das Glück der Mendelssohns. Geschichte einer deutschen Familie*. Berlin, 2005.

Landau, Wolf. *Die Petition des Vorstandes der israelitischen Gemeinde zu Dresden und ihr Schicksal in der II. Kammer*. Dresden, 1843.

Landmann, Michael. "Bausteine zur Biographie." *Buch des Dankes an Georg Simmel. Briefe, Erinnerungen, Bibliographie. Zu seinem 100. Geburtstag am 1. März 1958*. Ed. Kurt Gassen and Michael Landmann. Berlin, 1958.

Langewiesche, Dieter, and Heinz-Elmar Tenorth, eds. *Handbuch der deutschen Bildungsgeschichte*. Vol. 5: *1918–1945. Die Weimarer Republik und die nationalsozialistische Diktatur*. Munich, 1989.

Lederer, Emil. "Zur Soziologie des Weltkrieges." 1915. *Kapitalismus, Klassenstruktur und Probleme der Demokratie in Deutschland 1910–1940*. Ed. Jürgen Kocka. Göttingen, 1979. 119–45.

———. "Die Umschichtung des Proletariats." 1929. *Kapitalismus, Klassenstruktur und Probleme der Demokratie in Deutschland 1910–1940*. Ed. Jürgen Kocka. Göttingen, 1979. 172–85.

———. *Der Massenstaat. Gefahren der klassenlosen Gesellschaft*. Ed. and introd. Claus-Dieter Krohn. Graz, 1995. Originally published as *State of the Masses: The Threat of the Classless Society*. New York, 1940.

Lensch, Paul. *Die Sozialdemokratie. Ihr Ende und ihr Glück*. Leipzig, 1916.

———. *Drei Jahre Weltrevolution*. Berlin, 1917.

Lenz, Fritz. *Die Rasse als Wertprinzip. Zur Erneuerung der Ethik*. Munich, 1933. Originally published as *Zur Erneuerung der Ethik*. Munich, 1917.

Lenz, Gustav. *Über die geschichtliche Entstehung des Rechts. Eine Kritik an der historischen Schule*. Greifswald, 1854.

Lenz, Max. *Geschichte der Königlichen Friedrich-Wilhelms-Universität zu Berlin*. Vol. 2, part 1: *Ministerium Altenstein*. Halle an der Saale, 1910.

Leonhardt, Ludwig. *Heirat und Rassenpflege. Ein Berater für Eheanwärter*. Munich, 1934.

Lessing, Theodor. "Hindenburg." *Prager Tagblatt*, April 24, 1925.

———. *Ausgewählte Schriften*. Ed. Jörg Wollenberg. Vol. 2: *"Wir machen nicht mit!" Schriften gegen den Nationalismus und zur Judenfrage*. Bremen, 1997.

Lestschinsky, Jakob. *Das jüdische Volk im neuen Europa. Die wirtschaftliche Lage der Juden in Ost- und Zentraleuropa seit dem Weltkrieg*. Prague, 1934.

———. *Bilan de l'extermination*. Ed. Congrès Juif Mondial. Brussels, Paris, Geneva, 1946.

———. "Jewish Migrations, 1840–1956." *The Jews: Their History, Culture, and Religion*. Ed. Louis Finkelstein. Vol. 2. New York, 1960. 1536–96.

Leuschen-Seppel, Rosemarie. *Sozialdemokratie und Antisemitismus im Kaiserreich. Die Auseinandersetzung der Partei mit den konservativen und völkischen Strömungen des Antisemitismus 1871–1914*. Bonn, 1978.

Levy, J. *Fichte und die Juden*. Berlin, 1924.

Lewin, Reinhold. *Was verlor die deutsche Judenheit durch den Frieden von Versailles?* Berlin, ca. 1920.

Lichtenstaedter, Siegfried. *Jüdische Sorgen, jüdische Irrungen, jüdische Zukunft. Eindringliche Worte an meine Religions-Genossen zur Besinnung*. Winnenden bei Stuttgart, 1937.

———. *Zionismus und andere Zukunftsmöglichkeiten. Herausforderung zu einer Diskussion*. Leipzig, 1937.

Lichtenstaedter, Siegfried [Mehemed Emin Efendi]. *Das neue Weltreich. Ein Beitrag zur Geschichte des 20. Jahrhunderts. Psychologische und politische Phantasien*. Vol. 1: *Vom chinesischen Kriege bis zur Eroberung Konstantinopels*. Munich, 1901. Vol. 2: *Von der Eroberung Konstantinopels bis zum Ende Österreich-Ungarns*. Leipzig, 1903.

———. *Antisemitica. Heiteres und Ernstes, Wahres und Nüchternes*. Leipzig, 1926.

Lichtenstaedter, Siegfried [Ne'man]. "Die große Täuschung." *Völkerpsychologischer Beleuchtung. Offenes Schreiben an Herrn Geheimrat Friedrich Delitzsch*. Leipzig, 1922.

———. *Jüdische Politik. Betrachtungen, Mahnworte, Scheltworte, Trostworte*. Leipzig, 1933.

————. *Jüdische Fragen (Judentum du Judenheit, Lehre und Leben)*. Leipzig, 1935.

Liebeschütz, Hans. *Das Judentum im deutschen Geschichtsbild von Hegel bis Max Weber*. Tübingen, 1967.

Liebknecht, Wilhelm. *Rede über den Kölner Parteitag mit besonderer Berücksichtigung der Gewerkschaftsbewegung*. Bielefeld, 1893.

Lilla, Joachim. *Die Stellvertretenden Gauleiter der NSDAP im "Dritten Reich."* Bremerhaven, 2003.

List, Friedrich. "System der Gemeindewirtschaft." 1817. *Schriften, Reden, Briefe*. Vol. 1: *Der Kampf um die politische und ökonomische Reform 1815–1825*. Part 1: *Staatspolitische Schriften der Frühzeit*. Aalen, 1971. 149–204.

————. "Kommentar zu Staatskunde und Staatspraxis." 1818. *Schriften, Reden, Briefe*. Vol. 1: *Der Kampf um die politische und ökonomische Reform 1815–1825*. Part 2: *Handelspolitische Schriften der Frühzeit und Dokumente zum Prozess*. Aalen, 1971. 823–965.

Lloyd, Gordon, ed. *The Two Faces of Liberalism: How the Hoover-Roosevelt Debate Shapes the 21st Century*. Salem, MA: M&M Scrivener Press, 2006.

Loewenthal, Max J., ed. *Das jüdische Bekenntnis als Hinderungsgrund bei der Beförderung zum preußischen Reserveoffizier. Im Auftrage des Verbandes der Deutschen Juden*. Berlin, 1911.

Lösch, Niels C. *Rasse als Konstrukt. Leben und Werk Eugen Fischers*. Frankfurt am Main, 1997.

Lübbe, Hermann. "Terror. Über die ideologische Rationalität des Völkermords." *Weltbürgerkrieg der Ideologien. Antworten an Ernst Nolte. Festschrift zum 70. Geburtstag*. Ed. Thomas Nipperdey. Berlin, 1993. 304–11.

Ludwig, Emil. See Mussolini.

Mann, Heinrich. *Der Untertan*. 1914. Berlin, 1950.

Mann, Thomas. Untitled. *Die Lösung der Judenfrage. Eine Rundfrage*. Ed. Julius Moses. Berlin, 1907. 242–46.

————. *Der Zauberberg*. 1924. Frankfurt am Main, 1981.

————. *Zum Problem des Antisemitismus*. 1937. *Sieben Manifeste zur jüdischen Frage*. Ed. Walter A. Berendsohn. Darmstadt, 1966. 27–42.

————. *Deutsche Hörer! Fünfundfünfzig Radiosendungen nach Deutschland*. Oct. 1940–May 10, 1945. Leipzig, 1975.

————. *Deutschland und die Deutschen*. Stockholm, 1947.

Marcus, Alfred. *Die wirtschaftliche Krise der deutschen Juden. Eine soziologische Untersuchung*. Berlin, 1931.

Marr, Wilhelm. *Der Sieg des Judenthums über das Germanenthum. Vom confessionellen Standpunkt aus betrachtet*. Bern, 1879.

————. *Der Judenkrieg, seine Fehler und wie er zu organisieren ist. Antisemitische Hefte*, no. 1. Chemnitz, 1880.

Masaryk, Thomas G. *Zur russischen Geschichte und Religionsphilosophie. Soziologische Skizzen*. Jena, 1913.

Massing, Paul W. *Vorgeschichte des politischen Antisemitismus*. Frankfurt am Main, 1959.

May, Raphael Ernst. *Konfessionelle Militärstatistik*. Tübingen, 1919.

Mehring, Franz. *Herr Hofprediger Stöcker, der Socialpolitiker. Eine Streitschrift*. Bremen, 1882.

————. "Anti- und Philosemitisches." *Die Neue Zeit* 9 (1890–91): 585–88.

————. "Kapitalistische Agonie." *Die Neue Zeit* 10 (1891–92): 545–48.

————. "Im Wechsel der Zeiten." *Die Neue Zeit* 11 (1892–93): 1–4.

————. "Sauve qui peut." *Die Neue Zeit* 11 (1892–93): 161–64.

————. "Zu den preußischen Landtagswahlen." *Die Neue Zeit* 11 (1892–93): 801–04.

————. "Drillinge." *Die Neue Zeit* 12 (1893–94): 577–82.

————. "Einleitung." *Gesammelte Schriften von Karl Marx und Friedrich Engels 1841 bis 1850*. Ed. Franz Mehring. Vol. 1: *Von März 1841 bis März 1844*. Stuttgart, 1902. 331–59.

Meinecke, Friedrich. *Das Zeitalter der deutschen Erhebung (1795–1815)*. Bielefeld, 1906.

————. "Die deutsche November-Revolution. Ursachen und Tatsachen." *Staat und Persönlichkeit*. Berlin, 1933. 206–38.

————. *Die deutsche Katastrophe. Betrachtungen und Erinnerungen*. 1946. Wiesbaden, 1955.

Merkl, Peter H. *Political Violence under the Swastika*. Princeton, 1975.

Metternich, Klemens Wenzel Lothar von. "Die Deutsche Frage. Genesis, Verlauf und gegenwärtiger Stand derselben. Denkschrift an Erzherzog Johann, Reichsverweser, London, August 1848." *Aus Metternich's nachgelassenen Papieren*. Ed. Richard von Metternich-Winneburg. Vol. 8. Vienna, 1884. 443–53.

Michel, Wilhelm. *Verrat am Deutschtum. Eine Streitschrift zur Juden-frage.* Hannover, 1922.

Michels, Robert. *Sozialismus und Fascismus als politische Strömungen in Italien. Historische Studien.* Vol. 2: *Sozialismus und Fascismus in Italien.* Munich, 1925.

Mommsen, Theodor. "Auch ein Wort über unser Judenthum." *Der Berliner Antisemitismusstreit.* Ed. Walter Boehlich. Frankfurt am Main, 1988. 210–25.

Mommsen, Wilhelm, ed. *Deutsche Parteiprogramme.* Munich, 1960.

Mommsen, Wolfgang J. *Das Ringen um den nationalen Staat. Die Gründung und der innere Ausbau des Deutschen Reiches unter Otto von Bismarck. 1850 bis 1890.* Berlin, 1993.

Möller, Horst. *Parlamentarismus in Preußen 1919–1932.* Düsseldorf, 1985.

Müller, Curt. "Das Judentum in der deutschen Studentenschaft." *Cyclus akademischer Broschüren.* Vol. 10. Ed. Arnim Bouman. Leipzig, 1891.

Müller, Detlef K. *Datenhandbuch zur deutschen Bildungsgeschichte.* Vol. 2: *Höhere und mittlere Schulen.* Part 1: *Sozialgeschichte und Statistik des Schulsystems in den Staaten des Deutschen Reiches 1800–1945.* Göttingen, 1987.

Mussolini, Benito. *Mussolinis Gespräche mit Emil Ludwig.* Berlin, 1932.

Napoleon und Europa. Traum und Trauma. Edited by Bénédicte Savoy. Munich: Bundeskusthalle, with Prestel, 2010. Exhibition Catalog.

Nathan, Paul. "Die Enttäuschungen unserer Gegner." *Der Deutsche Krieg. Politische Flugschriften.* Vol. 11. Ed. Ernst Jäckh. Stuttgart, 1914.

Naumann, Friedrich. *National-sozialer Katechismus. Erklärung der Grundlinien des National-Sozialen Vereins.* Berlin, 1897.

———. *Mitteleuropa.* Berlin, 1915.

Němeček, Ottokar. *Zur Psychologie christlicher und jüdischer Schüler.* Langensalza, 1916.

Neumann, Sigmund. *Die Parteien der Weimarer Republik.* Introd. Karl Dietrich Bracher. Stuttgart, 1965. Originally published as *Die politischen Parteien in Deutschland.* Berlin, 1932.

Oehme, Walter, and Curt Caro. *Kommt "das Dritte Reich"?* Berlin, 1930.

Oettinger, Eduard Maria. *Offenes Billet-doux an den berühmten Hepp-Hepp-Schreier und Juden-Fresser Herrn Wilhelm Richard Wagner.* 2nd ed. Dresden, 1869.

Oppenheimer, Franz. *Die Judenstatistik des preußischen Kriegsministeriums.* Munich, 1922.

Osborn, Max. "Aus der immerhin besseren alten Zeit. Eine Erinnerung an Paul Singer." *Aufbau* (New York), Oct. 13, 1944.

Das Parteiprogramm. Wesen, Grundsätze und Ziele der NSDAP. Ed. and annotated by Alfred Rosenberg. Munich, 1922.

Paulsen, Friedrich. *Die deutschen Universitäten und das Universitätsstudium.* Berlin, 1902.

Philippson, Ludwig. "Die Gleichstellung der Juden." *Die Allgemeine Zeitung des Judenthums. Ein unparteiisches Organ für alles jüdische Interesse*, Feb. 5, 1849.

Planert, Ute. *Der Mythos vom Befreiungskrieg. Frankreichs Kriege und der deutsche Süden. Alltag, Wahrnehmung, Deutung 1792–1841.* Paderborn, 2007.

Plessner, Helmuth. *Grenzen der Gemeinschaft. Eine Kritik des sozialen Radikalismus.* 1924. Frankfurt am Main, 2001.

———. *Die verspätete Nation. Über die Verführbarkeit des bürgerlichen Geistes.* Stuttgart, 1959. Originally published as *Schicksal deutschen Geistes im Ausgang seiner bürgerlichen Epoche.* Zürich, 1935.

Pohlmann, Walter. *Das Judentum und seine Feinde.* Neuwied, 1893.

Pommerin, Reiner. *Sterilisierung der Rheinlandbastarde. Das Schicksal einer farbigen deutschen Minderheit.* Düsseldorf, 1979.

Die Preußische Staatsverwaltung und die Juden. Protestversammlung vom 10. Februar [1901] in Berlin. Stenographischer Bericht. Berlin, 1901.

Preußische Statistik, vol. 102. Königlichen Statistischen Bureau. Berlin, 1890.

Der Prozess gegen die Hauptkriegsverbrecher vor dem Internationalen Militärgerichtshof. Nürnberg 14. November 1945–1. Oktober 1946. Nuremberg, 1948.

Puschner, Marco. *Antisemitismus im Kontext der Politischen Romantik. Konstruktion des "Deutschen" und des "Jüdischen" bei Arnim, Brentano und Saul Ascher.* Tübingen, 2008.

Remmele, Adam. *Faschistische Treibhauskulturen. Eine belehrende Betrachtung über den Kampf zur Reichstagswahl 1930.* Karlsruhe, 1930.

Reuth, Ralf Georg. *Hitlers Judenhass. Klischee und Wirklichkeit.* Munich, 2009.

Richarz, Monika, ed. *Jüdisches Leben in Deutschland. Selbstzeugnisse zur Sozialgeschichte 1780–1871*. Stuttgart, 1976.

Rieger, Paul. *Ein Vierteljahrhundert im Kampf um das Recht und die Zukunft der deutschen Juden. Ein Rückblick auf die Geschichte des Centralvereins deutscher Staatsbürger jüdischen Glaubens in den Jahren 1893–1918*. Berlin, 1918.

Riemer, Friedrich Wilhelm. *Mitteilungen über Goethe, auf Grund der Ausgabe von 1841 und des handschriftlichen Nachlasses*. Ed. Arthur Pollmer. Leipzig, 1921.

Riesser, Gabriel. "Über die Stellung der Bekenner des mosaischen Glaubens in Deutschland. An die Deutschen aller Konfessionen." 1831. *Eine Auswahl aus seinen Schriften und Briefen*. Frankfurt am Main, 1913. 9–26.

———. *Vertheidigung der bürgerlichen Gleichstellung der Juden gegen die Einwürfe des Herrn Dr. H. E. G. Paulus. Den gesetzgebenden Versammlungen in Deutschland gewidmet*. Altona, 1831.

———. "Rede gegen Moritz Mohls Antrag zur Beschränkung der Rechte der Juden, gehalten in der deutschen Nationalversammlung zu Frankfurt am 29.8.1848." 1848. *Eine Auswahl aus seinen Schriften und Briefen*. Frankfurt am Main, 1913. 103–8.

Röpke, Wilhelm. *Der Weg des Unheils*. Berlin, 1931.

———. *Die deutsche Frage*. Erlenbach-Zürich, 1945.

Rosenberg, Arthur. "Treitschke und die Juden. Zur Soziologie der deutschen akademischen Reaktion." *Die Gesellschaft. Internationale Revue für Sozialismus und Politik* 7 (1930): 78–83.

Rosenstrauch, Hazel. *Wahlverwandt und ebenbürtig. Caroline und Wilhelm von Humboldt*. Frankfurt am Main, 2009.

Rumberg, Egon. *Die Rassenschande*. Düsseldorf, 1937.

Ruppin, Arthur. *Die Juden der Gegenwart. Eine sozialwissenschaftliche Studie*. Berlin, 1904.

———. *Soziologie der Juden*. Vol. 1: *Die soziale Struktur der Juden*. Berlin, 1930. Vol. 2: *Der Kampf der Juden um ihre Zukunft*. Berlin, 1931.

———. *Briefe, Tagebücher, Erinnerungen*. Ed. Schlomo Krolik. Afterword by Alex Bein. Königstein in Taunus, 1985.

Rürup, Reinhard. *Emanzipation und Antisemitismus. Studien zur "Judenfrage" der bürgerlichen Gesellschaft*. Göttingen, 1975.

Rybak, Jens. "Ernst Moritz Arndts Judenbilder. Ein unbekanntes Kapitel." *Über Ernst Moritz Arndts Leben und Wirken. Aufsätze.* Ed. der Ernst-Moritz-Arndt-Gesellschaft. Vols. 5–6. Groß Schoritz (Rügen), 1997. 102–47.

Sack, Eduard. "Gegen die Prügelpädagogen." 1878. *Die preußische Schule im Dienste gegen die Freiheit. Schulpolitische Kampfschriften.* Selected, introd., and ed. Karl-Heinz Günther. Berlin, 1961. 73–91.

———. "Schlaglichter zur Volksbildung." 1886. *Die preußische Schule im Dienste gegen die Freiheit. Schulpolitische Kampfschriften.* Selected, introd., and ed. Karl-Heinz Günther. Berlin, 1961. 157–98.

Samjatin, Jewgenij. *Wir.* 1920. Cologne, 1984.

Scheidemann, Philipp. "Wandlungen des Antisemitismus." *Die Neue Zeit* 2 (1906): 632–36.

Scheler, Max. "Das Ressentiment im Aufbau der Moralen." *Gesammelte Werke.* 1912. Vol. 3: *Vom Umsturz der Werte.* Bonn, 1972. 35–147.

Scheuer, Oskar Franz. *Burschenschaft und Judenfrage. Der Rassenantisemitismus in der deutschen Studentenschaft.* Berlin, 1927.

Scheur, Wolfgang. *Einrichtungen und Maßnahmen der sozialen Sicherheit in der Zeit des Nationalsozialismus.* Cologne, 1967.

Schieder, Theodor. "Faschismus und Imperium." *Geschichte des italienischen Volkes und Staates.* Ed. Michael Seidlmayer. Leipzig, 1940. 467–503.

Schildt, Axel. "Ein konservativer Prophet moderner nationaler Integration. Biographische Skizze des streitbaren Soziologen Johann Plenge." *Vierteljahrshefte für Zeitgeschichte* 35 (1987): 523–70.

Schmoller, Gustav. "Obrigkeitsstaat und Volksstaat, ein mißverständlicher Gegensatz." *Schmollers Jahrbuch für Gesetzgebung, Verwaltung und Volkswirtschaft im Deutschen Reiche* 40 (1916): 423–34.

Schnabel, Franz. *Deutsche Geschichte im neunzehnten Jahrhundert.* Vol. 1: *Die Grundlagen.* Freiburg im Breisgau, 1929. Vol. 2: *Monarchie und Volkssouveränität.* Freiburg im Breisgau, 1933. Vol. 3: *Erfahrungswissenschaften und Technik.* Freiburg im Breisgau, 1934.

Schoeck, Helmut. *Der Neid. Eine Theorie der Gesellschaft.* Freiburg im Breisgau, 1966.

Scholem Alejchem. *Tewje, der Milchmann.* 1894–1916. Dresden, 1967.

Scholtzhauer, Inge. *Das Philanthropin 1804–1942. Die Schule der Israelitischen Gemeinde in Frankfurt am Main.* Frankfurt am Main, 1990.

Schotthöfer, Fritz. *Il Fascio. Sinn und Wirklichkeit des italienischen Faschismus.* Frankfurt am Main, 1924.

Schottlaender, Rudolf. *Trotz allem ein Deutscher. Mein Lebensweg seit Jahrhundertbeginn.* Freiburg im Breisgau, 1986.

Schwarz, Israel. *Sendschreiben an das teutsche Parlament in Frankfurt am Main, für die Aussprechung der Judenemancipation, und ein offenes Wort an den christlichen Clerus.* Heidelberg, 1848.

Segall, Jakob. *Die beruflichen und sozialen Verhältnisse der Juden in Deutschland.* Berlin, 1912.

Seibt, Gustav. "Generation Bonaparte. Erbe der Gewalt." *Süddeutsche Zeitung,* Dec. 17, 2010.

Seldte, Franz. *Sozialpolitik im Dritten Reich 1933–1938.* Munich, 1939.

Sforza, Carlo. *Die feindlichen Brüder. Inventur der europäischen Probleme.* Berlin, 1933.

Sieburg, Friedrich. *Es werde Deutschland.* Frankfurt, 1933.

Sieferle, Rolf Peter. *Die konservative Revolution. Fünf biographische Skizzen.* Frankfurt am Main, 1995.

Silbergleit, Heinrich. *Die Bevölkerungs- und Berufsverhältnisse der Juden im Deutschen Reich.* Vol. 1. Berlin, 1931.

Silbermann, Alphons. *Der ungeliebte Jude. Zur Soziologie des Antisemitismus.* Zürich, 1981.

Silberner, Edmund. *Sozialisten zur Judenfrage. Ein Beitrag zur Geschichte des Sozialismus vom Anfang des 19. Jahrhunderts bis 1914.* Berlin, 1962.

Simon, F. *Wehrt Euch!! Ein Mahnwort an die Juden. Mit einem offenen Brief der Frau Baronin Bertha von Suttner.* Berlin, 1893.

Slezkine, Yuri. *Das jüdische Jahrhundert.* Göttingen, 2006.

Smith, Bradley F., and Agnes F. Peterson, eds. *Heinrich Himmler. Geheimreden 1933 bis 1945 und andere Ansprachen.* Introd. Joachim Fest. Frankfurt am Main, 1974.

Sombart, Werner. *Die Juden und das Wirtschaftsleben.* Leipzig, 1911.

———. *Die Zukunft der Juden.* Leipzig, 1912.

———. *Deutscher Sozialismus.* Berlin, 1934.

Speier, Hans. *Die Angestellten vor dem Nationalsozialismus. Ein Beitrag zum Verständnis der deutschen Sozialstruktur 1918–1933*. Göttingen, 1977.

Stapel, Wilhelm. *Antisemitismus*. Hamburg, 1920.

——. "Aphoristisches zur Judenfrage." *Der Jud ist schuld . . . ? Diskussionsbuch über die Judenfrage*. Ed. Mermann Bahr et al. Basel, 1932. 171–74.

Stein, Karl vom und zum. *Briefe und amtliche Schriften*. Vol. 5: *Juni 1814–Dezember 1818*. Edited by Manfred Botzenhardt. Stuttgart, 1964. Vol. 6: *Januar 1819–Mai 1826*. Edited by Alfred Hartlieb von Wallthor. Stuttgart, 1965. Vol. 9: *Historische und politische Schriften*. Edited by Walther Hubatsch. Stuttgart, 1972.

Stenographischer Bericht über die Hauptversammlung des Centralvereins deutscher Staatsbürger jüdischen Glaubens vom 4. Februar 1917. Berlin, 1917.

Sterling, Eleonore. *Er ist wie du. Aus der Frühgeschichte des Antisemitismus in Deutschland (1815–1850)*. Munich, 1956.

Stern, H. *Angriff und Abwehr. Ein Handbuch der Judenfrage*. 2nd ed. Berlin, 1924.

Stoecker, Adolf. *Das moderne Judenthum in Deutschland, besonders in Berlin. Zwei Reden, in der christlich-sozialen Arbeiterpartei gehalten*. Berlin, 1880.

Thon, Jakob, and Arthur Ruppin. *Der Anteil der Juden am Unterrichtswesen in Preußen*. Berlin, 1905.

Toury, Jacob. *Deutschlands Stiefkinder. Ausgewählte Aufsätze zur deutschen und deutsch-jüdischen Geschichte*. Gerlingen, 1997.

Treitschke, Heinrich von. "Das constitutionelle Königthum in Deutschland (Heidelberg 1869–1871)." *Historische und politische Aufsätze*. Vol. 3: *Freiheit und Königthum*. 7th ed. Leipzig, 1915. 427–561.

——. "Unsere Aussichten." *Preußischen Jahrbücher* 44 (1879): 559–76.

——. *Ein Wort über unser Judenthum. Separatabdruck aus dem 44., 45. und 46. Bande der Preußischen Jahrbücher*, 4th exp. ed., Berlin, 1881.

——. *Deutsche Geschichte im Neunzehnten Jahrhundert*. Vol. 1: *Bis zum zweiten Pariser Frieden*. 3rd ed. Leipzig, 1882. Vol. 2: *Bis zu den Karlsbader Beschlüssen*. Leipzig, 1882. Vol. 3: *Bis zur März-Revolution*.

Leipzig, 1894. Vol. 4: *Bis zum Tode Friedrich Wilhelms III.* Leipzig, 1889. Vol. 5: *Bis zur Märzrevolution.* Leipzig, 1894.

Tröbst, Hans. "Mustapha Kemal Pascha und sein Werk." Part 6 (Conclusion). *Heimatland. Vaterländisches Wochenblatt, Organ des Deutschen Kampfbundes,* Oct. 15, 1923. 7–8.

———. *Soldatenblut. Vom Baltikum zu Kemal Pascha.* Leipzig, 1925.

Unruh, Friedrich Franz von. *National-Sozialismus. Mit dem Anhang von Carl Busemann, Das Wirtschaftsprogramm.* Frankfurt am Main, 1931.

VEJ. Die Verfolgung und Ermordung der europäischen Juden durch das nationalsozialistische Deutschland 1933–1945. Ed. Götz Aly (vols. 1 and 2), Wolf Gruner (vol. 1), Susanne Heim, Ulrich Herbert, Hans-Dieter Kreikamp, Horst Möller, Dieter Pohl, and Hartmut Weber. Vol. 1: *Deutsches Reich 1933–1937.* Edited by Wolf Gruner. Munich, 2008. Vol. 2: *Deutsches Reich 1938–August 1939.* Edited by Susanne Heim. Munich, 2009. Vol. 7: *Besetzte sowjetische Gebiete unter deutscher Militärverwaltung, Baltikum und Transnistrien unter deutscher und rumänischer Zivilverwaltung.* Edited by Bert Hoppe. Munich, 2011.

Villers, *Brief an die Gräfin F. de B., enthaltend eine Nachricht von den Begebenheiten, die zu Lübeck an dem Tage, Donnerstag den 6ten November 1806, und folgenden vorgefallen sind.* Amsterdam, 1807.

Virchow, Rudolf. *Ueber den Hungertyphus und einige verwandte Krankheitsformen. Vortrag, gehalten am 9. Februar 1868 zum Besten der Typhuskranken in Ostpreußen.* Berlin, 1868.

Voegelin, Erich. *Rasse und Staat.* Tübingen, 1933.

———. *Die Rassenidee in der Geistesgeschichte von Ray bis Carus.* Berlin, 1933.

Vogt, Martin, ed. Herbst im "Führerhauptquartier." *Berichte Werner Koeppens an seinen Minister Alfred Rosenberg.* Koblenz, 2002.

Volkov, Shulamit. *Die Juden in Deutschland 1780–1918.* Munich, 2000.

Wagner, Richard. *Das Judenthum in der Musik.* Leipzig, 1869. 1st ed. under the pseudonym K. Freigedank, 1850. 9–32.

Wassermann, Henry, and Eckhart G. Franz. " 'Kauft nicht beim Juden.' Der politische Antisemitismus des späten 19. Jahrhunderts in Darmstadt." *Juden als Darmstädter Bürger, Darmstadt 1984.* Ed. Eckhart G. Franz. Darmstadt, 1984. 123–36.

Wassermann, Jakob. *Mein Weg als Deutscher und Jude.* 1921. Munich, 1994.

———. *Lebensdienst. Gesammelte Studien, Erfahrungen und Reden aus drei Jahrzehnten.* Leipzig, 1928.

Wawrzinek, Kurt. *Die Entstehung der deutschen Antisemitenparteien (1873–1890).* Berlin, 1927.

Weinryb, Bernard D. *Der Kampf um die Berufsumschichtung. Ein Ausschnitt aus der Geschichte der Juden in Deutschland.* Berlin, 1936.

Weizmann, Chaim. *Trial and Error: The Autobiography of Chaim Weizmann.* New York, 1949.

Wehler, Hans-Ulrich. *Deutsche Gesellschaftsgeschichte.* Vol. 4: *Vom Beginn des Ersten Weltkriegs bis zur Gründung der beiden deutschen Staaten 1914–1949.* Munich, 2003.

Weltsch, Felix. *Judentum und Nationalismus.* Berlin, 1920.

Wilhelm II. *Ereignisse und Gestalten aus den Jahren 1878–1918.* Leipzig, 1922.

Winkler, August Heinrich. *Weimar 1918–1933. Die Geschichte der ersten deutschen Demokratie.* Munich, 1993.

Wirth, Max. *Geschichte der Handelskrisen.* Frankfurt am Main, 1874. 4th rev. ed., 1890.

World Jewish Congress. *Memorandum to the United Nations Special Committee on Palestine.* New York, 1947.

York-Steiner, Heinrich. *Die Kunst als Jude zu leben. Minderheit verpflichtet.* Leipzig, 1928.

———. "Wie entsteht der Antisemitismus der Deutschen?" *Der Jud ist schuld . . . ? Diskussionsbuch über die Judenfrage.* Ed. Herman Bahr et al. Basel, 1932. 393–98.

Zandman, Felix. *Never the Last Journey.* New York, 1995.

Zollschan, Ignaz. *Der Rassenwahnsinn als Staatsphilosophie. Mit einem Vorwort von Julian Huxley.* Heidelberg, 1949.

Zweig, Arnold. *Caliban oder die Politik der Leidenschaft. Versuch über die menschlichen Gruppenleidenschaften dargetan am Antisemitismus.* Potsdam, 1927.

INDEX

ABOUT THE AUTHOR

GÖTZ ALY is the author of *Hitler's Beneficiaries* and *Into the Tunnel*, among other books. One of the most respected historians of the Third Reich and the Holocaust, he has received the National Jewish Book Award, Germany's prestigious Heinrich Mann Prize, and numerous other honors.